KILSYTH PRIMARY SCHOOL

SESSION 19 60 19 61

.... SECOND .... PRIZE

Class 6A

JAMES PATRICK

Joan M. Matthews Teacher

WILLIAM WALKER, B.A., Headmaster

EVERY BOY'S
HANDBOOK

EVERY BOY'S HANDBOOK

Edited by
ROBERT BATEMAN

PAUL HAMLYN
LONDON

Published by

PAUL HAMLYN

SPRING HOUSE - SPRING PLACE
LONDON NW5

CONTENTS

THE WORLD: USEFUL FACTS AND FIGURES

PEOPLE AND PLACES

PEOPLE AND THE NEW WORLD

PEOPLE ON THE MOVE

PEOPLE OF OUR TIME

PEOPLE AND LANGUAGE

PEOPLE AND SCIENCE

PEOPLE AND THE ARTS

PEOPLE AND SPORT

PEOPLE AND LEISURE

LIST OF PLATES

Following page 72

Following page 88

Following page 136

THE WORLD:
USEFUL FACTS AND FIGURES

These tables of sizes, distances, heights and depths, numbers and locations of various things in the world we live in should help in settling many school and family arguments.

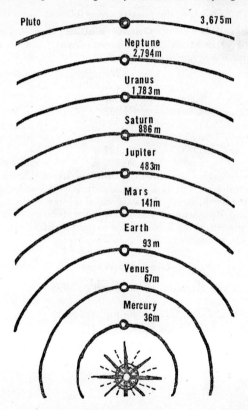

Pluto — 3,675m

Neptune 2,794m

Uranus 1,783m

Saturn 886m

Jupiter 483m

Mars 141m

Earth 93m

Venus 67m

Mercury 36m

The Solar System

The sun — the centre of our solar system — has a diameter of about 865,000 miles. The earth is one of nine planets which revolve round the sun. Here are these planets, together with their distances from the sun (in millions of miles).

Other facts about the planets are as follows:

Planet	Diameter in Miles	One Revolution around Sun (days)	One Rotation on Axis
Mercury	3,008	88	88 days
Venus	7,600	225	not certain
Earth	7,927	365¼	23 h. 56 m.
Mars	4,200	687	24 h. 37 m.
Jupiter	88,439	4,332	9 h. 50 m.
Saturn	75,060	10,759	10 h. 14 m.
Uranus	30,875	30,687	10 h. 49 m.
Neptune	33,000	60,127	15 h. 40 m.
Pluto	3,600	90,400	unknown

The moon — the earth's satellite — has a diameter of 2,160 miles, and it is approximately 239,000 miles away from the earth. Research has revealed no sign of life on the moon, and no definite traces have been discovered on any of the planets — but studies point to possible life of some sort on Mars, probably in the vegetable category.

Land and Water

Much more than half the world's surface is ocean. In fact, the land area is only 56,000,000 square miles out of a total of 197,000,000. The four great oceans are:

Name	Area (millions of sq. miles)
Pacific	64
Atlantic	31.5
Indian	28.35
Arctic	5.5

The six continents are:

Name	Area (millions of sq. miles)
Asia	17
Africa	11.7
North America	9
South America	7
Europe	3.8
Australia	2.975

Ocean Deeps

Position	Name	Depth (feet)
Mariana Trench	Challenger Deep	37,800
Tonga Trench		34,885
Philippine Trench	Galathea Deep	34,580
Kurile Trench	Vityaz Deep	34,045
Japanese Trench	Ramapo Deep	34,035
Kermadec Trench		32,788
Guam Trench		31,614
Puerto Rico Trench	Milwaukee Deep	30,246
New Britain Trench	Planet Deep	29,987

Great Seas and Lakes

Name and Location	Area (sq. miles)
Mediterranean Sea (Southern Europe, Africa, Asia Minor)	1,100,000
South China Sea (China, East Indies)	960,000
Behring Sea (Alaska, Siberia)	878,000
Caribbean Sea (Central America, West Indies)	750,000
Gulf of Mexico (United States, Mexico)	716,000
Sea of Okhotsk (Siberia)	589,000
Hudson Bay (Canada)	475,000
Sea of Japan (Japan, U.S.S.R., Korea)	389,000

North Sea (North-Western Europe)   221,000
Red Sea (Africa, Arabia)   178,000
Caspian Sea (U.S.S.R., Persia)   170,000
Black Sea (U.S.S.R., Turkey, Eastern Europe)   166,000
Baltic Sea (Scandinavia, U.S.S.R.)   163,000
Lake Superior (U.S.A., Canada)   31,820
Lake Victoria (East Central Africa)   26,200
Aral Sea (U.S.S.R.)   24,635
Lake Huron (U.S A., Canada)   23,010
Lake Michigan (U.S.A.)   22,400
Lake Tanganyika (East Africa)   12,700

Large Islands

Name	Area (sq. miles)
Greenland	840,000
New Guinea	345,000
Borneo	290,000
Madagascar	228,000
Baffin Land (Canada)	197,700
Sumatra	163,000
Great Britain	89,000
Honshiu (Japan)	87,500
Ellesmere (Canada)	77,000
Celebes	72,500
South Island (New Zealand)	58,500
Java	48,400
North Island (New Zealand)	44,500
Cuba	44,000
Newfoundland (Canada)	42,750
Luzon (Philippine Islands)	41,000
Iceland	40,000

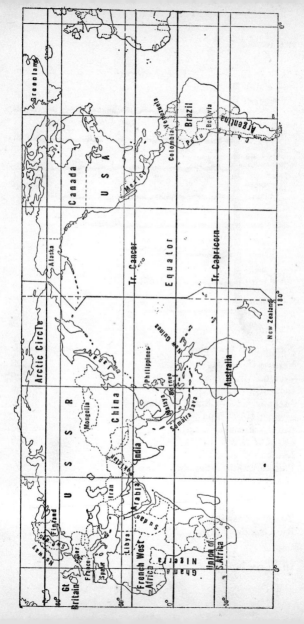

Great Rivers

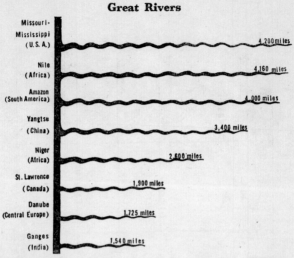

Missouri-
Mississippi
(U.S.A.) — 4,200 miles

Nile
(Africa) — 4,160 miles

Amazon
(South America) — 4,000 miles

Yangtsu
(China) — 3,400 miles

Niger
(Africa) — 2,600 miles

St. Lawrence
(Canada) — 1,900 miles

Danube
(Central Europe) — 1,725 miles

Ganges
(India) — 1,540 miles

Other great rivers are:

Name and Location	Length (miles)
Yenisei (Siberia)	3,300
Congo (Africa)	2,900
Lena (Siberia)	2,850
Mekong (Indo-China, Thailand)	2,800
Hwang Ho (China)	2,700
Amur (Siberia, China)	2,700
Ob (U.S.S.R.)	2,600
Mackenzie (Canada)	2,500
Paraná (South America)	2,450
Murray (Australia)	2,310
Volga (U.S.S.R.)	2,300
La Plata (South America)	2,300
Yukon (Alaska)	2,000
Rio Grande (Mexico, U.S.A.)	1,800

Sao Francisco (Brazil)	1,800
Euphrates (Iraq)	1,700
Indus (Pakistan)	1,700
Brahmaputra (India)	1,680
Zambesi (Africa)	1,600

High Waterfalls

Name and Location	Height (feet)
Angel Falls (Venezuela)	3,212
Yosemite (California)	2,825
Kukenaam (Venezuela)	2,000
Sutherland (New Zealand)	1,904
Tugela (South Africa)	1,800
Ribbon (California)	1,612
Gavarnie (France)	1,385
Takkakaw (Canada)	1,200
Geissbach (Switzerland)	1,150
Wollomombie (Australia)	1,100
Vettisfos (Norway)	900
Chirombo (East Africa)	880
King Edward VIII (British Guiana)	840
Gersoppa (India)	830
Glomach (Scotland)	370
Victoria (Rhodesia)	360
Niagara (U.S.A., Canada)	167

Active Volcanoes

Name and Location	Height (feet)
Cotopaxi (Andes, Ecuador)	19,344
Wrangell (Alaska)	14,000
Mauna Loa (Hawaii)	13,675
Erebus (Antarctica)	13,200
Iliamna (Aleutian Islands)	11,000
Etna (Sicily)	10,700

Chillan (Andes, Chile)	10,500
Paricutín (Mexico)	9,000
Asamayama (Japan)	8,200
Hekla (Iceland)	5,100
Vesuvius (Italy)	3,858
Stromboli (Italy)	3,000

Principal Mountains

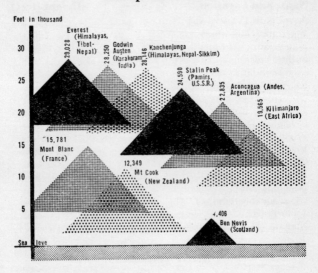

Other high mountains are:

Name and Location	Height (feet)
Makalu (Himalayas, Tibet—Nepal)	27,790
Nanga Parbat (Himalayas, India)	26,660
Illimani (Andes, Bolivia)	21,185
Chimborazo (Andes, Ecuador)	20,577

McKinley (Alaska)	20,300
Logan (St Elias, Canada)	19,850
Elbrus (Caucasus, U.S.S.R.)	18,468
St Elias, (St Elias, Alaska—Canada)	18,008
Popocatepetl (Mexico)	17,883

Natural Resources of the World

The pattern of modern civilisation is based upon what the earth can provide. Lands in which the earth is barren, or the climate too extreme, attract few people unless salable minerals can be mined; but rich, fertile areas are usually densely populated. In the following paragraphs some of the staple needs of man are listed, with details of the areas in which they are found.

Meat and Dairy Produce. Most peoples of the world are meat eaters, and though cattle for meat can be raised on rough grassland, rich pasture is needed for dairy cattle, the source of milk, from which butter and cheese are made. The great beef-producing countries are the United States, Canada, Argentina and Australia. The major dairying nations are New Zealand, Australia, the United States, Denmark and Holland.

Sheep and Wool Produce. The big sheep-producing countries are Australia, New Zealand, Argentina and Russia. The ideal sheep for economic breeding is a cross between the English strain, raised for its tender meat, and the Merino, or Mediterranean breed, noted for its wool and leather.

Cereals. Man has been developing cereals from the original wild grasses of the world since he first began to cultivate the soil. The principal cereals are wheat, oats, barley, rice, rye and maize. The great wheat areas of the world are Canada, the United States, Argentina, Australia and Eastern Europe. Asia is the source of most of the world's rice.

Tea. Tea is grown mainly in India, China, Ceylon and Japan, with the greatest export trade being carried out by

23

India, which sends millions of pounds in weight every year to the major tea-drinking countries.

Coffee. The coffee plant, which takes five years to grow to a crop-yielding size, is grown mainly in Brazil, Colombia and East Africa.

Cocoa. The cocoa bean was brought back to Europe from Central America in the fifteenth century, by the first explorers. Today the principal growing area is West Africa, which produces enormous quantities every year for making chocolate and cocoa powder.

Sugar. There are two sources of sugar. These are sugar cane and sugar beet. Sugar cane is a tropical plant of which the stems yield a syrupy juice. This is boiled to purify and crystallise it. The juice of the sugar beet, a vegetable grown in temperate climates, is refined in a similar way. The principal sugar cane area is the West Indies.

Tobacco. Grown wild by the natives of North America, tobacco was brought to Europe in the sixteenth century. The main plantations are in the southern United States, but tobacco is also grown extensively in Rhodesia and the Middle East, and to a limited extent in many other areas for local use.

Cotton. Sub-tropical areas are best for cotton production, and the principal cotton countries are the United States, in its southern states, the West Indies, Egypt, India, China and southern Russia.

Rubber. Though some countries now produce much of their rubber by synthetic processes, rubber is still a major source of agricultural revenue for countries bordering the Equator. The main growing area is Malaya, to which the original rubber trees were brought from Brazil. Rubber is collected by cutting narrow grooves in the bark and allowing the natural rubber, or 'latex' to drip into a cup attached to the tree.

Minerals. Mineral ores are the source of the metals man needs, and most of them are found at considerable depth.

Open-cast mining is used for surface lodes of minerals, but most mines are deep shafts with underground galleries penetrating hundreds of feet into the heart of the lode. Gold is found mainly in South Africa, Australia and North and South America. Copper and lead are found in every continent, silver in Central and South America and the Far East and iron in most parts of the world.

Fuel. Coal, the source of so many useful by-products, is found extensively and in high quality in Britain, most of Europe and the Eastern seaboard of the United States. Poorer qualities exist in many other parts of the world. The major oil-producing areas are the United States, Canada, Venezuela and the Middle East.

Fisheries. Sea fishing is carried on in all parts of the world, but the areas which produce more than is needed for local consumption are the Grand Banks off Newfoundland, famous for cod, the herring fisheries off Iceland and stretching southward as far as the Portuguese coast and the salmon areas of the North Pacific.

PEOPLE AND PLACES

The First Men: Who were the first men? After a succession
of ice ages lasting for hundreds of thousands of years, bleak
millions of years in which the earth was inhabited by enormous reptiles, further iceages, and also a long period dominat-
ed by early men, who had learned to use primitive tools
and clothe themselves, the first true men seem to have
emerged about fifty thousand years ago. They were hunters;
they used spears and throwing-stones, wore skins and furs
and painted on the walls of their caves — paintings which
remain to be seen today in the caves of France and Spain.

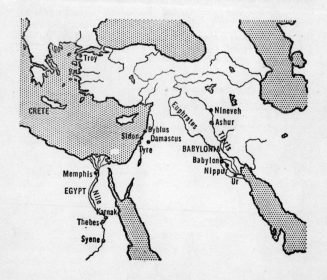

About eight thousand years ago, man had improved to a level at which he made finely polished stone implements, and cultivated fields of corn. Then, about six thousand years ago, came the first civilisations — in the Nile Valley and in Mesopotamia between the Rivers Tigris and Euphrates. Empires and city-states spread across Arabia, into Turkey and thence to Europe; sailors made their first perilous journeys upon the Mediterranean, taking months of labour and danger to cover distances which a modern liner traverses between sunrise and dusk.

Empire followed empire—Egyptian, Greek, Roman, Chinese — and slowly men grouped themselves by race, religion and way of life into the nations of the present day, while the world's population rose from a few million to the present total of some two thousand five hundred million.

Countries of the World. The lists which follow cannot be completely accurate, as not all countries have been fully surveyed and not every area has a census of population, but they are reliable enough for most purposes.

British Commonwealth

(* = actual population)

Country	Population in Millions	Capital	Population in Thousands
Europe			
United Kingdom	51.0	London	8,346
Gibraltar	24,000*	—	—
Malta	0.3	Valetta	19
Asia			
Aden	0.8	Aden	33
Brunei	55,000*	Brunei	11
Ceylon	8.1	Colombo	425
Cyprus	0.5	Nicosia	68

27

Hong Kong	2.2	Victoria	887
India	357.0	Delhi	1,100
Malaya	6.2	Kuala Lumpur	300
North Borneo	0.3	Jesselton	12
Pakistan	75.8	Karachi	1,126
Sarawak	0.6	Kuching	45
Singapore	1.3	—	—

Africa

Basutoland	0.6	Maseru	3
Bechuanaland	0.3	(Administered from Mafeking, Union of South Africa)	—
British Cameroons	1.4	Buea	3
Gambia	0.3	Bathurst	21
Ghana	5.0	Accra	136
Kenya	6.7	Nairobi	100
Mauritius and Dependencies	0.6	Port Louis	90
Nigeria	34.8	Lagos	267
Rhodesia and Nyasaland	7.8	Salisbury	184
St Helena and Dependencies	5,368*	Jamestown	1
Seychelles	39,000*	Victoria	9
Sierra Leone	2.2	Freetown	65
South West Africa	0.4	Windhoek	14
Swaziland	0.2	Mbabane	2
Tanganyika	8.5	Dar es Salaam	99
Uganda	5.5	Entebbe	8
Union of South Africa	14.5	Pretoria / Cape Town	330 / 480
Zanzibar	0.3	Zanzibar	45

North America

| Canada | 17.0 | Ottawa | 285 |

Central America and West Indies

Bahamas	0.1	Nassau	50
Barbados	0.2	Bridgetown	13
Bermuda	42,000*	Hamilton	3
British Honduras	88,800*	Belize	22
Jamaica	1.6	Kingston	150
Leeward Islands	0.1	—	—
Trinidad and Tobago	0.7	Port of Spain	120
Windward Islands	0.3	—	—

South America

British Guiana	0.5	Georgetown	115
Falkland Islands	2,294*	Stanley	1

Australasia and Oceania

Australia	10.0	Canberra	33
Fiji	0.3	Suva	32
Gilbert and Ellice Islands	39,000*	Tarawa	3
Nauru	3,600*	—	—
New Hebrides	55,500*	Vila	1
New Zealand	2.3	Wellington	143
Papua—New Guinea	1.7	Port Moresby	3
Solomon Islands	0.1	Honiara	2
Tonga	56,000*	Nukualofa	6
Western Samoa	100,000*	Apia	16

Foreign Countries

(* = actual population)

Country	Population in Millions	Capital	Population in Thousands
Europe			
Albania	1.3	Tirana	60
Andorra	5,200*	Andorra-la-Vella	600*
Austria	7.0	Vienna	1,766

Belgium	8.8	Brussels	971
Bulgaria	7.0	Sofia	434
Czechoslovakia	13.5	Prague	978
Denmark	4.4	Copenhagen	975
Finland	4.2	Helsinki	394
France	44.8	Paris	2,850
Germany, East	17.3	Berlin (East)	1,200
Germany, West	49.3	Bonn	134
Greece	7.9	Athens	565
Hungary	9.7	Budapest	1,058
Iceland	0.1	Reykjavik	57
Ireland, Republic of	2.9	Dublin	522
Italy	52.65	Rome	1,688
Liechtenstein	15,800*	Vaduz	3
Luxembourg	0.3	Luxembourg	64
Monaco	20,000*	Monaco	2
Netherlands	11.3	⎰Amsterdam	860
		⎱The Hague	600
Norway	3.4	Oslo	441
Poland	28.2	Warsaw	650
Portugal	8.7	Lisbon	790
Roumania	17.4	Bucharest	1,042
San Marino	13,000*	San Marino	2
Spain	29.6	Madrid	1,527
Sweden	7.2	Stockholm	753
Switzerland	5.1	Berne	154
Turkey (Europe)	1.7	—	—
U.S.S.R. (Europe)	166.9	Moscow	4,839
Vatican City State	940*	Vatican City	940*
Yugoslavia	16.9	Belgrade	470

Asia

Afghanistan	12.0	Kabul	250
Bhutan	0.6	Punakha	unknown
Burma	17.8	Rangoon	740
Cambodia	4.2	Phnom Penh	375

China, People's Republic of	590.1	Peking	2,768
Formosa (Nationalist China)	10.0	Taipei	503
Indonesia	80.0	Djakarta	1,200
Iraq	6.5	Baghdad	552
Israel	2.0	Jerusalem	153
Japan	92.2	Tokyo	9,100
Jordan	1.4	Amman	110
Korea (North)	8.7	Pyongyang	286
Korea (South)	21.3	Seoul	1,221
Laos	2.5	Vientiane	25
Lebanon	1.4	Beirut	450
Mongolia	1.0	Ulan Bator	100
Nepal	8.5	Katmandu	175
Oman	0.5	Muscat	5
Persia	19.0	Teheran	990
Philippine Islands	21.6	Manila	1,180
Saudi Arabia	7.0	{Riyadh	80
		{Mecca	150
Syria**	3.9	Damascus	335
Thailand	23.1	Bangkok	1,179
Tibet	1.3	Lhasa	25
Turkey (Asia)	20.8	Ankara	287
U.S.S.R. (Asia)	60.3	—	—
Vietnam (North)	14.7	Hanoi	297
Vietnam (South)	12.0	Saigon	1,900
Yemen	4.5	{Sana	50
		{Taiz	12

Africa

Algeria	9.3	Algiers	417
Angola	4.1	Luanda	61
Cameroun	3.3	Yaoundé	32
Central African Republic	1.1	Bangui	80
Chad	2.5	Fort Lamy	43

Congo, Republic of (formerly Belgian)	13.2	Léopoldville	284
Congo, Republic of (formerly French)	7.0	Brazzaville	100
Dahomey	1.7	Porto Novo	30
Egypt**	22.2	Cairo	2,368
Ethiopia	18.0	Addis Ababa	250
French Somaliland	66,000*	Djibouti	17
Gaboon	0.4	Libreville	17
Guinea	3.0	Conakry	100
Ivory Coast	2.5	Abidjan	105
Liberia	1.3	Monrovia	45
Libya	1.1	Tripoli	142
Madagascar	4.4	Tananarive	183
Mauritania	0.6	Nouakchott	—
Morocco	9.6	Rabat	170
Mozambique	5.7	Lourenço Marques	48
Niger	2.5	Niamey	15
Portuguese Guinea	0.5	Bissau	6
Ruanda-Urundi	4.6	Usumbura	18
Senegal†	2.3	Dakar	234
Somalia	2.0	Mogadiscio	63
Spanish Guinea	0.2	Santa Isabel	9
Spanish West Africa	0.2	—	—
Sudan	10.3	Khartoum	87
Sudanese Republic†	3.7	Bamako	100
Togo	1.0	Lomé	39
Tunisia	3.7	Tunis	370
Upper Volta	3.3	Ouagadougou	30

North America

Mexico	33.3	Mexico City	2,234
United States	175.0	Washington, D. C.	802

** *Egypt and Syria together form the United Arab Republic.*
† *Senegal and the Sudanese Republic form the Federation of Mali.*

Central America and West Indies

Costa Rica	1.2	San José	118
Cuba	6.0	Havana	780
Dominican Republic	2.3	Ciudad Trujillo	181
Guadeloupe	0.2	Basse-Terre	11
Guatemala	3.2	Guatemala	285
Haiti	3.5	Port-au-Prince	152
Honduras	1.5	Tegucigalpa	72
Martinique	0.2	Fort-de-France	66
Netherlands Antilles	0.2	Willemstad	44
Nicaragua	1.2	Managua	109
Panamá	1.0	Panamá	128
Puerto Rico	2.2	San Juan	224
El Salvador	2.1	San Salvador	180
Virgin Islands, U.S.	24,000*	Charlotte Amalie	11

South America

Argentina	19.3	Buenos Aires	3,555
Bolivia	3.8	La Paz	320
		Sucre	40
Brazil	63.1	Rio de Janeiro	2,725
Chile	7.3	Santiago	1,507
Colombia	12.6	Bogotá	640
Ecuador	3.6	Quito	211
French Guiana	29,000*	Cayenne	11
Paraguay	1.4	Asunción	202
Peru	8.9	Lima	926
Surinam (Netherlands Guiana)	0.2	Paramaribo	67
Uruguay	3.0	Montevideo	810
Venezuela	5.8	Caracas	878

The World's Largest Cities

Name	Population
Tokyo, Japan	9,100,539
London, England	8,346,137
New York, U.S.A.	8,074,000
Shanghai, China	6,204,417
Moscow, U.S.S.R.	4,839,000
Chicago, U.S.A.	3,620,962
Buenos Aires, Argentina	3,555,000
Berlin, Germany	3,351,000
Paris, France	2,850,189
Bombay, India	2,840,000
Leningrad, U.S.S.R.	2,814,000
Peking, China	2,768,150
Rio de Janeiro, Brazil	2,725,274
Tientsin, China	2,694,000
Calcutta, India	2,548,677
Osaka, Japan	2,547,321
Sao Paulo, Brazil	2,500,000
Cairo, Egypt	2,368,000
Mexico City, Mexico	2,233,941
Los Angeles, U.S.A.	2,104,663

The World's Tallest Buildings

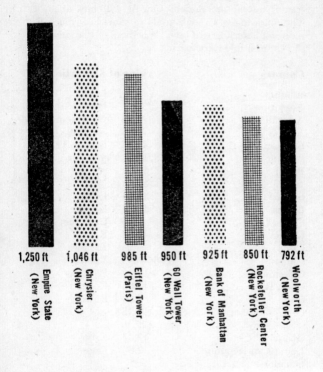

1,250 ft	1,046 ft	985 ft	950 ft	925 ft	850 ft	792 ft
Empire State (New York)	Chrysler (New York)	Eiffel Tower (Paris)	60 Wall Tower (New York)	Bank of Manhattan (New York)	Rockefeller Center (New York)	Woolworth (New York)

Foreign Money

The exact value of money is constantly changing. There was a time when £1 sterling would buy just 20 French francs, but at the present time it will buy about 1,375. The following is a rough guide to show how much foreign money £1 sterling will buy. (Where more than one figure is shown, multiple rates are in use.)

Country	Value of £1 Sterling	
Albania	140	Leks
Argentina	230	Pesos
Australia	1.25	Australian Pounds
Austria	72.78	Schillings
Belgium	140	Belgian Francs
Bolivia	33,000	Bolivianos
Brazil	{525* / 52.25	Cruzeiros
Bulgaria	19.04	Levas
Burma	13.33	Kyat
Canada	2.75	Canadian Dollars
Ceylon	13.33	Rupees
Chile	2.95	Escudos
China	6.86—6.93	Yuan
Colombia	19—20	Pesos
Costa Rica	15.60—18.60	Colones
Cuba	2.80	Pesos
Czechoslovakia	{39.18* / 20.16	Koruny
Denmark	19.34	Krone
Dominican Republic	2.80	Pesos
Ecuador	{50* / 42.50	Sucres
Egypt	0.97	Egyptian Pounds
Ethiopia	7	Ethiopian Dollars
Finland	894	Markka

France	13.75	New Francs
Germany (East)	6.22	Ostmarks
Germany (West)	11.69	Marks
Greece	84	Drachmae
Guatemala	280.28	Quetzales
Haiti	14	Gourdes
Honduras (Republic of)	5.61	Lempiras
Hong Kong	16	Hong Kong Dollars
Hungary	32.87	Forints
Iceland	106.7	Krone
India	13.33	Rupees
Indonesia	128	Rupiahs
Iraq	1	Dinar
Ireland	1	Irish Pound
Israel	5.04—6.04	Israeli Pounds
Italy	1,739	Lire
Japan	1,000	Yen
Korea (South)	1,800	Hwan
Foreign Money (cont'd)		
Lebanon	8.89	Lebanese Pounds
Luxembourg	140.20	Luxembourg Francs
Malaya	8	Malayan Dollars
Mexico	35	Pesos
Netherlands	10.58	Florins
New Zealand	1	New Zealand Pound
Nicaragua	19.25—20	Cordobas
Norway	20	Krone
Pakistan	13.33	Pakistan Rupees
Panamá	2.80	Balboas
Paraguay	342	Guaranies
Persia	214.20	Rials
Peru	77—79	Soles
Philippine Islands	5.61	Pesos
Poland	{67.38* {11.20	Zlotys

37

Portugal	80.23	Escudos	3d
Rhodesia	1	Rhodesian Pound	£1
Roumania	$\begin{cases}33.60* \\ 16.80\end{cases}$	Lei	
El Salvador	7—7.08	Colones	
Spain	169	Pesetas	
Sweden	14.51	Kronor	
Switzerland	12.10	Swiss Francs	1/8
Thailand	59	Bahts	4d
Turkey	$\begin{cases}25.27* \\ 7.84\end{cases}$	Turkish Pounds	
Union of South Africa	1	South African Pound	£1
Uruguay	31.50	Pesos	
U. S. A.	2.80	Dollars	7/-
U.S.S.R.	$\begin{cases}27.60* \\ 11.20\end{cases}$	Roubles	1/9
Venezuela	9.36	Bolívars	
Yugoslavia	$\begin{cases}1,120* \\ 840\end{cases}$	Dinars	½d

= Tourist rate

British Money

Notes

£5, £1, 10/-

Gold Coins

- £5   (no longer minted)
- £2   (no longer minted)
- £1   (sovereign; no longer minted for distribution in U.K.
- 10/- (half-sovereign; no longer minted)

'Silver' Coins (Those minted since 1946 are of cupro-nickel.

- 5/- (crown)
- 4/- (double florin; no longer minted)

38

2/6	(half-crown)
2/-	(florin)
1/-	(shilling)
6d.	(sixpence)
4d.	(groat; no longer minted)
3d.	(threepence; no longer minted)

Nickel-Brass Coins

3d.

'*Copper*' Coins (actually bronze since 1860)

1d.	(penny)
½d.	(halfpenny)
¼d.	(farthing; no longer minted)

All gold coins dated 1838 or later, silver and cupro-nickel dated 1816 or later and bronze dated 1860 or later are legal tender (valid for making payments), but if you offer more than £2 in silver it can be refused and notes demanded; similarly 2/- is the legal limit for nickel-brass 3d. coins, and 1/- the limit for bronze. £5 notes dated previous to September 2, 1944, are not legal tender.

The Seven Wonders of the World

It would be a hard task for anyone to name the Seven Wonders of the Modern World, but certainly among the candidates would be nuclear power, the jet engine, television, radar and some of the almost miraculous discoveries of recent years in medicine.

The Seven Wonders of the Ancient World were:

The Pyramids of Egypt, of which the biggest, the Great Pyramid of Cheops, was originally more than 480 feet in height.

The Hanging Gardens of Babylon, near Baghdad. These were terraced gardens, irrigated by means of huge storage tanks on the uppermost terraces.

39

The Tomb of Mausolus at Halicarnassus, in Asia Minor.

The Temple of Diana (Artemis) at Ephesus, a great marble temple dating from 500 B.C.

The Statue of Jupiter (Zeus) at Olympia, built of marble and inlaid with gold.

The Colossus of Rhodes, a bronze statue (about 105 feet high) with its legs astride the harbour entrance at Rhodes.

The Pharos at Alexandria, the world's first real lighthouse.

Religions of the World

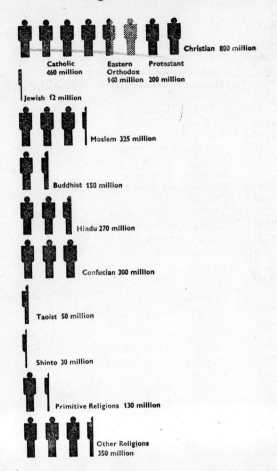

Christian 800 million

Catholic
460 million

Eastern
Orthodox
140 million

Protestant
200 million

Jewish 12 million

Moslem 325 million

Buddhist 150 million

Hindu 270 million

Confucian 300 million

Taoist 50 million

Shinto 30 million

Primitive Religions 130 million

Other Religions
350 million

41

Great Dates in History

B. C.

4241	Egyptians use first 365-day calendar.
3500	Primitive cuneiform writing in use by Sumerians.
c. 3400	First Egyptian Dynastic Period.
c. 2900	The Great Pyramid of Egypt built by Cheops.
1300	Phoenicians open up trade throughout the Mediterranean.
1230	Exodus of the Israelites from Egypt.
1194	Fall of Troy.
961	Building of the Temple at Jerusalem begun.
776	First Olympic Games held in Greece.
753	Founding of Rome.
490	Greeks defeat Persians at Marathon.
488	Death of Buddha.
335—23	The campaigns of Alexander the Great.
149	Carthage destroyed by Scipio.
55	Julius Caesar invades Britain.
4	Actual date of the birth of Christ.

A. D.

30	Crucifixion.
43	Conquest of Britain by Rome begun.
70	Destruction of Jerusalem.
79	Vesuvius erupts, destroying Pompeii and Herculaneum.
122	Building of Hadrian's Wall.
407	Romans leave Britain.
476	Fall of the Roman Empire in the West.
569	Birth of Mohammed in Mecca.
711	Moors overrun Spain.
732	Moors driven from France.
1000	Norsemen reach Labrador.
1066	Normans conquer Britain.

1095	The Crusades begin.
1215	The Magna Carta signed by King John.
1216	First Parliament in England.
1271	Beginning of Marco Polo's travels.
1337	Hundred Years' War begins.
1348	The Black Death sweeps Europe.
1440	Printing with movable type begun in Germany.
1453	Eastern Roman Empire falls to Turks.
1455—85	Wars of the Roses.
1476	First printing press in England.
1492	Columbus discovers America.
1492	Moors driven from Spain.
1500	Portuguese discover Brazil.
1519—22	First voyage round the world, by Magellan.
1534	Reformation in England.
1536	Dissolution of the monasteries in England.
1572	Massacre of St. Bartholomew in France.
1577—80	Drake's voyage round the world.
1588	Drake defeats Spanish Armada.
1605	Gunpowder Plot to blow up English Parliament.
1607	First permanent colony established in Virginia.
1618—48	Thirty Years' War.
1620	*Mayflower* colonists land in New England.
1642	New Zealand and Tasmania discovered.
1665	Great Plague of London.
1666	Great Fire of London.
1707	Act of Union unites England and Scotland.
1715	First Jacobite Rebellion.
1745	Second Jacobite Rebellion, 'The Forty-five'.
1756	Beginning of Seven Years' War.
1760	British defeat French in Canada.
c. 1760	Beginning of Industrial Revolution.
1770	Captain Cook discovers New South Wales.
1775—83	American War of Independence.
1776	American Declaration of Independence.
1789	French Revolution begins.

1796	Napoleonic Wars begin.
1804	Napoleon becomes Emperor of France.
1805	Battle of Trafalgar.
1815	Battle of Waterloo.
1832	First Reform Act in Parliament.
1833	Britain abolishes slavery.
1840	Introduction of penny post in Britain.
1848	Gold discovered in California.
1853—56	Crimean War.
1857	Indian Mutiny.
1861—65	American Civil War.
1863	United States abolishes slavery.
1867	Dominion of Canada established.
1869	Suez Canal opens.
1870—71	Franco-Prussian War.
1877—78	Russo-Turkish War breaks power of Turkey in Europe.
1899— 1902	Boer War.
1903	First successful aeroplane flight, by Wright brothers.
1904—05	Russo-Japanese War.
1909	Blériot makes first cross-Channel flight.
1909	Peary reaches North Pole.
1911	Amundsen reaches South Pole.
1912	Ocean liner *Titanic* sinks, 1513 lost.
1914	World War I begins.
1915	Ocean liner *Lusitania* torpedoed, 1500 lost.
1917	United States enters World War I.
1917	Russian Revolution.
1918	End of World War I.
1919	Alcock and Brown make first non-stop trans-atlantic flight.
1920	First meeting of League of Nations.
1922	Mussolini marches on Rome.
1924	Death of Lenin.

1926	General Strike takes place in Britain.
1927	Lindbergh makes first solo flight across Atlantic.
1929	Start of the Great Slump.
1931	Japan occupies Manchuria.
1933	Hitler attains power in Germany.
1935	Italy invades Ethiopia.
1936—39	Civil War in Spain.
1937	Japan begins war on China.
1938	Germany annexes Austria.
1938	Munich Agreement.
1939	Outbreak of World War II.
1940	Germany invades Denmark, Norway, Netherlands, Belgium and Luxembourg.
1940	Dunkirk evacuation.
1940	Paris taken by Germans.
1940	Battle of Britain.
1941	Russia and United States enter World War II.
1942	All of France occupied by Germans.
1943	Russians halt German advance at Stalingrad.
1943	Allies invade Italy.
1944	Allies invade France.
1945	Germany surrenders.
1945	Hitler dies.
1945	First atomic bomb dropped on Japan.
1945	Japan surrenders.
1945	United Nations established.
1947	India attains independence.
1948	State of Israel proclaimed.
1949	North Atlantic Treaty signed.
1950—53	Korean War.
1952	First British atomic test.
1952	Americans test H-bomb.
1953	Conquest of Mount Everest.
1955	Britain starts building atomic power stations.
1956	Suez Canal dispute.

1957	Russians launch first space satellites.
1958	Americans enter space exploration race.
1959	Russians launch first artifical planet.
1959	Russians launch first rocket to reach moon and photograph its far side.

Exploration and Discoveries of the Past Five Hundred Years

1484	Mouth of Congo River, by Diogo Cam.
1488	Cape of Good Hope, by Bartholomeu Diaz.
1492	West Indies, by Christopher Columbus.
1497	East coast of Canada, by John Cabot.
1498	Cape route to India, by Vasco da Gama.
1498	South America, by Christopher Columbus.
1513	Pacific Ocean, by Vasco Nuñez de Balboa.
1519	Magellan Strait, by Ferdinand Magellan.
1534	St Lawrence River, by Jacques Cartier.
1541	Mississippi River, by Hernando de Soto.
1605—06	Australia, by Willem Jansz.
1610	Hudson Bay (Canada), by Henry Hudson.
1616	Baffin Bay (Canada), by William Baffin.
1642	New Zealand and Tasmania, by Abel Janszoon Tasman.
1778	Hawaii, by Captain James Cook.
1820	Antarctic mainland, by Edward Bransfield.
1855	Victoria Falls, by David Livingstone.
1858	Source of the Nile, by John Hanning Speke.
1865	Matterhorn summit first reached, by Edward Whymper.
1908	North Pole first reached, by Robert E. Peary.
1911	South Pole first reached, by Roald Amundsen.
1953	Everest summit first reached, by Sir Edmund Hillary and Sherpa Tensing.

The United Nations

The history of the world has been almost continuously one of war. There has seldom been a year without war in some quarter of the globe. In 1944, towards the end of World War II, a conference was held at Washington between statesmen of the United States, Britain, Soviet Union and China — the four 'Great Powers' on the Allied side in the War — to plan a world-wide organisation of countries pledged to prevent war. The first full meeting of the United Nations was held in 1945, at San Francisco, and the building of the present headquarters, in New York, was begun soon afterwards. The members of the United Nations are (in order of seating):

Afghanistan	Dominican	Israel
Albania	Republic	Italy
Argentina	Ecuador	Japan
Australia	El Salvador	Jordan
Austria	Ethiopia	Laos
Belgium	Federation of	Lebanon
Bolivia	Malaya	Liberia
Brazil	Finland	Libya
Bulgaria	France	Luxembourg
Burma	Ghana	Mexico
Byelorussian S.S.R.	Greece	Morocco
Cambodia	Guatemala	Nepal
Cameroun	Guinea	Netherlands
Canada	Haiti	New Zealand
Ceylon	Honduras	Nicaragua
Chile	Hungary	Norway
China (Formosa)	Iceland	Pakistan
Colombia	India	Panamá
Costa Rica	Indonesia	Paraguay
Cuba	Iran (Persia)	Peru
Czechoslovakia	Iraq	Philippines
Denmark	Ireland	Poland

Portugal	Tunisia	and Syria)
Roumania	Turkey	United Kingdom
Saudi Arabia	Ukrainian S.S.R.	United States
Spain	Union of South	Uruguay
Sudan	Africa	Venezuela
Sweden	U. S. S. R.	Yemen
Thailand	United Arab	Yugoslavia
Togo	Republic (Egypt	

The General Assembly, which meets in September each year, consists of all members. Any important issue brought before the Assembly is settled by a two-thirds majority vote; lesser issues require only a simple majority.

The Security Council is made up of eleven members and is in continuous session to prevent international disputes. There are five permanent members: United Kingdom, United States, U. S. S. R., France and Formosa. The General Assembly chooses the remaining members, electing them for a period of two years. The Council reaches decisions by a majority of seven votes to four, but in any major issue five of the votes must be those of the permanent members. If any one of these members votes against the majority, therefore, this vote is in effect a veto, and no settlement can be reached.

There are four other sections of the United Nations Organisation: the Economic and Social Council, the Trusteeship Council, the International Court of Justice and the Secretariat.

The United Nations also runs various agencies, including organisations to provide world banking and trade facilities. Four of these organisations are:

FAO — Food and Agriculture Organisation. This exists to improve nutrition, food production and rural economy.

WHO — World Health Organisation. Its aim is to improve the health of people in all countries through medical research, diet improvement and better hygiene.

UNESCO — United Nations Educational, Scientific and Cultural Organisation. Its purpose is to promote, through education, greater rights and freedoms for all people, irrespective of race, language or religion.

UNHCR — United Nations High Commission for Refugees. This exists to provide international help and protection for all who because of political, religious or racial persecution have had to leave their own countries and become exiles.

The United Nations Association is a public society which anyone may join. Its purpose is to promote friendship, understanding and co-operation among the peoples of the world and to win support for all that the United Nations is trying to do.

Other Alliances

So far, the United Nations has had only partial success as a form of 'world government', and nations have still felt it necessary to group themselves for mutual defence. The main groups are as follows:

NATO — North Atlantic Treaty Organisation. This consists of Belgium, Canada, Denmark, France, Greece, Iceland, Italy, Luxembourg, Netherlands, Norway, Portugal, Turkey, United Kingdom, United States and West Germany.

SEATO — South-East Asia Treaty Organisation. The members are Australia, France, New Zealand, Pakistan, Philippines, Thailand, United Kingdom and United States.

Warsaw Pact — This consists of Albania, Bulgaria, Czechoslovakia, East Germany, Hungary, Poland, Roumania and U. S. S. R.

Central Treaty Organisation (formerly Baghdad Pact) — This is a Middle East defensive group consisting of Pakistan, Persia, Turkey and the United Kingdom.

Monarchs of the World

Almost all countries of the world today have a parliamentary system — that is, a council of people elected to rule.

By far the majority of nations have at their head a President, in most cases elected every few years. Those which still have hereditary monarchs are:

Country	Ruler	Came to Throne
Afghanistan	King Mohamed Zahir Shah	1933
Belgium	King Baudouin	1951
Cambodia	King Norodom Suramarit	1955
Denmark	King Frederik IX	1947
Ethiopia	Emperor Haile Selassie	1930
Great Britain	Queen Elizabeth II	1952
Greece	King Paul I	1947
Japan	Emperor Hirohito	1926
Jordan	King Hussein	1952
Libya	King Idris I	1951
Liechtenstein	Prince Franz Joseph II	1938
Luxembourg	Grand Duchess Charlotte	1919
Monaco	Prince Rainier	1949
Nepal	King Mahendra Bir Bikram Shah	1955
Netherlands	Queen Juliana	1948
Norway	King Olaf	1957
Persia	Shah Mohammed Reza Pahlevi	1941
Saudi Arabia	King Saud Ibn Abdul Aziz	1953
Sweden	King Gustaf VI	1950
Thailand	King Bhumibol Adulyadej	1946
Yemen	King Ahmed bin Yahya Muhammed	1948

The British Commonwealth

This is a free and equal association of twelve nations: Australia, Canada, Ceylon, Ghana, India, the Federation of Malaya, New Zealand, Nigeria, Pakistan, the Federation of Rhodesia and Nyasaland, the Union of South Africa and the United Kingdom, together with colonies, protectorates and trust territories. The Queen is the Head of State for all of these with the exception of India and Pakistan, which, being republics, do not owe allegiance to her but recognise her as the Head of the Commonwealth.

The Royal Family

Her Majesty Queen Elizabeth II succeeded her father, King George VI, at his death on February 6, 1952. Her Coronation was on June 2, 1953. She was born on April 21, 1926, and on November 20, 1947, she married Prince Philip, son of Prince Andrew of Greece. Prince Philip, Duke of Edinburgh, was born on June 10, 1921. Their elder son, Prince Charles Philip Arthur George, Prince of Wales, the heir to the Throne, was born on November 14, 1948. Their daughter, Princess Anne Elizabeth Alice Louise, was born on August 15, 1950. Their younger son, Prince Andrew Albert Christian Edward, was born on February 19, 1960.

The other immediate members of the Royal Family are: Queen Elizabeth the Queen Mother, born August 4, 1900, widow of the late King George VI; Princess Margaret Rose, sister of the Queen, born August 21, 1930.

The order of succession to the throne is:

> The Prince of Wales
> Prince Andrew
> Princess Anne
> Princess Margaret
> The Duke of Gloucester and his sons
> The Duke of Kent, his brother, and his sister.

Kings and Queens of England

Name	Born		Reign	
			From	*To*
Saxons and Danes				
Egbert	*c.*	775	827	839
Ethelwulf		—	839	858
Ethelbald		—	858	860
Ethelbert		—	860	866
Ethelred I		—	866	871
Alfred the Great	*c.*	849	871	901
Edward the Elder	*c.*	870	901	925
Athelstan	*c.*	895	925	940
Edmund I	*c.*	921	940	946
Edred	*c.*	925	946	955
Edwy	*c.*	943	955	559
Edgar		944	959	975
Edward the Martyr	*c.*	963	975	978
Ethelred II, the Unready	*c.*	968	978	1016
Edmund II, Ironside	*c.*	980	1016	1016
Canute		994	1017	1035
Harold I	*c.*	1016	1035	1040
Hardicanute	*c.*	1018	1040	1042
Edward the Confessor	*c.*	1004	1042	1066
Harold II	*c.*	1020	1066	1066
House of Normandy				
William I		1027	1066	1087
William II		1057	1087	1100
Henry I		1068	1100	1135
Stephen		1104	1135	1154
House of Plantagenet				
Henry II		1133	1154	1189
Richard I		1157	1189	1199
John		1166	1199	1216
Henry III		1207	1216	1272

Edward I	1239	1272	1307
Edward II	1284	1307	1327
Edward III	1312	1327	1377
Richard II	1367	1377	1399
Henry IV	1366	1399	1413
Henry V	1388	1413	1422
Henry VI	1421	1422	1461
Edward IV	1442	1461	1483
Edward V	1470	1483	1483
Richard III	1452	1483	1485

House of Tudor

Henry VII	1457	1485	1509
Henry VIII	1491	1509	1547
Edward VI	1537	1547	1553
Jane (Lady Jane Grey)	1537	1553	1553
Mary I	1516	1553	1558
Elizabeth I	1533	1558	1603

House of Stuart

James I	1566	1603	1625
Charles I	1600	1625	1649

Commonwealth created May 19, 1649

Oliver Cromwell	1599	1653	1658
Richard Cromwell	1626	1658	1659

House of Stuart (Restoration)

Charles II	1630	1660	1685
James II	1633	1685	1688
William III }	1650	1689	{1702
Mary II }	1662		{1694
Anne	1665	1702	1714

House of Hanover

George I	1660	1714	1727
George II	1683	1727	1760

53

George III	1738	1760	1820
George IV	1762	1820	1830
William IV	1765	1830	1837
Victoria	1819	1837	1901

House of Saxe-Coburg

Edward VII	1841	1901	1910

House of Windsor

George V	1865	1910	1936
Edward VIII	1894	1936	1936
George VI	1895	1936	1952
Elizabeth II	1926	1952	

Kings and Queens of Scotland

Name	Reign	
	From	*To*
Malcolm III (Canmore)	1057	1093
Donald Bane	1093	1094
Duncan II	1094	1094
Donald Bane (restored)	1094	1097
Edgar	1097	1107
Alexander I	1107	1124
David I	1124	1153
Malcolm IV	1153	1165
William I	1165	1214
Alexander II	1214	1249
Alexander III	1249	1286
Margaret	1286	1290
John Baliol	1292	1296
Robert I (Bruce)	1306	1329
David II	1329	1371
Robert II	1371	1390
Robert III	1390	1406
James I	1406	1437

James II	1437	1460
James III	1460	1488
James IV	1488	1513
James V	1513	1542
Mary (Queen of Scots)	1542	1567
James VI (became James I of England in 1603)	1567	1625

Royal Salutes

A Royal Salute of sixty-two guns is fired at the Tower of London each year on the anniversaries of the Queen's Birth, Accession to the Throne and Coronation. Forty-one guns are fired when the Queen opens or dissolves Parliament in person, when she passes through London in procession, and on the birth of a Royal child.

The Union Jack

The Union Jack is a flag composed of three crosses. These are the crosses of St Andrew (blue and white), St Patrick (red and white) and St George (red and white). The first two are diagonal, the third vertical and horizontal. At the time it was adopted (1606) the flag contained only the crosses of St George and St Andrew, as it signified the accession of James VI of Scotland to the English Throne as James I. The cross of St Patrick (Ireland) was introduced when the Act of Union came into force in 1800. The flag is flown on government and public buildings in Britain on fourteen days of the year. Twelve of these are Royal anniversaries and the others are Empire Day (May 24) and Remembrance Sunday (November 10). It is also flown at the opening and closing of Parliament. It is flown at half-mast on occasions of the death of members of the Royal Family, certain foreign rulers, or prime ministers of Great Britain.

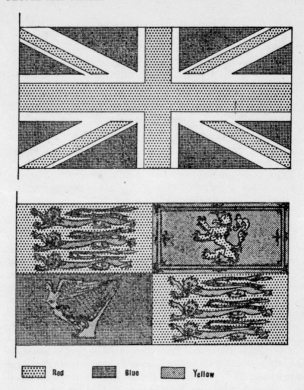

Red   Blue   Yellow

The Royal Standard

The Royal Standard is the personal flag of the Queen and is flown only on buildings in which the Queen is actually present. It is divided into four quarters. In the first and fourth are the three lions passant of England, in the second, the lion rampant of Scotland, and in the third, the harp of Ireland.

56

The White, Red and Blue Ensigns

The White Ensign, bearing the cross of St George on a white background, with the Union Jack filling the upper corner nearest the flagstaff, is the flag of the Royal Navy and the Royal Yacht Squadron.

The Red Ensign (the Red Duster) is a red flag with the Union Jack filling the upper corner nearest the flagstaff. It is flown by British merchant vessels.

The Blue Ensign is a blue flag with the Union Jack in the upper corner nearest the flagstaff. It is flown by the Royal Naval Reserve and by certain selected yacht clubs.

British Parliamentary Government

The Queen, though Head of the British Commonwealth, takes a purely formal part in government, which is carried on in each Commonwealth nation by a Prime Minister and Cabinet drawn from the membership of its Parliament. The Queen opens Parliament in Britain by making a speech from the Throne in the House of Lords, and the same ceremony has been carried out by Her Majesty in Commonwealth nations, though as she is normally resident in Britain this is usually the task of the Governor-General, who is the Queen's representative.

The method of parliamentary government varies considerably from one Commonwealth country to the next, but the pattern is based upon that of Britain, in which the Cabinet usually consists of seventeen Ministers, not more than fifteen of whom may be members of the House of Commons. There may be, in addition, twenty-three Parliamentary Secretaries, at least two of whom must be members of the House of Lords. The head of the Cabinet is the Prime Minister, whose appointment is made personally by the Queen on the recommendation of 'elder statesmen'- senior politicians with a long record in public life.

Britain's Prime Ministers

Date	Name	Party
1721	Sir Robert Walpole	Whig
1742	Earl of Wilmington	Whig
1743	Henry Pelham	Whig
1754	Duke of Newcastle	Whig
1756	Duke of Devonshire	Whig
1757	Duke of Newcastle	Whig
1762	Earl of Bute	Tory
1763	George Grenville	Whig
1765	Marquess of Rockingham	Whig
1766	William Pitt (the Elder)	Whig
1767	Duke of Grafton	Whig
1770	Lord North	Tory
1782	Marquess of Rockingham	Whig
1782	Earl of Shelburne	Whig
1783	Duke of Portland	Coalition
1783	William Pitt (the Younger)	Tory
1801	Henry Addington	Tory
1804	William Pitt (the Younger)	Tory
1806	Lord Grenville	Whig
1807	Duke of Portland	Tory
1809	Spencer Perceval	Tory
1812	Earl of Liverpool	Tory
1827	George Canning	Tory
1827	Viscount Goderich	Tory
1828	Duke of Wellington	Tory
1830	Earl Grey	Whig
1834	Viscount Melbourne	Whig
1834	Sir Robert Peel	Tory
1835	Viscount Melbourne	Whig
1841	Sir Robert Peel	Tory
1846	Lord John Russell	Whig
1852	Earl of Derby	Tory
1852	Earl of Aberdeen	Peelite

1855	Viscount Palmerston	Liberal
1858	Earl of Derby	Conservative
1858	Viscount Palmerston	Liberal
1865	Lord John Russell	Liberal
1866	Earl of Derby	Conservative
1868	Benjamin Disraeli	Conservative
1868	William E. Gladstone	Liberal
1874	Benjamin Disraeli	Conservative
1880	William E. Gladstone	Liberal
1885	Marquess of Salisbury	Conservative
1886	William E. Gladstone	Liberal
1886	Marquess of Salisbury	Conservative
1892	William E. Gladstone	Liberal
1894	Earl of Rosebery	Liberal
1895	Marquess of Salisbury	Conservative
1902	A. J. Balfour	Conservative
1905	Sir H. Campbell-Bannerman	Liberal
1908	Herbert Asquith	Liberal Coalition
1916	David Lloyd George	Coalition
1922	Andrew Bonar Law	Conservative
1923	Stanley Baldwin	Conservative
1924	J. Ramsay MacDonald	Labour
1924	Stanley Baldwin	Conservative
1929	J. Ramsay Mac Donald	Labour; Coalition
1935	Stanley Baldwin	Coalition
1937	Neville Chamberlain	Coalition
1940	Winston Churchill	Coalition
1945	Clement R. Attlee	Labour
1951	Sir Winston Churchill	Conservative
1955	Sir Anthony Eden	Conservative
1957	Harold Macmillan	Conservative

Government Departments

The following are some principal Ministries of the Government, each with the title of the Minister or Cabinet Minister at its head:

Admiralty. The Royal Navy and the maintaining of security on sea routes used by British shipping. (First Lord of the Admiralty)

Agriculture, Fisheries and Food. Farming, fishing, the maintaining and improving of food supplies, and animal health. (Minister of Agriculture)

Air Ministry. The Royal Air Force. (Secretary of State for Air)

Aviation. All civil airlines, aerodromes and aviation and missile research. (Minister of Aviation)

Colonial Office. The government of all Colonies administered directly from London. (Secretary of State for the Colonies)

Defence. The overall responsibility for national defence by the co-ordination of air, naval and military preparedness. (Minister of Defence)

Education. The organisation of the State educational system, from primary schools to universities and adult education. (Minister of Education)

Foreign Office. All matters relating to foreign countries. (Secretary of State for Foreign Affairs)

Health. The running of the National Health Service. All matters concerning medicine, nursing, hospitals and public hygiene. (Minister of Health)

Home Office. Law enforcement. The control of fire, police, prison and immigration services. (Home Secretary)

Housing and Local Government. Housing and new towns, control of the use of land and relations between central and local government. (Minister of Housing and Local Government)

Labour. All matters connected with employment. (Minister of Labour)

Pensions and National Insurance. The administration of unemployment, health and industrial injuries insurance, family allowances, widows' and retirement pensions. (Minister of Pensions and National Insurance)

Post Office. The operation of the postal collection and delivery services and telephone and telegraph services, collection of national insurance payments and certain revenues, payment of allowances and pensions and operation of the National Savings Scheme. (Postmaster-General)

Power. The provision of gas, electricity, coal, oil and petrol supplies, and the development of nuclear power. (Minister of Power)

Scottish Office. All matters of particular concern to Scotland. (Secretary of State for Scotland)

Trade, Board of. Matters affecting British industry and trade, other than those handled by the Ministries of Agriculture, Fisheries and Food, and Works. (President of the Board of Trade).

Transport. Road, rail and sea transport. (Minister of Transport)

Treasury. All matters relating to finance and the national budget. (Prime Minister and First Lord of the Treasury).

Works. Public buildings and monuments, parks, and building materials. (Minister of Works)

How Laws are Made and Who Makes Them

New laws are discussed and voted upon in the two Houses of Parliament. The House of Lords, presided over by the Lord High Chancellor, has a membership of about eight hundred, comprising Royal princes, archbishops, dukes, marquesses, earls, viscounts, bishops, barons and law lords. The House of Commons, directed by a Speaker, is an elected assembly of six hundred and thirty men and women who are paid an annual salary for full-time attendance. Each represents a constituency (or area of the country) which elected him or her by a straight majority vote at the last General Election or a later By-election caused by the death or retirement of the previous representative. The normal span of a Parliament is five years, though at any time the Queen may upon the advice of the Prime Minister dissolve Parliament and proclaim a General Election. It is also

61

possible that the Government may be defeated in the House of Commons on a major issue. It may then be forced to resign, in which case either the next strongest party forms a government, or a new election is sought.

All but a handful of the Members of the House of Commons belong to one or other of the main political parties, and after a General Election it is the party with most Members which forms the Government. At certain times of national crisis, two parties may unite to form a Coalition Government.

New Laws start as Bills. Any Member of the Lords or Commons can introduce a Bill, though the majority are brought in by the Government, based on its plans as outlined in the Queen's Speech at the Opening of Parliament. The Bill has to pass through three Readings before it is considered to be agreed by the House of Commons. It then goes forward to the House of Lords. If it is a Financial Bill the House of Lords must pass it without making any changes, but the Lords can reject any other Bill, which means it has to go back through the Commons for further consideration. If the Commons then return it to the Lords after the lapse of a year, the Lords' rejection does not prevent it being passed and forwarded to the Queen for her Assent, which in practice is automatic.

General Elections Results

The strength of Britain's political parties can be learned from the following table of voting in recent General Elections:

Party	Votes	Seats in the House of Commons
1951		
Conservative*	13,724,418	321
Labour	13,948,385	295
Liberal	730,551	6
Communist	21,640	0
Others	177,329	3

1955

Conservative*	13,311,938	345
Labour	12,405,246	277
Liberal	722,395	6
Communist	33,144	0
Others	288,031	2

1959

Conservative*	13,750,965	365
Labour	12,195,765	258
Liberal	1,661,262	6
Communist	30,897	0
Others	223,949	1 (Independent)

* *and associated parties*

Awards and Rewards

Most countries reward their great men and women by decorations for gallantry in war or titles for loyal and useful service in times of peace. In Britain, for example, a brilliant discovery by a scientist may gain him a knighthood or baronetcy.

The greatest international award is the Nobel Prize. Dr Alfred Nobel, the Swedish scientist who invented dynamite, left well over a million pounds to provide a fund which would award annual prizes of nearly fourteen thousand pounds to the most deserving man or woman working in each of the following activities: Physics Research, Chemistry Research, Physiology and Medicine, Literature, Promotion of Peace.

British Awards for Gallantry

The Victoria Cross. This was first awarded in January 1856, and the bronze crosses were made from guns captured from the enemy during the Crimean War. The last of this metal

Victoria Cross

George Cross

Distinguished Service Order

Distinguished Conduct Medal

Distinguished Service Cross

George Medal

Military Cross

Air Force Cross

Distinguished Flying Cross

Distinguished Flying Medal

Air Force Medal

Albert Medal

Military Medal

Queen's Police Medal

 Red   Blue   Purple   Claret

was used up in 1942, and since then the crosses have been made of gun-metal from the Royal Mint. The cross is worn before all other decorations. It is one-and-a-half inches across, and bears the Royal Crown surmounted by a lion. It carries the inscription 'For Valour', and has a claret ribbon. The cross is awarded to anybody serving with or under the command of the armed forces who performs an act of great bravery in the presence of the enemy.

The George Cross. First awarded in 1940, this decoration is a silver cross with a dark blue ribbon. The inscription is 'For Gallantry', and the design shows St George and the Dragon. It is awarded to civilians, and it is only given to members of the fighting services for the greatest gallantry in circumstances in which military awards could not normally be granted.

The Distinguished Service Order is awarded to officers of the armed services or the Merchant Navy.

The Distinguished Service Cross is for Royal Naval officers below the rank of captain, and warrant officers.

The Military Cross is awarded to Army and Colonial Army captains, lieutenants and regimental sergeant-majors.

The Distinguished Flying Cross is for Royal Air Force and Fleet Air Arm officers and warrant officers for gallantry while flying in operations against the enemy.

The Air Force Cross is for acts of gallantry in the air but not in operations against the enemy.

The Albert Medal is given for gallantry in saving life at sea or on land.

The Distinguished Conduct Medal is awarded to warrant officers, non-commissioned officers and men of the Army and Royal Air Force.

The Conspicuous Gallantry Medal is for warrant officers and men of the Royal Navy, Merchant Navy or Royal Air Force.

The George Medal is given for acts of gallantry.

The Queen's Police and Fire Services Medal for Gallantry.

65

The Edward Medal is for heroic acts by miners or quarrymen, or by those engaged in rescuing them.

The Distinguished Service Medal is for chief petty officers, petty officers and men of the Royal Navy, and equivalent ranks in the Royal Marines and Merchant Navy.

The Military Medal is awarded to warrant officers, non-commissioned officers and men and women of the Army.

The Distinguished Flying Medal is awarded for gallantry to non-commissioned officers and men of the Royal Air Force while flying in operations against the enemy.

British Military Insignia

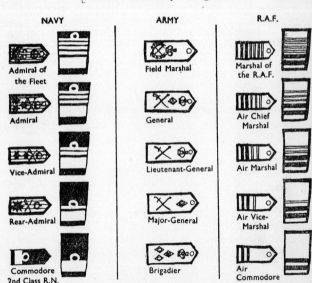

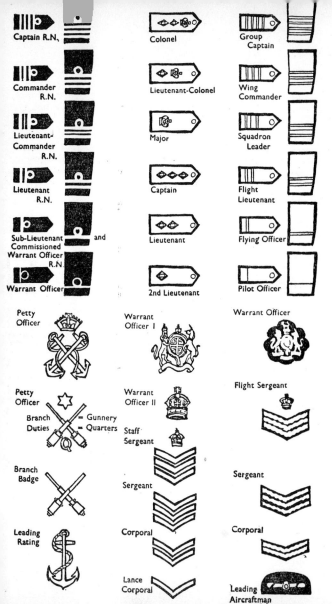

Captain R.N,

Commander R.N.

Lieutenant-Commander R.N.

Lieutenant R.N.

Sub-Lieutenant and Commissioned Warrant Officer R.N.

Warrant Officer

Colonel

Lieutenant-Colonel

Major

Captain

Lieutenant

2nd Lieutenant

Group Captain

Wing Commander

Squadron Leader

Flight Lieutenant

Flying Officer

Pilot Officer

Petty Officer

Petty Officer

Branch Duties = Gunnery = Quarters

Branch Badge

Leading Rating

Warrant Officer I

Warrant Officer II

Staff Sergeant

Sergeant

Corporal

Lance Corporal

Warrant Officer

Flight Sergeant

Sergeant

Corporal

Leading Aircraftman

The Duke of Edinburgh's Award

This is a scheme begun in 1956 for boys between the ages of fifteen and eighteen, to encourage development of character. There are three awards — bronze, silver and gold — for attaining certain standards over a wide range of activities. To gain an award a boy must demonstrate his ability in self-reliance by planning and carrying out cross-country journeys, his fitness by reaching certain athletic standards, his competence in carrying out first aid and camp work and his progress in his own chosen hobby. The scheme is run by Sir John Hunt, leader of the British Everest Expedition. Boys intending to take part can obtain details through their schools or youth clubs.

PEOPLE AND THE
NEW WORLD

It was in the fifteenth century that the people of Europe began to look for new lands in which they could find broader commercial scope and, later, personal freedom. The American continent had been discovered by Scandinavian seamen five centuries earlier, but no settlements had remained. Voyagers such as Christopher Columbus believed that a westward course would lead them to India, and so when they reached America they called it the Indies.

Settlement in North, South and Central America was rapid. The Spanish and Portuguese colonised the South, the French and English the North. The struggles for power lasted for more than a century before the present boundaries and governments became settled. Britain at one time controlled all of eastern North America, but this direct government from London came to an end with the establishment of the United States as an independent nation during the War of 1775—1783 and the creation of Canada as a Dominion in 1867.

The development of the New World has been man's greatest achievement, for it required a mass migration of countless thousands of people from Europe and Africa to colonise such an enormous area as North America, which had previously been inhabited only by wandering indigenous tribes, wrongly called 'Indians'. Two hundred years ago the United States was a group of British colonies on the Eastern seaboard, still struggling to win a living from a new

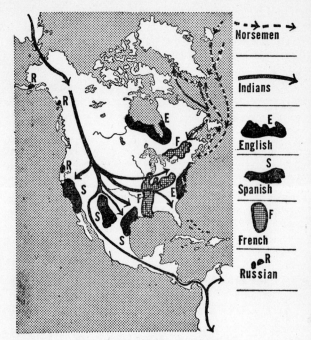

American early settlements

country, to cut back the forests and plough the land in order to grow crops which would pay for their imports from Europe. Today the United States is the wealthiest nation in the world, with one of the highest standards of living. In material assets, it has more cars, telephones, television sets, radios, etc., per thousand of its population than any other nation. Canada, though slower to develop, has raised its standard of living in very much the same way.

Canada

Canada is made up of twelve provinces and territories, listed below with their dates of admission as provinces:

Province or Territory	Capital	Date of Admission	Population
Alberta	Edmonton	1905	1,255,000
British Columbia	Victoria	1871	1,500,000
Manitoba	Winnipeg	1870	849,000
New Brunswick	Fredericton	1867	558,000
Newfoundland	St. John's	1949	447,000
Nova Scotia	Halifax	1867	700,000
Ontario	Toronto	1867	5,983,000
Prince Edward Island	Charlottetown	1873	107,000
Quebec	Quebec	1867	4,800,000
Saskatchewan	Regina	1905	885,000
Northwest Territories	—	—	18.000
Yukon Territory	Whitehorse	—	10,000

Growth of the United States in population

♦ = 5 million people

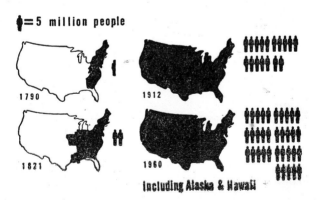

Including Alaska & Hawaii

71

The United States

The United States is made up of fifty States and the Federal District (Washington, D. C.). These are as follows:

Name and Abbreviation	Capital	Date of Admission to the Union
Alabama (Ala.)	Montgomery	1819
Alaska	Juneau	1959
Arizona (Ariz.)	Phoenix	1912
Arkansas (Ark.)	Little Rock	1836
California (Calif.)	Sacramento	1850
Colorado (Colo.)	Denver	1876
Connecticut (Conn.)	Hartford	1788*
Delaware (Del.)	Dover	1787*
District of Columbia (D. C.)	Washington	1791
Florida (Fla.)	Tallahassee	1845
Georgia (Ga.)	Atlanta	1788*
Hawaii	Honolulu	1959
Idaho	Boise	1890
Illinois (Ill.)	Springfield	1818
Indiana (Ind.)	Indianapolis	1816
Iowa (Ia.)	Des Moines	1846
Kansas (Kans.)	Topeka	1861
Kentucky (Ky.)	Frankfort	1792
Louisiana (La.)	Baton Rouge	1812
Maine (Me.)	Augusta	1820
Maryland (Md.)	Annapolis	1788*
Massachusetts (Mass.)	Boston	1788*
Michigan (Mich.)	Lansing	1837
Minnesota (Minn.)	St Paul	1858
Mississippi (Miss.)	Jackson	1817
Missouri (Mo.)	Jefferson City	1821
Montana (Mont.)	Helena	1889
Nebraska (Nebr.)	Lincoln	1867

Queen Elizabeth — world's largest liner

United States

Liberté

Queen Mary   *Oriana*

Flandre

Caronia   *Rotterdam*

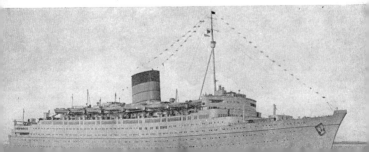

Old *Mauretania*

New *Mauretania*

Nevada (Nev.)	Carson City	1864
New Hampshire (N. H.)	Concord	1788*
New Jersey (N. J.)	Trenton	1787*
New Mexico (N. Mex.)	Santa Fe	1912
New York (N. Y.)	Albany	1788*
North Carolina (N. C.)	Raleigh	1789*
North Dakota (N. Dak.)	Bismarck	1889
Ohio	Columbus	1803
Oklahoma (Okla.)	Oklahoma City	1907
Oregon (Oreg.)	Salem	1859
Pennsylvania (Pa.)	Harrisburg	1787*
Rhode Island (R. I.)	Providence	1790*
South Carolina (S. C.)	Columbia	1788*
South Dakota (S. Dak.)	Pierre	1889
Tennessee (Tenn.)	Nashville	1796
Texas (Tex.)	Austin	1845
Utah	Salt Lake City	1896
Vermont (Vt.)	Montpelier	1791
Virginia (Va.)	Richmond	1788*
Washington (Wash.)	Olympia	1889
West Virginia (W. Va.)	Charleston	1863
Wisconsin (Wis.)	Madison	1848
Wyoming (Wyo.)	Cheyenne	1890

One of the Thirteen Original States

Presidents of the United States

In the American system of government the President combines his Presidential powers with many of those held by a Prime Minister under a system such as that in most Commonwealth countries, and is, therefore, a man of great personal influence during his term of office. The Presidents of the United States have been:

Name	Party	Came to Office
George Washington	Federalist	1789
John Adams	Federalist	1797
Thomas Jefferson	Democratic-Republican	1801
James Madison	Democratic-Republican	1809
James Monroe	Democratic-Republican	1817
John Quincy Adams	Coalition	1825
Andrew Jackson	Democratic	1829
Martin Van Buren	Democratic	1837
William Henry Harrison	Whig	1841
John Tyler	Whig	1841
James Knox Polk	Democratic	1845
Zachary Taylor	Whig	1849
Millard Fillmore	Whig	1850
Franklin Pierce	Democratic	1853
James Buchanan	Democratic	1857
Abraham Lincoln	Republican	1861
Andrew Johnson	Republican	1865
Ulysses Simpson Grant	Republican	1869
Rutherford Birchard Hayes	Republican	1877
James Abram Garfield	Republican	1881
Chester Alan Arthur	Republican	1881
Grover Cleveland	Democratic	1885 and 1893
Benjamin Harrison	Republican	1889
William McKinley	Republican	1897
Theodore Roosevelt	Republican	1901
William Howard Taft	Republican	1909
Woodrow Wilson	Democratic	1913
Warren Gamaliel Harding	Republican	1921
Calvin Coolidge	Republican	1923
Herbert Clark Hoover	Republican	1929
Franklin Delano Roosevelt	Democratic	1933
Harry S. Truman	Democratic	1945
Dwight D. Eisenhower	Republican	1953

Central and South America and the Caribbean

The countries of Central and South America are independent with the exception of British Honduras, British and French Guiana and Surinam (Netherlands Guiana). They are:

Name	Date of Gaining Independence
Argentina	1816
Bolivia	1825
Brazil	1822
Chile	1818
Colombia	1819
Costa Rica	1821
Ecuador	1822
Guatemala	1821
Honduras	1821
Mexico	1810
Nicaragua	1821
Panamá	1903
Paraguay	1811
Peru	1821
El Salvador	1821
Uruguay	1825
Venezuela	1821

The three independent Caribbean countries are:

Cuba	1902
Dominican Republic	1821
Haiti	1804

PEOPLE ON THE MOVE

Two hundred years ago man's fastest way of getting from place to place or sending a message was on horseback. The following information shows how much the picture has changed.

Man's Fastest Speed

The fastest speed yet reached by man is probably over 2,000 miles an hour, in an American rocket plane, but complete details about this have not yet been published. The official record is 1,404.19 miles an hour, set up by Captain W. W. Irwin of the U. S. Air Force, flying over the Mojave Desert in California, on May 16, 1958. Flights such as this are made at high altitudes.

Land Speed Record

The fastest speed on land is a record of 403.135 miles an hour, set up by the late John Cobb, of Britain, on September 16, 1947, on Bonneville Salt Beds, U. S. A.

Water Speed Record

The water speed record of 260.35 miles an hour, set up on Coniston Water in Lancashire on May 14, 1959, stands to the credit of Donald Campbell, son of the late Sir Malcolm Campbell, holder of both land and water speed records in the nineteen-thirties.

Great Ships; The Blue Riband of the Atlantic

The fifteenth-century voyages of Columbus to America took many weeks of hardship; today it takes five days to cross from Britain to the United States and would take less than four days at maximum speeds. For nearly a century there has been keen competition between the great seafaring nations for the Blue Riband — the Championship of the Atlantic. The following table shows the progress of the Blue Riband since 1900.

Year	Direction	Ship	Tonnage	Time		
				d.	h.	m.
1900	West-East	Deutschland (German)	16,502	5	7	38
1904	West-East	Kaiser Wilhelm II (German)	19,361	5	8	16
1909	East-West	Lusitania (British)	31,550	4	11	42
1909	East-West	Mauretania (British)	31,938	4	10	51
1929	West-East	Bremen (German)	51,650	4	14	30
1929	East-West	Bremen		4	17	42
1930	East-West	Europa (German)	51,656	4	17	6
1933	East-West	Bremen		4	17	43
1933	East-West	Rex (Italian)	50,000	4	13	58
1934	West-East	Empress of Britain (British)	42,348	4	6	58
1935	East-West	Normandie (French)	80,000	4	3	2
1936	East-West	Queen Mary (British)	81,237	4	0	27
1936	West-East	Queen Mary		3	23	57
1937	East-West	Normandie		3	23	2
1938	East-West	Queen Mary		3	21	48
1938	West-East	Queen Mary		3	20	42
1952	West-East	United States (American)	53,330	3	10	40
1952	East-West	United States		3	12	12

The largest merchant ship afloat is the ocean liner *Queen Elizabeth* (British: 83,673 tons). The ten largest ocean liners in the world are the *Queen Elizabeth*, *Queen Mary* (British: 81,237 tons), *United States* (American: 53,330 tons), *Liberté* (French: 51,839 tons), *Oriana* (British: 40,000 tons), *Rotterdam* (Netherlands: 38,650 tons), *Windsor Castle* (British:

38,000 tons), *Nieuw Amsterdam* (Netherlands: 36,667 zons),
Mauretania (British: 35,655 tons) and *Caronia* (British:
34,172 tons).

Great Ship Canals

	Year Opened	Length (miles)	Width (feet)	Depth (feet)
Gota (Sweden)	1832	115	47	10
Suez (Egypt)	1869	100	197	34
Albert (Belgium)	1939	80	53	16½
Kiel (Germany)	1895	61	144	37
Panamá (Canal Zone)	1914	50	110	45
				(min.)
Elbe (Germany)	1900	41	72	10
Manchester (England)	1894	35	120	28—30
Welland (Canada)*	1887	27	80	25
Amsterdam (Netherlands)	1876	16½	88	23
Corinth (Greece)	1893	4	72	26

Reconstructed, and reopened 1931

Railways

The first steam railway locomotive was tried out in 1804
at Merthyr Tydfil in Wales, but the first to be successful was
the famous *Puffing Billy*, installed at Wylam Colliery near
Newcastle-on-Tyne in 1813, and in use until 1872 when it
was bought by the government to be kept as a museum piece.
In 1825 the Stockton and Darlington Railway was opened
for goods traffic using a locomotive supplied by George
Stephenson. Stephenson was the successful winner four years
later, with his locomotive *Rocket*, of a competition to choose
the locomotive for the Liverpool and Manchester Railway.
Stephenson's locomotive drew thirty passengers at up to
twenty-nine miles an hour. Today there are probably nearly
a million miles of railway in the world, and the French have
a locomotive capable of speeds over 200 miles an hour.

British Railways

British Railways have 50,914 miles of track and 5,264 passenger stations. Over 1,000,000,000 originating passenger journeys are made in a year. Other facts about British Railways are:

Number of bridges	63,100
Number of tunnels	1,049
Locomotives (including steam, diesel and electric)	17,381
Passenger carriages	42,003
Goods wagons	1,020,197
Ships working in conjunction with system	121
Largest station in area	Clapham Junction (27³/₄ acres)
Station with largest number of platforms	Waterloo (21)
Longest platform	Manchester (Victoria and Exchange, 2,194 ft)
Track with highest altitude	Druimuachdar (1,484 feet above sea level)

The six Regions of British Railways are:

London Midland Region (formerly the London Midland and Scottish Company in the areas of England and Wales)

Western Region (formerly the Great Western Railway)

Southern Region (formerly the Southern Railway)

Eastern Region (formerly the Southern area of the London and North Eastern Railway)

North Eastern Region (formerly the North Eastern area of the London and North Eastern Railway)

Scottish Region (formerly the Scottish areas of the London Midland and Scottish and the London and North Eastern Railways)

79

Great Railway Tunnels

Name	Location	Length (miles)
City — Northern	London	$17\frac{1}{4}$
West End — Northern	London	16
Simplon No. 1	Switzerland	$12\frac{1}{4}$
Simplon No. 2	Switzerland	$12\frac{1}{4}$
Apennine	Italy	$11\frac{1}{2}$
St Gotthard	Switzerland	$9\frac{1}{4}$
Loetschberg	Switzerland	9
Mont Cenis	France	$8\frac{1}{2}$
Cascade	South Dakota, U. S. A.	$7\frac{3}{4}$
Arlberg	Austria	$6\frac{1}{3}$
Moffat	Colorado, U. S. A.	6
Shimizu	Japan	6
Kvineshei	Norway	$5\frac{3}{4}$
Rimutaka	New Zealand	$5\frac{1}{2}$
Otira	New Zealand	$5\frac{1}{4}$
Tauern	Austria	$5\frac{1}{4}$
Connaught	British Columbia, Canada	5
Ste Marie-aux-Mines	France	$4\frac{1}{2}$
Severn	England	$4\frac{1}{4}$

Principal Railway Gauges of the World

Gauge	Where in Use
5 ft 6 in.	Spain, Portugal, Argentina, Chile, India, Ceylon, Pakistan
5 ft 3 in.	Ireland, Brazil, Victoria (Australia), South Australia
5 ft 0 in.	U. S. S. R.
4 ft $8\frac{1}{2}$ in.	Great Britain, Europe (except Portugal, Spain, U. S. S. R.), Canada, U. S. A., Mexico, Uruguay, Peru, North Africa, Middle East, Egypt, Turkey, Australian Commonwealth, New South Wales (Australia), China, Korea

3 ft 6 in.	South and Western Australia, Queensland (Australia), New Zealand, Tasmania, South Africa, East and West Africa, Indonesia, Sudan, Sweden, Norway, Japan, Newfoundland (Canada), Costa Rica, Nicaragua, Honduras
3 ft 5¼ in.	Algeria, Jordan, Syria
3 ft 3⅜ in.	South America, East and West Africa, Malaya, Burma, Thailand, Indo-China, Indonesia
3 ft 0 in.	Ireland, South America, El Salvador, Guatemala, Panamá
2 ft 11 in.	Sweden
2 ft 6 in.	India, Ceylon
2 ft 0 in.	South America, India, Pakistan, Wales

Some Principal Wheel Notations for British and American Steam Locomotives

Wheels	Notation	Type
oO	2-2-0	Planet
oOo	2-2-2	Jenny Lind
ooOo	4-2-2	Bicycle
OO	0-4-0	Four-wheel Switch
OOo	0-4-2	
ooOO	4-4-0	American
oOOo	2-4-2	Columbia
ooOOo	4-4-2	Atlantic
OOoo	0-4-4	Four-coupled
OOooo	0-4-6	Four-coupled
ooOOoo	4-4-4	Jubilee
OOO	0-6-0	Six-wheel Switch
OOOo	0-6-2	
oOOO	2-6-0	Mogul
ooOOO	4-6-0	Ten-wheel
oOOOo	2-6-2	Prairie
ooOOOo	4-6-2	Pacific
OOOoo	0-6-4	Six-coupled

OOOooo	0-6-6	Six-coupled
oOOOoo	2-6-4	Adriatic
ooOOOoo	4-6-4	Hudson
OOOO	0-8-0	Eight-wheel
oOOOO	2-8-0	Consolidation
ooOOOO	4-8-0	Twelve-wheel
oOOOOo	2-8-2	Mikado
ooOOOOo	4-8-2	Mountain
oOOOOoo	2-8-4	Berkshire
ooOOOOoo	4-8-4	Northern
oOOOOO	2-10-0	Decapod
ooOOOOO	4-10-0	Mastodon
oOOOOOo	2-10-2	Santa Fe
ooOOOOOo	4-10-2	Overland
oOOOOOoo	2-10-4	Texas
ooOOOOOOo	4-12-2	Union Pacific
oOOO OOOo	2-6-6-2	

Navigation

How does a ship find its way across thousand of miles of ocean and yet arrive at the harbour mouth as unerringly as a car steered home to its garage?

A nautical chart looks much like a road map, except that the roads are 'sea lanes', with lightships, buoys, shoals and sandbanks instead of towns, railways, church towers and hilltops. And, of course, the lines of latitude and longitude are clearly marked.

Before leaving port, the ship's navigator marks out his route on the chart. This chart is generally on what is known as 'Mercator's Projection', which means all the lines of longitude, or meridians, run parallel, whereas in reality of course, they meet at the Poles. The compass points to *Magnetic* North, which is a variable number of miles away from *True* North, so that in working out the course the navigator must allow for this variation. This may be ten or more degrees — and it is found on the 'compass rose', a compass diagram printed on the chart at frequent intervals, or published in nautical tables.

For a course due East — 90° — with a variation of 10° East the *Magnetic* course would be 80°. But before setting this for the helmsman, the navigator checks his deviation card — a note of any errors in the compass when it was last tested. Suppose the deviation is 2° West; then that would have to be *added* to the figure of 80° to give the final compass course that the helmsman will follow.

But the helm alone won't keep a ship on its course, so at sea the navigator uses the chronometer and sextant to check at regular intervals. The time of the ship's clocks is changed as it travels East or West of the Greenwich Meridian (0° longitude), and the difference between the ship's clocks (showing local time) and the chronometer (showing Greenwich time) tells the navigator his longitude. This is a simple calculation: there are 360° of longitude, and the earth turns once on its axis in every 24 hours; 360 divided by 24 gives us 15 — which means one hour of 'sun's progress' equals 15°. When it is noon at Greenwich, it is 1 p. m. if you are 15° East, and 11 a. m. if you are 15° West.

Latitude is checked by a sextant. This is a device for measuring angles, and as we know from generations of navigation just where the sun ought to be at a given latitude on any particular occasion, and where each of the principal stars should appear at night, a check of the angle between the sun, moon or stars and the horizon provides a figure which need only be looked up in a standard book of tables carried by every ship.

This, of course, is the method out at sea, where no landmarks are available to help in navigation. Along the coast the task of the officer on the bridge is much easier, for he can take bearings of lighthouses, church spires, prominent hilltops and other easily recognisable points marked on his chart. Where the bearings intersect is the ship's position.

Radio is another important aid to the navigator. He can take bearings from radio beacons — fixed points which send out radio signals in the same way that a lighthouse transmits intermittent beams of light. And, most important of all, he can use radar, a British invention which makes it possible for the navigator to know where ships, wrecks, buoys and other dangers are in relation to his own vessel. The radar set sends out ultra-short-wave impulses in all directions; any of these striking an object sends back an echo to the set, and this appears as a bright dot on the monitor screen.

Distances by Sea

Using normal shipping routes, these are the distances of some of the world's principal seaports from Britain.

Name	Distance (miles)	Name	Distance (miles)
Alexandria (Egypt)	2,950	Mombasa (Kenya)	5,980
Basra (Iraq)	6,053	Montreal (Canada)	2,760
Bombay (India)	5,910	New York (U.S.A.)	3,118
Cape Town (South Africa)	5,978	Rangoon (Burma)	7,590
Copenhagen (Denmark)	683	Rio de Janeiro (Brazil)	5,030
Gothenburg (Sweden)	584	Sydney (Australia)	12,201
Hong Kong	9,743	Tunis (North Africa)	2,050
Karachi (Pakistan)	5,730	Valparaiso (Chile)	7,207
Manila (Philippine Islands)	9,650	Wellington (New Zealand)	11,096
Marseilles (France)	1,833	Yokohama (Japan)	11,536

Notable Bridges of the World

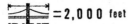

= 2,000 feet

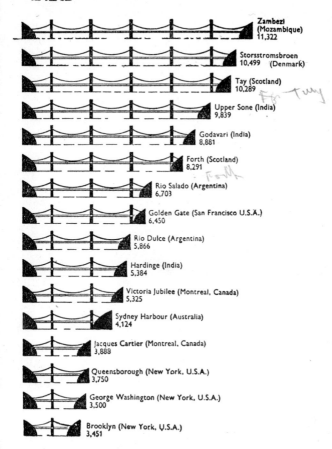

Zambezi (Mozambique) 11,322

Storsstromsbroen 10,499 (Denmark)

Tay (Scotland) 10,289

Upper Sone (India) 9,839

Godavari (India) 8,881

Forth (Scotland) 8,291

Rio Salado (Argentina) 6,703

Golden Gate (San Francisco U.S.A.) 6,450

Rio Dulce (Argentina) 5,866

Hardinge (India) 5,384

Victoria Jubilee (Montreal, Canada) 5,325

Sydney Harbour (Australia) 4,124

Jacques Cartier (Montreal, Canada) 3,888

Queensborough (New York, U.S.A.) 3,750

George Washington (New York, U.S.A.) 3,500

Brooklyn (New York, U.S.A.) 3,451

Distances by Air

These are the distances of principal world cities from London by air, using the shortest routes.

Name	Distance (miles)	Name	Distance (miles)
Aden	4,104	Madrid (Spain)	775
Amsterdam (Netherlands)	231	Melbourne (Australia)	11,934
Athens (Greece)	1,501	Montreal (Canada)	3,310
Baghdad (Iraq)	3,063	Moscow (U.S.S.R.)	1,549
Berlin (Germany)	593	Munich (Germany)	588
Bombay (India)	4,901	Nairobi (Kenya)	4,429
Brussels (Belgium)	218	New York (U.S.A.)	3,500
Chicago (U.S.A.)	4,127	Nicosia (Cyprus)	2,028
Colombo (Ceylon)	5,854	Oslo (Norway)	722
Copenhagen (Denmark)	609	Paris (France)	215
Djakarta (Indonesia)	8,337	Prague (Czechoslovakia)	670
Geneva (Switzerland)	468	Rome (Italy)	908
Gibraltar	1,085	San Francisco (U.S.A.)	6,169
Hong Kong	8,102	Singapore	7,678
Johannesburg (South Africa)	6,277	Stockholm (Sweden)	899
Karachi (Pakistan)	4,428	Teheran (Persia)	3,419
Kingston (Jamaica)	5,207	Tel Aviv (Israel)	2,230
Kuala Lumpur (Malaya)	7,883	Tokyo (Japan)	10,066
Lagos (Nigeria)	3,401	Venice (Italy)	703
Lisbon (Portugal)	972	Vienna (Austria)	791
		Warsaw (Poland)	914

Local Time throughout the World

As you travel eastwards from Greenwich, the longitude time (see under Navigation) is one hour later for every

15°; to the west it is an hour earlier. But for convenience local clocks don't always show the correct longitude time, otherwise travellers inside even a quite small country would be constantly confused. In Britain, all clocks show Greenwich time; only in big countries such as Canada, the U. S. S. R., the United States, etc., are time zones necessary.

Here are the local times in various big cities of the world when it is noon at Greenwich:

City	Time		City	Time	
Adelaide (Austra-			Chicago (U.S.A.)	6	a.m.
lia)	9.30	p.m.	Colombo		
Algiers (Algeria)		noon	(Ceylon)	5.30	p.m.
Amsterdam			Copenhagen		
(Netherlands)	1	p.m.	(Denmark)	1	p.m.
Ankara (Turkey)	2	p.m.	Dakar (Senegal)	11	a.m.
Athens (Greece)	2	p.m.	Djakarta		
Belgrade			(Indonesia)	8	p.m.
(Yugoslavia)	1	p.m.	Dublin (Ireland)		noon
Berlin (Germany)	1	p.m	Edinburgh		
Bombay (India)	5.30	p.m.	(Scotland)		noon
Boston (U.S.A.)	7	a.m.	Gibraltar	1	p.m.
Brussels (Belgium)	1	p.m.	Guatemala City		
Bucharest			(Guatemala)	6	a.m.
(Rumania)	2	p.m.	Guayaquil		
Budapest			(Ecuador)	7	a.m.
(Hungary)	1	p.m.	Halifax (Canada)	8	a.m.
Buenos Aires			Havana (Cuba)	7	a.m.
(Argentina)	9	a.m.	Helsinki (Finland)	2	p.m.
Cairo (Egypt)	2	p.m.	Hobart		
Calcutta (India)	5.30	p.m.	(Tasmania)	10	p.m.
Canton (China)	8	p.m.	Hong Kong	8	p.m.
Cape Town			Honolulu (U.S.A.)	2	a.m.
(South Africa)	2	p.m.	Johannesburg		
Caracas			(South Africa)	2	p.m.
(Venezuela)	7.30	a.m.			

Karachi			Peking (China)	8	p.m.
(Pakistan)	5	p.m.	Perth (Australia)	8	p.m.
Kingston			Prague (Czecho-		
(Jamaica)	7	a.m.	slovakia)	1	p.m.
La Paz (Bolivia)	8	a.m.	Rangoon (Burma)	6.30	p.m.
Leningrad			Reykjavik		
(U.S.S.R.)	2	p.m.	(Iceland)	11	a.m.
Léopoldville			Rio de Janeiro		
(Congo)	1	p.m.	(Brazil)	9	a.m.
Lima (Peru)	7	a.m.	Rome (Italy)	1	p.m.
Lisbon (Portugal)		noon	San Francisco		
Madrid (Spain)	1	p.m.	(U.S.A.)	4	a.m.
Manila (Philip-			Santiago (Chile)	8	a.m.
pine Islands)	8	p.m.	Shanghai (China)	8	p.m.
Mecca (Saudi			Singapore	7.30	p.m.
Arabia)	3	p.m.	Sofia (Bulgaria)	2	p.m.
Melbourne			Stockholm		
(Australia)	10	p.m.	(Sweden)	1	p.m.
Mexico City			Sydney		
(Mexico)	6	a.m.	(Australia)	10	p.m.
Montevideo			Teheran (Persia)	3.30	p.m.
(Uruguay)	9	a.m.	Tel Aviv (Israel)	2	p.m.
Montreal			Tokyo (Japan)	9	p.m.
(Canada)	7	a.m.	Toronto (Canada)	7	a.m.
Moscow			Vancouver		
(U.S.S.R.)	2	p.m.	(Canada)	4	a.m.
Nairobi (Kenya)	3	p.m.	Vienna (Austria)	1	p.m.
New Orleans			Warsaw (Poland)	1	p.m.
(U.S.A.)	6	a.m.	Wellington (New		
New York			Zealand)		midnight
(U.S.A.)	7	a.m.	Winnipeg		
Oslo (Norway)	1	p.m.	(Canada)	6	a.m.
Panamá City			Zürich		
(Panamá)	7	a.m.	(Switzerland)	1	p.m.
Paris (France)	1	p.m.			

Brooklyn Bridge — New York

Sydney Harbour Bridge — Australia

Golden Gate Bridge — San Francisco

French Electric Locomotive *BB-9004* can reach 205.6 m. p. h.

Fastest Steam Locomotive, British *Bristolian*

Canadian Diesel

British *Stirling No. 1* (1870) saw 37 years' service

U. S. Streamlined 'Pacific' Type Steam Locomotive

British 'Pacific' Type Steam Locomotive

Aircraft Spotting

When travelling by air you can easily tell the country of origin of other aircraft you see around you by their registration marks. All planes other than military aircraft carry two groups of letters on the wings. The first group indicates the country of origin, thus 'G-ABC' would be a British aircraft with the distinguishing letters 'ABC'. The national markings are these:

Marking	Country	Marking	Country
AN	Nicaragua	HI	Dominican Republic
AP	Pakistan		
B	Formosa	HK	Colombia
CB	Bolivia	HL	Korea
CC	Chile	HP	Panamá
CCCP	U.S.S.R.	HS	Thailand
CF	Canada	HZ	Saudi Arabia
CN	Morocco	I	Italy
CR	Portuguese Colonies	JA	Japan
		JY	Jordan
CS	Portugal	LG	Guatemala
CU	Cuba	LN	Norway
CX	Uruguay	LV	Argentina
CZ	Monaco	LX	Luxembourg
D	Germany	LZ	Bulgaria
EC	Spain	N	U.S.A.
EI	Ireland	OB	Peru
EL	Liberia	OD	Lebanon
EP	Persia	OE	Austria
ET	Ethiopia	OH	Finland
F	France	OK	Czecho-slovakia
G	Great Britain		
HA	Hungary	OO	Belgium (and Colonies)
HB	Switzerland		
HC	Ecuador	OY	Denmark
HH	Haiti	PH	Netherlands

PI	Philippine Islands	XA, XB, XC	Mexico
PJ	Netherlands Antilles	XH	Honduras
PK	Indonesia	XT	China(People's Republic)
PP, PT	Brazil	XY, XZ	Burma
PZ	Surinam	YA	Afghanistan
SA	Libya	YE	Yemen
SE	Sweden	YI	Iraq
SN	Sudan	YJ	New Hebrides
SP	Poland	YK	Syria
SU	Egypt	YR	Roumania
SX	Greece	YS	El Salvador
TC	Turkey	YU	Yugoslavia
TF	Iceland	YV	Venezuela
TI	Costa Rica	ZA	Albania
VH	Australia	ZK	New Zealand
VQ, VP, VR	British Colonies and Protectorates	ZP	Paraguay
		ZS	Union of South Africa
VT	India	3W	Vietnam
		4R	Ceylon
		4X	Israel

Car Spotting

If you're keen on car spotting, carry your Handbook with you when you're on a journey. The following tables will help you to identify cars from overseas, for cars travelling outside their countries of registration carry special identification letters as well as their normal registration plates. The national markings are:

Marking	Country	Marking	Country
A	Austria	AUS	Australia*
ADN	Aden*	B	Belgium
AL	Albania	BDS	Barbados*
AND	Andorra	BG	Bulgaria

BH	British Honduras	FL	Liechtenstein
BL	Basutoland*	GB	Great Britain*
BP	Bechuanaland*	GBA	Alderney*
BR	Brazil	GBG	Guernsey*
BRG	British Guiana*	GBJ	Jersey*
BRN	Bahrain*	GBM	Isle of Man*
BRU	Brunei*	GBY	Malta*
BS	Bahamas*	GBZ	Gibraltar
BUR, BA	Burma*	GCA, G	Guatemala
C	Cuba*	GN	Ghana
CDN	Canada	GR	Greece
CH	Switzerland	H	Hungary
CL	Ceylon*	HK	Hong Kong*
CNB	British North Borneo*	I	Italy
		IL	Israel
CO	Colombia	IND	India*
CR	Costa Rica	IR	Persia
ČS	Czechoslovakia	IRQ	Iraq
CY	Cyprus*	IS	Iceland*
D	Germany (Federal Republic)	JA	Jamaica*
		JOR	Jordan
DK	Denmark	K	Cambodia
DOM	Dominican Republic	KWT	Kuwait
		L	Luxembourg
E	Spain (also Colonies and Protectorates)	MA	Morocco
		MC	Monaco
		MEX	Mexico
EAK	Kenya*	MS	Mauritius*
EAT	Tanganyika*	N	Norway
EAU	Uganda*	NA	Netherlands Antilles
EAZ	Zanzibar*		
EIR	Ireland*	NGN	Netherlands New Guinea*
EQ	Ecuador		
ET	Egypt	NIC	Nicaragua
F	France (also Colonies and Protectorates)	NL	Netherlands
		NP	Nyasaland*

91

NR	Northern Rhodesia*	SU	U. S. S. R.
P	Portugal (also Colonies and Protectorates)	SWA	South West Africa
		SY	Seychelles*
		SYR	Syria
PA	Panamá	T	Thailand*
PAK	Pakistan*	TD	Trinidad and Tobago*
PE	Peru		
PI	Philippine Islands	TN	Tunisia
PL	Poland	TR	Turkey
PY	Paraguay*	U	Uruguay
R	Roumania	USA	U.S.A.
RA	Argentina	V	Vatican City
RC	China (People's Republic)	VN	Vietnam
		WAG	Gambia*
RCH	Chile	WAL	Sierra Leone*
RH	Haiti	WAN	Nigeria*
RI	Indonesia	WD	Dominica (Windward Islands)*
RL	Lebanon		
RSM	San Marino	WG	Grenada (Windward Islands)*
S	Sweden*		
SD	Swaziland*	WL	St Lucia (Windward Islands)*
SF	Finland		
SGP	Singapore*	WV	St Vincent (Windward Islands)*
SK	Sarawak*		
SME	Surinam	YU	Yugoslavia
SP	Somalia	YV	Venezuela
SR	Southern Rhodesia*	ZA	Union of South Africa*

Countries where driving on the left prevails.

Signalling

Travel and communications require efficient systems of signalling. In 1588, when the Spanish Armada threatened to attack Britain, huge bonfires were built on hilltops across the country, and it was arranged that if invasion came these bonfires would be lit in turn to pass the warning. Later came signal stations on hilltops, relaying messages by means of mirrors reflecting the sun. These were in use by the Royal Navy for sending messages between London and Portsmouth Dockyard from 1795 until 1847. During the last thirty years before the electric telegraph replaced these signal stations, the system in use was the Semaphore Code, using a mast with two arms. Semaphore is now used mainly as a method of flag signalling by scouts, campers and mountaineers.

Semaphore Code

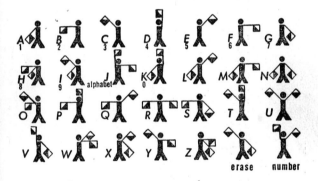

Before starting a Semaphore message it is customary to hoist the letters 'VOX' or 'I' in International Code flags. Transmission is opened by giving the Alphabetical Sign, then waiting for the signal 'C' in reply as an indication to go ahead. When numbers are to be sent, the Numerical Sign is made; on return to ordinary letters the Alphabetical Sign is given.

93

International Code

Ships at sea communicate by radio, Morse Code transmitted by signal lamps or the International Code of flag signals. The flag signals are shown opposite:

The flags marked 'Substitutes' are used to repeat a flag which is already in a hoist. An abbreviated code is used for single-flag hoists, to transmit the following standard messages:

A : I am undergoing speed trials.
B : I have explosives on board.
C : Yes.
D : Keep clear, I am in difficulties.
E : I am altering course to starboard.
F : I am disabled.
G : I require a pilot.
H : Pilot is on board.
I : I am altering course to port.
J : I am sending a message by Semaphore.
K : Stop at once.
L : Stop, I wish to communicate with you.
M : A doctor is on board.
N : No.
O : Man overboard.
P (The Blue Peter): I am about to sail.
Q : Quarantine flag.
R : I have stopped.
S : I am going astern.
T : Do not pass ahead of me.
U : You are in danger.
V : I need help.
W : Send a doctor.
X : Stop, and watch for my signals.
Y : I am carrying mails.
Z : I am calling a shore station.
RY (flying from the masthead): Crew have mutinied.

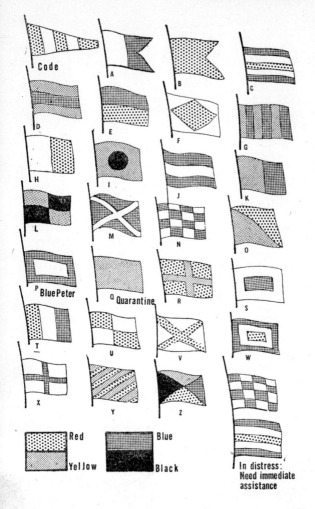

Code
A
B
C
D
E
F
G
H
I
J
K
L
M
N
O
P Blue Peter
Q Quarantine
R
S
T
U
V
W
X
Y
Z

Red
Yellow
Blue
Black

In distress:
Need immediate
assistance

95

The following combinations of two letters on the halyards hoisted to the yardarm signify:

AD : I must abandon my ship.
CG : Alight as near to me as possible.
IX : Seriously damaged in collision.
KA : Vessel is very seriously damaged.
KT : Do you have a line-throwing apparatus?
NC : I am in distress and need immediate assistance.

Morse Code

An American artist, Samuel F. B. Morse (1791—1872), invented the Code that bears his name, to simplify the method of sending messages by telegraph — of which he has equal claim with Britain's Professor Wheatstone to be the inventor. Morse can be sent on a hand key by a skilled operator at up to twenty-five words a minute, but automatic transmitters can exceed this many times, and also 'scramble' the coded message by variations of speed so that only a receiving set equipped with the same system of speed controls can interpret it.

The Code consists of dots and dashes, a dash being equal to three dots. A gap equal to one dot is left between each symbol; twice as much is left between each letter, and a longer break, preferably at least the length of a dash, between words.

The International Morse Code is as follows:

A	. —	H	. . . .
B	— . . .	I	. .
C	— . — .	J	. — — —
D	— . .	K	— . —
E	.	L	. — . .
F	. . — .	M	— —
G	— — .	N	— .

O	— — —	Z	— — . .
P	. — — .	1	. — — — —
Q	— — . —	2	. . — — —
R	. — .	3	. . . — —
S	. . .	4	. . . . —
T	—	5	. . . . .
U	. . —	6	— . . . .
V	. . . —	7	— — . . .
W	. — —	8	— — — . .
X	— . . —	9	— — — — .
Y	— . — —	0	— — — — —

Full stop	. — . — . —
Semicolon	— . — . — .
Comma	— — . . — —
Colon	— — — . . .
Question	. . — — . .
Apostrophe	. — — — — .
Hyphen	— . . . . —
Bracket	— . — — . —
Inverted commas	. — . . — .
Underline	. . — — . —
Double dash	— . . . —
Distress signal (S.O.S.)	. . . — — — . . .
Attention signal	— . — . —
Invitation to transmit	— . —
Wait	. — . . .
Break	— . . . —
Understood	. . . — .
Error	. . . .
Received	. — .
Position report	— . — .
End of message	. — . — .
Finish of transmission	. . . — . —

97

Ground Signals

Pilots having to make a forced landing can send messages to passing aircraft by using the signals below. They can be made from cloth, sticks, stones or even trampled snow. They should be at least eight feet in length.

I	Serious injuries. Send doctor	**I>**	Will attempt take-off
II	Send medical supplies	**L7**	Aircraft badly damaged
X	Unable to proceed	**△**	Probably safe to land here
F	Send food and water	**L**	Require fuel and oil
⌄	Send firearms and ammunition	**LL**	All is well
□	Send map and compass	**N**	No
¦	Require signal lamp or radio	**Y**	Yes
K	Show direction to proceed	**⌐L**	Send engineer
↑	Am proceeding this direction	**W**	Not understood

Radio

Though the Morse Code is often sent by signal lamp, its main use is in telegraphy and wireless telegraphy. Telegraphy has been in use for well over a century, but it was not until 1887—88 that a German scientist succeeded in sending wireless messages from one side of his laboratory to the other. In 1896 Guglielmo Marconi (1874—1937) patented a much improved transmitter and receiver, and by 1903 communication had been established between Britain and America. Within a few years a vast network of ship and shore stations grew up. In the nineteen-twenties came broadcasting or radio telephony. Broadcasting in Britain, at first carried on by private business concerns in their own research works, began as a public service on November 14, 1922.

Broadcasting Stations

The following broadcasting stations can be heard in Britain by listeners using three-waveband sets of reasonably high power:

Long Wave

Metres	Place	Kilowatts
1935	Brasov (Rumania)	150
1829	Allouis-Cher (France)	250
1734	Moscow (U. S. S. R.)	500
1648	Reykjavik (Iceland)	100
1571	Motala (Sweden)	150
1500	Droitwich (England) (B. B. C. Light Programme)	400
1376	Oslo (Norway)	200
1322	Warsaw (Poland)	500
1224	Kalundborg (Denmark)	150
1181	Lahti (Finland)	200

Medium Wave

Metres	Place	Kilowatts
561	Beromünster (Switzerland)	150
539	Helsinki (Finland)	100
530	Athlone (Ireland)	100
522	Tel Aviv (Israel)	50
514	Vienna (Austria)	150
506	Sundsvall (Sweden)	150
505	Sofia (Bulgaria)	60
498	Lyons (France)	100
495	Nicosia (Cyprus)	20
484	Brussels (Belgium)	150
470	Prague (Czechoslovakia)	120
464	Daventry (England) (Network 3 and Third Programme)	150
457	Florence (Italy)	180
445	Rennes (France)	150
439	Belgrade (Yugoslavia)	150
434	Moorside Edge (England) (B.B.C. North of England Home Service)	150
428	Istanbul (Turkey)	150
422	Marseilles (France)	150
412	Athens (Greece)	150
402	Hilversum (Netherlands)	120
397	Lisbon (Portugal)	135
393	Sottens (Switzerland)	150
388	Stockholm (Sweden)	150
371	Burehead/Westerglen (Scotland) (B.B.C. Scottish Home Service)	100
367	Cairo (Egypt)	300
363	Tetuan (Morocco)	20
359	Nancy (France)	150
355	Rome (Italy)	150
351	Bucharest (Roumania)	150
348	Paris (France)	150

344	Moscow (U. S. S. R.)	150
341	Washford (England)	
	(B.B.C. Welsh Home Service)	100
334	Milan (Italy)	150
330	Baghdad (Iraq)	200
330	Brookman's Park (England)	
	(B.B.C. London Home Service)	140
324	Brussels (Belgium)	100
318	Toulouse (France)	100
309	Hamburg (Germany)	100
306	Algiers (Algeria)	200
306	Gothenburg (Sweden)	150
303	Berlin (Germany)	300
298	Hilversum (Netherlands)	120
295	Odessa (U.S.S.R.)	20
288	Dresden (Germany)	240
285	Start Point (England)	
	(B.B.C. West of England Home Service)	120
280	Paris (France)	100
276	Droitwich (England)	
	(B.B.C. Midland Home Service)	100
271	Vilnius (U.S.S.R.)	150
261	Lisnagarvey (N. Ireland)	
	(B.B.C. Northern Ireland and North of England Home Service)	100
261	Stagshaw (England)	100
259	Strasbourg (France)	150
251	Munich (Germany)	150
249	Bordeaux (France)	100
247	Brookman's Park, Moorside Edge and Westerglen (England)	
	(B.B.C. Light Programme)	50
245	Madrid (Spain)	20
243	Bratislava (Czechoslovakia)	100
228	Stavanger (Norway)	100
224	Crowborough (England)	
	(B.B.C. European Service)	150

222	Riga (U.S.S.R.)	20
218	Lille (France)	100
208	Luxembourg	150
205	Monte Carlo (Monaco)	400

Short Wave

The short wavebands are used where reception is wanted at great distances, and many nations operating overseas services employ them for transmissions to reach the other side of the world. In general, at night the average receiver will pick up signals most clearly on the longest wavebands; in daylight the shortest are likely to bring in the best results.

Principal Stations on the 49-metre band are: Tokyo (Japan), Boston (U. S. A.), New York (U. S. A.), Vancouver (Canada), Dixon (U. S. A.), Léopoldville (Congo), Delhi (India), Latin American Stations.

Principal Stations on the 31-metre band are: Ankara (Turkey), Mexico City (Mexico), Radio Australia, San Francisco (U. S. A.), Montevideo (Uruguay), Honolulu (U. S. A.), New York (U.S.A.), Manila (Philippines), Taipei (Formosa).

Principal Stations on the 25-metre band are: Léopoldville (Congo), Djakarta (Indonesia), Radio Australia, Wellington (New Zealand).

Principal Stations on the 19-metre band are: Colombo (Ceylon), Delhi (India), Radio Australia, Rio de Janeiro (Brazil), Peking (China), Karachi (Pakistan).

Principal Stations on the 16-metre band are: Radio Australia, Boston (U. S. A.), Delhi (India), Peking (China), Karachi (Pakistan), Bethany (U. S. A.).

Also in use in many countries are VHF (Very High Frequency) stations, broadcasting on wavelengths of about three metres. VHF broadcasts in Britain can be picked up on sets designed for the purpose as follows:

Home Service	Wrotham transmitter	93.5 Megacycles
Network Three	Wrotham transmitter	91.3 Megacycles
Third Programme	Wrotham transmitter	91.3 Megacycles
Light Programme	Wrotham transmitter	89.1 Megacycles

Nineteen other VHF stations are also in operation in Britain.

British Overseas Broadcasting provides a total of nearly five hundred and fifty hours of transmissions every week. The General Overseas Service is mainly designed for audiences in the Commonwealth and for Forces serving abroad, and the contents of the programmes are very largely repeat perfomances selected from the Home Service and the Light Programme.

The European Service broadcasts to the Continent in English, French, Spanish, Italian, Greek, Turkish, Finnish, Czech, Hungarian, Polish, Russian, Roumanian, Bulgarian, Yugoslav, Albanian, German, Hebrew, Serbo-Croat, Slovak and Slovene.

The Overseas Service is directed to Australia, New Zealand, the Pacific Islands, South Africa, Rhodesia, West and East Africa, the West Indies, the Falkland Islands, Asia, the Far East and Latin America. The service is divided into five groups: Pacific, South African, North American, Far Eastern and Latin American.

Television

Britain pioneered television broadcasting with the world's first public service, in November, 1936. The service closed down throughout the War; since the War transmitters have been set up in most major countries throughout the world.

Television in Britain is now organised in two groups: the B. B. C., providing a national service, and the I. T. A. (Independent Television Authority), controlling a number of programme companies which derive their income from the sale of advertising time between programmes. These companies are: Associated Rediffusion, Associated Television, A. B. C. Television, Granada Television, Scottish Television, Television West and Wales, Southern Television, Tyne and Tees Television, Anglian Television and Ulster Television. All of these operate independently, joining together at certain times to present 'networked' programmes. The news is provided by a separate company, Independent Television News.

The spread of television has brought about a demand for a high-speed service of 'newsfilm' recording each day's events. Newsfilm is now circulated between Britain, America, Canada, France, Australia, Russia, Spain, Sweden and Italy, using passenger airlines and relays of motorcycle dispatch riders between airports and television stations. In addition, to provide an international network, major events can be televised, at the moment they happen, to most countries in Europe through 'Eurovision', a system linking transmitters and studios in up to a dozen countries at a time.

The Press

The first known newspaper printed in Britain was *The Corante, or Weekly Newes from Italy, Germany, Hungarie, Spaine and France,* published in 1621. For more than two centuries, both in Britain and other countries, newspapers were crippled by heavy taxation and severe penalties for failing to follow official Government policy, but in the middle of the last century these restrictions ended.

Daily papers are, in general, *national* in small countries, and *regional* in large ones. In Britain, a daily paper printed in London can be sold in the north of Scotland in the morning, but this is obviously impossible in Australia, Canada or the United States, where each major city has its own daily paper circulating within a range of two or three hundred miles.

Britain's national papers are:

Daily Papers

Name	Affiliation	Date Started
The Times	Independent	1785
News Chronicle	Independent	1846
Daily Telegraph and Morning Post	Conservative	1855
Daily Mail	Independent	1896
Daily Express	Independent	1900
Daily Mirror	Independent	1903
Daily Sketch	Independent	1909
Daily Herald	Labour	1912
Daily Worker	Communist	1932
Guardian (published in Manchester)	Liberal	1821

Sunday Papers

Observer	Independent	1791
Sunday Dispatch	Independent	1801
Sunday Times	Independent	1822
News of the World	Independent	1843
Reynolds's News	Labour	1850
People	Independent	1881
Sunday Graphic	Conservative	1915
Sunday Pictorial	Independent	1915
Sunday Express	Independent	1918
Empire News (published in Manchester)	Conservative	1884

PEOPLE OF OUR TIME

Who are the 'people of our time'? Obviously they are those who in one way or another are leaving their mark upon the world for good or evil, and whose activities may in some way affect *you*. The following are some whose names have made news in recent years.

ADENAUER, Dr Konrad. Chancellor of the West German Republic since 1949 and leader of the largest political Party in West Germany, the Christian Democrats. Formerly Lord Mayor of Cologne. Born 1876.

ANOUILH, Jean. Leading French dramatist, many of whose plays have appeared on the English stage. Born 1910.

ARMSTRONG, Louis. American jazz musician. He formed a band in 1930 and has been widely known since then. Born 1900.

ARRAU, Claudio. Pianist. Began performing at the age of five and won his first scholarship at the age of seven. Now lives in the United States. Born 1903.

ATTLEE, 1st Earl (Clement Richard Attlee), K. G., P. C., O. M., C. H., F. R. S. Britain's Labour Party Prime Minister from 1945 until 1951. Went into Parliament a few years after War service in 1914—19, and held various posts in previous Labour Governments. Was a member of the War Cabinet in World War II. Born 1883.

AUDEN, Wystan Hugh. Leading twentieth-century English poet, resident in the United States. Has been Professor of Poetry at the University of Oxford since 1956. Born 1907.

BADER, Group Captain Douglas Robert Steuart, C.B.E., D.S.O., D.F.C. Became famous as the legless pilot of World War II. Lost both legs in a flying accident in 1931, the year after he joined the R.A.F; rejoined in 1939, and was captured by the Germans in 1941. Was released in 1945, and now works with Shell Petroleum Company. Born 1910.

BANNISTER, Dr Roger Gilbert, C.B.E. Fisrt man to run a mile inside of four minutes (3 m. 49 s.), at Oxford, May 6, 1954, aided by Chris Charaway and Chris Brasher. Was Oxford University Athletics President 1949. Born 1929.

BARBIROLLI, Sir John (Giovanni Battista), F.R.A.M. One of the leading orchestral conductors of the present day. Has appeared for many years in Britain, the United States and Australia. Born 1899.

BARRAULT, Jean-Louis. Leading French actor and theatrical producer. Worked as producer with *Comédie Française*, 1940—46. Now directs his own company. Born 1910.

BEATON, Cecil Walter Hardy, C. B. E. Photographer and theatrical designer. Has designed costumes and scenery for many ballet and theatrical productions both in London and New York. Born 1904.

BEAVERBROOK, 1st Baron (William Maxwell Aitken), P. C. One of the most amazing figures in modern journalism; has been for many years the power behind two leading British newspapers, the *Daily Express* and *Sunday Express*, both of which he built up to a mass circulation. Has held several political posts, including that of Minister of Supply during World War II. Born 1879.

BECKETT, Samuel. Author and playwright. Born in Dublin. Has lived in France since 1932. He is the author of such works as *Waiting for Godot, Endgame, Molloy* and *Malone Dies*. Born 1906.

BEECHAM, Sir Thomas, Bt, C.H. Orchestral conductor and founder in 1946 of the Royal Philharmonic Orchestra. He is recognised as the 'Grand Old Man' of British conducting. Born 1879.

BEN-GURION, David. Prime Minister of Israel. An active Zionist in his youth, he settled in Israel in 1906. Has been a prominent figure in Israeli politics and in the Jewish Labour movement for much of his life. Born 1886.

107

BOULT, Sir Adrian Cedric. Orchestral conductor. Has been director of Music for the B.B.C., and Conductor of the B.B.C. Symphony Orchestra. From 1950 to 1957 he was Conductor of the London Philharmonic Orchestra. Born 1889.

BRANDO, Marlon. American actor and film star, whose performance in the play *A Streetcar Named Desire* first brought him considerable critical acclaim. Has appeared in such films as *The Wild One, Julius Caesar, On the Waterfront* and *Teahouse of the August Moon*. Born 1924.

BRITTEN, (Edward) Benjamin, C.H. Composer, best known for such operas as *Peter Grimes, Billy Budd* and *The Turn of the Screw*. Born 1913.

BUTLER, Rt Hon. Richard Austen, C.H., M.P. British Home Secretary, Lord Privy Seal and Leader of the House of Commons since 1955. Has been successively Minister of Education, Minister of Labour and Chancellor of the Exchequer. Has been M.P. for Saffron Walden since 1929. Born 1902.

CALLAS, Maria (Signora G.B. Meneghini). Leading soprano; Prima Donna at La Scala Opera House, Milan. Educated in New York and Athens, she has sung in opera houses throughout the world. Born 1923.

CANTERBURY, Archbishop of (Most Rev. and Rt Hon. Geoffrey Fisher, P.C., G.C.V.O.). For many years headmaster of Repton Scholl, Dr Fisher became Bishop of Chester in 1932. Appointed Bishop of London in 1939 and Archbishop of Canterbury in 1945. In his early years was a keen rugger player and oarsman. Born 1887.

CASALS, His Excellency Pablo. One of the greatest violoncellists of our time, he is also a composer and conductor. He has received many honours. Born in Spain, 1876.

CASTRO, Dr Fidel. Prime Minister of Cuba. In 1958 he led a successful rebellion against the Batista government. Born 1917.

CHAPLIN, Charles Spencer (Charlie). Film actor and producer. Began his career in the London music halls, but became famous through the early silent film comedies which he made in Hollywood. Some of his best-known films are *The Kid*, *The Gold Rush*, *City Lights*, *Modern Times*, *The Great Dictator*, *Monsieur Verdoux* and *Limelight*. His silent film *The Gold Rush* (1926) is generally recognised as one of the ten greatest films of all time. Now lives in Switzerland. Born 1889.

CHIANG KAI-SHEK, Generalissimo. President of Nationalist China (Formosa) since 1948. Was leader of all China during World War II, but in the Civil War which followed he was defeated on the mainland by the Communist forces. Born 1887.

CHOU EN-LAI, General. Leader in the Chinese People's Republic, where he has been Prime Minister since 1949. Born 1898.

CHURCHILL, Rt Hon. Sir Winston Leonard Spencer, K.G., O.M., C.H., M.P. Was Britain's Prime Minister during the war years from 1940 to 1945, and again from 1951 until his retirement in 1955. Served with the British Forces in the Sudan in 1898, and was a correspondent in the Boer War, during which he was captured and made a dramatic escape. Entered Parliament in 1900; left the Conservative Party to join the Liberal Party in 1904; held numerous government posts, and though on active service for part of World War I, spent the remaining years as Minister of Munitions. Lost his seat in Parliament in the 1922 General Election, but was elected again in 1924 and rejoined the Conservative Party. Was Chancellor of the Exchequer in the Baldwin Government, 1924—29. Was First Lord of the Admiralty, 1939—40, and was appointed Prime Minister in May 1940, during the War crisis. Rallied Britain with his remarkable war speeches. In 1945, when the end of the war was in sight, he prepared to form a new government, but his Party was defeated. Became Prime

Minister again in 1951, but retired in 1955, remaining M.P. for Woodford. His history of the Second World War and his book *A History of the English-Speaking Peoples* are widely read, and his painting is often seen in exhibitions. Born 1874.

COCKCROFT, Sir John (Douglas), O.M., K.C.B., C.B.E. Physicist. First widely known for his work in splitting the atom in 1932. Has been Director of the Atomic Energy Research Establishment, Harwell, since 1946, and was awarded the Nobel Prize for Physics in 1951. Born 1897.

COCTEAU, Jean. French poet and author. Has also produced a number of films. Born 1889.

COMPTON, Denis Charles Scott, C.B.E. Regarded as one of the greatest British sporting figures in the last twenty years, Compton has represented England at both cricket and soccer, playing in more than seventy Tests and nearly a dozen international soccer matches. Won a League Championship Medal with Arsenal in 1947—48 and a Cup Winner's Medal in 1949—50. Knee trouble led to his retirement from sport in 1958. Born 1918.

CORTOT, Alfred. Pianist. Was awarded the Gold Medal of the Royal Philharmonic Society. Born Switzerland, 1877.

COWARD, Noel. British playwright and actor, who has also succeeded as a composer. Born 1899.

CROSBY, Harry Lillis (Bing). American film star and singer. Has maintained his popularity for some thirty years. His record sales total many millions. Probably his greatest successes were the films in which he appeared with Bob Hope — *Road to Singapore, Road to Moroco, Road to Utopia*, etc. Born 1904.

CURZON, Clifford (Michael). Pianist; well known throughout Europe and America. Born 1907.

DE GAULLE, General Charles André Joseph Marie. President of France since December 1958. Was Commander-in-Chief of the Free French Forces during World War II. After the war he retired from military and political leadership, but in 1958 he was made Prime Minister with special powers, to avert a crisis in France over the rebellion in Algeria. Born 1890.

DIEFENBAKER, Rt Hon. John George, P.C., Q.C. Has been Prime Minister of Canada since June 1957 and Leader of the Canadian Progressive Conservative Party since December 1956. He was Chairman at the first Commonwealth Conference. Born 1895.

DISNEY, Walter E. Film cartoonist and producer. Created Mickey Mouse and Donald Duck. His full-length cartoon films include *Snow-White and the Seven Dwarfs*, *Pinocchio* and *Fantasia*. Has made several nature films, including *The Living Desert* and *The Vanishing Prairie*. Born 1901.

DIXON, Sir Pierson (John), G.C.M.G., C.B. British diplomat and Permanent Representative of Great Britain in the United Nations since 1954. Born 1904.

EDEN, Rt Hon. Sir (Robert) Anthony, K.G., M.C. Was Britain's Prime Minister from April 1955 until his resignation in January 1957. Was Foreign Secretary 1935—38 and 1940—45, and was Leader of the House of Commons 1942—45. Served as Foreign Secretary and Deputy Prime Minister 1951—55. Born 1897.

EISENHOWER, Dwight David. President of the United States 1953—1960. Was Supreme Commander Allied Expeditionary Force in Western Europe during World War II. Was responsible for the overall planning of the Anglo-American invasion in 1944 which liberated France. Born 1890.

ELIOT, Thomas Stearns, O.M. Leading twentieth-century poet, dramatist and literary critic. American by birth, he resides in Britain. Was awarded the Nobel Prize for Literature in 1948. Born 1888.

EVANS, Dame Edith (Dame Edith Mary Booth), D.B.E. One of Britain's leading actresses. Her first London appearance was in 1912, and since then she has played leading roles in a great many successful productions. Born 1888.

111

EVATT, Rt Hon. Herbert Vere, P.C. Australian politician. Leader of the Labour Party in Parliament at Canberra. During World War II was Australia's representative on the War Cabinet in London. Born 1894.

FAULKNER, William. Leading American author, much of whose writings is set in his native Mississippi. Received Nobel Prize for Literature in 1950 and Pulitzer Prize in 1955. Born 1897.

FIELDS, Gracie, C.B.E. Actress and singer. Began life as a Lancashire cotton-mill worker, but soon became well known as a singer of popular songs, particularly in Lancashire dialect. Has toured most countries and appeared in a number of films. Born 1898.

FONTEYN, Dame Margot, D.B.E. Prima Ballerina of the Sadler's Wells Ballet in London. Has danced leading roles in both classical and modern ballet in many countries. Born 1919.

FORSTER, Edward Morgan, C.H. British author. Awarded the James Tait Black Prize and *Prix Femina Vie Heureuse* for his novel *A Passage to India*. Born 1879.

FRANCO Bahamonde, General Don Francisco. Head of Spanish State. Led the anti-Government forces in Spain from 1936 to 1939, and has been Chief of State since then, serving as Regent pending the return of the Spanish Royal Family. Born 1892.

FUCHS, Sir Vivian Ernest. World-famous explorer and scientist. Has been Director of the Falkland Islands Dependencies Scientific Bureau since 1950. He led the Commonwealth Trans-Antarctic Expedition, 1955—58. He has received many scientific awards, including the Founder's Gold Medal of the Royal Geographical Society in 1951, the Polar Medal in 1953 and the Special Gold Medal of the Royal Geographical Society in 1958. Born 1908.

GAITSKELL, Rt Hon. Hugh Todd Naylor, C.B.E., M.P. Leader of the Parliamentary Labour Party since 1955. During the Labour Government's period of office he was

Minister of Fuel and Power, and later Chancellor of the Exchequer. Born 1906.

GIELGUD, Sir (Arthur) John. Has been a leading British actor for nearly forty years, playing leading roles in many well-known plays and a number of Shakespearean productions. Has appeared in such films as *Julius Caesar* and *Richard III*. Born 1904.

GREENE, Graham. Author of many well-known novels, including *Brighton Rock*, *The Heart of the Matter*, *The End of the Affair*, *The Quiet American* and *Our Man in Havana*. Several of his novels have been filmed. Born 1904.

GRIMOND, Joseph, M.P. Politician, and Leader of the Liberal Party since 1956. Born 1913.

GROMYKO, Andrei A. U.S.S.R. Minister of Foreign Affairs. Was Ambassador to the United States 1943—46 and Ambassador to Britain 1952—53. Born 1909.

GRONCHI, Giovanni. President of Italy since 1955. An active anti-Fascist during World War II, he entered politics as Catholic trade union leader. Born 1887.

GUINNESS, Sir Alec, C.B.E. Actor, famous principally for his great ability in character roles. In the film *Kind Hearts and Coronets* he took six different parts, ranging from a naval officer to an elderly woman. His other films include *The Lavender Hill Mob*, *The Captain's Paradise*, *Father Brown*, *The Prisoner* and *The Bridge on the River Kwai*. Born 1914.

HAMBOURG, Mark. British pianist and composer. Made his London début in 1890. Born Russia, 1879.

HAMMARSKJÖLD, Dag. Swedish statesman and Secretary-General of the United Nations since 1953. Has made personal visits to many trouble spots in the interests of peace. Born 1905.

HEIFETZ, Jascha. Violinist. Made his first public appearance at the age of four and a half. Fist played in London in 1920. Born Russia, 1901.

HELPMANN, Robert Murray. Australian-born ballet dancer, actor and producer. Was leading male dancer of the Sadler's Wells Ballet Company for many years; later appeared in films, including *Henry V, The Red Shoes* and *Tales of Hoffman*. Born 1909.

HEMINGWAY, Ernest. American author and journalist. His novel of World War I, *A Farewell to Arms*, brought him international fame. Won the Pulitzer Prize for *The Old Man and the Sea*, 1953. Was awarded the Nobel Prize for Literature in 1954. Other books, some of which have been filmed, include *Fiesta, To Have and Have Not, Death in the Afternoon* and *For Whom the Bell Tolls*. Born 1898.

HEPWORTH, Barbara. British sculptor. Has exhibited in Europe and the United States. She executed work for the Festival of Britain. Born 1903.

HESS, Dame Myra, D.B.E. British pianist. Studied at the Royal Academy of Music and made her London début at the age of seventeen.

HILLARY, Sir Edmund, K.B.E. New Zealand mountaineer and explorer. With Sherpa Tensing, reached the summit of Mount Everest in 1953. In 1955—58 took part in the Trans-Antarctic Expedition with Sir Vivian Fuchs of Britain. Born 1919.

HIROHITO. Emperor of Japan. Came to the Throne in 1926, and until the end of World War II, was regarded by most Japanese more as a God than Emperor. Since then, however, has made a genuine attempt to encourage democratic government in his country. Born 1901.

HITCHCOCK, Alfred Joseph. British-born film director. Has made many highly successful thrillers, first in Britain and later in Hollywood. In recent years has concentrated on short films for television. Born 1899.

HOME, 14th Earl of. (Alexander Frederick Douglas-Home). British Secretary of State for Foreign Affairs since 1960. Was Leader of the House of Lords from 1957. Born 1903.

HOPE, Bob (Leslie Townes Hope). American radio, stage and film actor, born in Britain. Appeared with Bing Crosby in a highly successful series of films, of which *Road to Singapore* was the first. His weekly radio show in the United States has been a favourite for many years. Born 1904.

HUNT, Colonel (Hon. Brig.) Sir (Henry Cecil) John, C.B.E., D.S.O. Leader of the British Expedition to Mount Everest, 1952—53. Served in the British Army for many years. Since 1956, has been in charge of the Duke of Edinburgh's Award Scheme. Born 1910.

HUTTON, Sir Leonard. England's cricket captain in 1953 when the Ashes were won from Australia. His career in cricket lasted from 1934, when he played his first County Championship match for Yorkshire, until 1956, when he retired from the game. In 1938 he set up a Test record of 364 at the Oval against Australia. He shares with Australia's Sir Donald Bradman the distinction of being recognised as the most consistent Test batsman of recent times. Born 1916.

HUXLEY, Aldous (Leonard). British author now living in the United States. He is well known for such novels as *Point Counter Point, Brave New World* and *The Genius and the Goddess*. Born 1894.

KAYE, Danny. American comedian and film actor, who has also carried out world-wide work on behalf of the United Nations Children's Fund. Some films in which he has appeared are *The Secret Life of Walter Mitty, The Inspector General* and *The Five Pennies*. Born 1913.

KEMSLEY, 1st Viscount (James Gomer Berry), C.B.E. Newspaper proprietor. Until recently he was Chairman of Kemsley Newspaper Ltd and Editor-in-Chief of the *Sunday Times*. Born 1883.

KENNEDY, John F. U. S. statesman and author. Has been Democratic Party Senator from Massachusetts since 1953. Democratic candidate for the Presidency in 1960. Born 1917.

115

KHRUSHCHEV, Nikita Sergeyevich. Senior executive in the Government of the U.S.S.R. His official title is 'Chairman of the Council of Ministers of the U.S.S.R.'. He joined the Party in 1918 and took up his present post on the resignation of Georgi Malenkov. Visited Britain in 1956. Born 1894.

KOESTLER, Arthur. Author. Has been a foreign correspondent, and was a war correspondent in the Spanish Civil War. In World War II he served in the French Foreign Legion and then in the British Pioneer Corps. His books include *Darkness at Noon*, *The Yogi and the Commissar* and *The Sleepwalkers*. Born Hungary, 1905.

KREISLER, Fritz. Violinist. First performed in London in 1902. Born Austria, 1875.

LAUGHTON, Charles. Stage and film actor. Two of his most popular films were *The Private Life of Henry VIII* and *Mutiny on the Bounty*, both of which are still screened in repertory theatres after more than twenty years. Born 1899.

LENNOX-BOYD, Rt Hon. Alan Tindal. Secretary of State for the Colonies 1954—1960. Has been Parliamentary Secretary of several ministries, Minister of State for Colonial Affairs and Minister of Transport and Civil Aviation. Born 1904.

LLOYD, Rt Hon. (John) Selwyn (Brooke) C.B.E., Q.C., M.P. Chancellor of the Exchequer since 1960. Was Secretary of State for Foreign Affairs 1955—1960. Originally a barrister, he entered politics and became Minister of State in 1951, Minister of Supply in 1954 and Minister of Defence in 1955. Born 1904.

LOVELL, Prof. Alfred Charles Bernard, O.B.E., F.R.S. Physicist and astronomer. Since 1951 has been Director of Jodrell Bank Experimental Station, Cheshire. Born 1913.

MacARTHUR, General of the Army Douglas. American military figure, formerly Commander-in-Chief of U.S. Forces Far East Command and Supreme Commander

Allied Powers in Japan. He was Commander-in-Chief of United Nations forces in Korea until 1951, when he was retired from all commands by President Truman. Born 1880.

MACLEOD, Rt Hon. Iain Norman, M.P. Secretary of State for the Colonies since 1960. Formerly Minister of Labour. Born 1913.

MACMILLAN, Rt Hon. (Maurice) Harold, M.P. Prime Minister of Britain since January 1957. Was Minister of Housing and Local Government 1951—54, Minister of Defence 1954—55, Foreign Secretary 1955 and Chancellor of the Exchequer 1955—57. Born 1894.

MAKARIOS III (Michael Mouskos). Greek Orthodox Archbishop. President of the Republic of Cyprus since August, 1960. Born 1913.

MAO TSE-TUNG. Chinese statesman. Chairman of the Communist Party of the Chinese People's Republic and former Chairman of the Central People's Government Council of China. Born 1893.

MASEFIELD, John, O. M. Author and poet. He has been the British Poet Laureate since 1930. Born 1878.

MAUGHAM, (William) Somerset, C. H. Author and playwright. Some of his best-known novels are *Of Human Bondage, The Moon and Sixpence, Cakes and Ale* and *The Razor's Edge*. Born 1874.

MENUHIN, Yehudi. Violinist. Began playing at the age of five, and was hailed as an infant prodigy. Has performed in most countries. Born 1916.

MENZIES, Rt Hon. Robert Gordon, C.H. Prime Minister of Australia since 1949. Was originally a barrister and served previously as Prime Minister, 1939—41. Born 1894.

MIRZA, Major-General Iskander, C.I.E., O.B.E. President of Pakistan since 1956. Received his military training at Sandhurst and served in the British Army before entering politics. His handling of the dispute over the frontier state of Kashmir, claimed by India, did much to prevent

117

war between the two Commonwealth nations. Born 1899.

MOISEIWITSCH, Benno, C.B.E. British pianist. First performed in London in 1909. Born Russia, 1890.

MONROE, Marilyn (Norma Jeane Baker). Popular American film actress; has appeared in such films as *The Asphalt Jungle*, *Bus Stop* and *The Prince and the Showgirl* in which she shared the lead with Sir Laurence Olivier. Born 1928.

MONTGOMERY OF ALAMEIN, 1st Viscount (Field Marshal Bernard Law Montgomery), K. G., G.C.B., D.S.O. Military leader. Retired from the British Army in 1958 after a widely controversial career. Commanded the Eighth Army during the North African and Sicilian campaigns of 1942—43 in World War II. Later, he played a major role in the command of the troops invading France in 1944. Was Deputy Supreme Allied Commander in Europe 1951—58. Born 1887.

MOORE, Henry. Leading twentieth-century sculptor. Studied at the Leeds School of Art and at the Royal College of Art, London. His first London exhibition was in 1928. Born 1898.

MORRISON, Rt Hon. Herbert Stanley, C.H., M.P. Statesman. He has served as Leader of the London County Council, Minister of Transport, Minister of Supply and Home Secretary and Minister of Home Security. From 1945 to 1951 he was Deputy Prime Minister, and Lord President of the Council and Leader of the House. He was made a Life Peer in September 1959. Born 1888.

MOUNTBATTEN OF BURMA, 1st Earl (Admiral of the Fleet Louis Mountbatten), K.G., P.C., G.C.B., G.C.S.I., G.C.I.E., G.C.V.O., D.S.O. Chief of the Defence Staff since 1959. Entered the Royal Navy in 1913. Had a distinguished record in World War II. Was Viceroy of India in 1947, and Commander in Chief of the Mediterranean Fleet, 1942—54. Was First Sea Lord and Chief of Naval Staff, 1955—59. Born 1900.

NASSER, Gamal Abdel. President of the United Arab Republic. Led the movement which forced King Farouk into exile in 1952, and took over the Presidency of Egypt after General Naguib was deposed in 1954. In 1956 nationalised the Suez Canal. In 1958 announced the formation of the United Arab Republic, comprising Egypt and Syria, with himself as President. Born 1918.

NEHRU, Shri Jawaharlal. Prime Minister of India since 1947. Was originally a barrister, and became a close associate of Gandhi in the movement for Indian independence. Led the National Interim Government while India was emerging as a Commonwealth State. Has attempted to steer his country between the conflicting policies of the Eastern and Western nations. Born 1889.

NIXON, Richard. Vice-President of the United States 1953—61. Originally a lawyer, he served in the Navy during World War II, went into Congress in 1947, and became a Senator in 1951. Born 1913.

NKRUMAH, Rt Hon. Kwame. Prime Minister of Ghana. Was imprisoned 1950—51, during his campaign to win self-government for his country. Became Prime Minister of the Gold Coast Colony in 1952, and remained in office when the colony became Ghana. Born 1909.

NUFFIELD, 1st Viscount (William Richard Morris), G.B.E., C.H. Car manufacturer and philanthropist. From the profits of his vast manufacturing organisation, he has given millions of pounds for scientific research, education, improvement of recreation in the services and social welfare. Born 1877.

OISTRAKH, David Fyodorovich. Russian violinist, known throughout Europe and the Americas. His first London performance was in 1954. Born 1908.

OLIVIER, Sir Laurence Kerr. Leading British actor for more than thirty years. Has won fame in Shakespearean roles both in Britain and America, and has acted in film versions of several of Shakespeare's plays. Born 1907.

PENNEY, Sir William George, O. B. E. Atomic scientist, responsible for the creation and testing of Britain's first atomic bomb, at Monte Bello, in 1952, and for later work on the hydrogen bomb. Has been Director of the Atomic Weapons Research Establishment, Aldermaston, since 1953. Born 1909.

PICASSO, Pablo Ruiz. Leading twentieth-century artist. Born in Spain, he has spent most of his life in France where he has led many new art movements, notably the Cubist Movement. His paintings have been exhibited throughout the world. Born 1881.

POPE JOHN XXIII (Angelo Giuseppe Roncalli). Was ordained as a priest in August 1904 and made a Cardinal in 1953, when he was also nominated Patriarch of Venice. In November 1958 he was crowned Pope. Born 1881.

REDGRAVE, Sir Michael Scudamore, C.B.E. Actor. Has performed with the Old Vic and at the Stratford Memorial Theatre and has also appeared in films. Born 1908.

RICHARDS, Sir Gordon. During thirty-four years as a jockey, rode more winners than anyone else in British horse-racing history. Despite his thousands of successes, it was not until 1953 that he won the Derby, riding Pinza, and the following year he had to retire after an injury while racing. Has since become a racing trainer. Born 1904.

RICHARDSON, Sir Ralph David. Actor. Has been on the British stage for nearly forty years, and has also appeared in several films. Has toured the United States and Commonwealth countries. Born 1902.

ROBESON, Paul Le Roy. American concert singer and actor. Has been recording folk songs and Negro spirituals for more than thirty years. Has also made many concert appearances and has acted leading roles in a number of plays. He has appeared in several films. Born 1898.

ROOSEVELT, Anna Eleanor (Mrs F. D. Roosevelt). Member of American Association for United Nations, in charge of organisation. Former United States Representative to United Nations. She is the widow of former President Franklin Delano Roosevelt. Born 1884.

RUSSELL, 3rd Earl (Bertrand Arthur William Russell, O.M. Philosopher, mathematician and writer. The most famous of his many works is *History of Western Philosophy*. Born 1872.

SARGENT, Sir (H.) Malcolm (W.). Was Chief Conductor of the B. B. C. Symphony Orchestra 1950—57. He is Conductor-in-Chief of Promenade Concerts. Born 1895.

SCHWEITZER, Dr. Albert, Hon. O. M. Primarily a medical missionary at Lambaréné in the Gaboon Republic, he is also a noted authority on music, an organist and an author. Founded a hospital at Lambaréné. Won the Nobel Peace Prize in 1952. Born 1875.

SHOSTAKOVICH, Dmitry Dmitrievich. Russian composer. Some of his best-known music has been written for films and theatrical productions. Born 1906.

SITWELL, Dame Edith, D.B.E. Poet; sister of Sir Osbert Sitwell and Sacheverell Sitwell. Has published a number of books of poetry since 1915. Born 1887.

SITWELL, Sir Osbert. 5th Bt, C.H., C.B.E. Poet, essayist, novelist and short-story writer. First published his work with his sister Edith in 1916. Born 1892.

STEVENSON, Adlai E. U. S. Statesman, well known in many countries. He was Governor of Illinois 1949—53. In 1952 and 1956 he was the Democratic Party's candidate for the Presidency. Born 1900.

STRAVINSKY, Igor. Composer. Born in Russia but became a United States citizen in 1945. His music for such ballets as *Petrouchka* and *The Fire Bird* helped to make him famous. Born 1882.

THORNDIKE, Dame Sybil, D.B.E. Actress prominent on the London stage for half a century. Married to actor Sir Lewis Casson. Born 1882.

TITO. President (Josip Broz). Head of state in Yugoslavia, he is a veteran Communist and took part in the Russian

Revolution. Spent many years in prison in his own country for conspiracy against the monarchy. Became a Partisan leader during World War II and became Marshal of Yugoslavia in 1943. Has not aligned his country either with the West or the East, but has paid State visits to Britain and Russia. Born 1892.

TOYNBEE, Arnold Joseph. Historian. He is famous for his ten-volume work *A Study of History*. Born 1889.

ULANOVA, Galina Sergeyevna. Russian dancer. She has been Prima Ballerina at the Bolshoi Theatre, Moscow, since 1944. Born 1910.

USTINOV, Peter Alexander. British actor, playwright and film producer; has taken part in many of his own plays and films, including the very successful *Private Angelo*. Born 1921.

VERWOERD, Hendrik Frensch. Prime Minister of the Union of South Africa since 1958. He is a farmer in Transvaal. Born 1901.

WAUGH, Evelyn Arthur St John. Author. Some of his best-known novels are *Vile Bodies, Black Mischief, Scoop, Put Out More Flags* and *The Loved One*. Born 1903.

WELENSKY, Sir Roland (Roy), K.C.M.G. Prime Minister and Minister of External Affairs and Defence of the Federation of Rhodesia and Nyasaland since 1956. Born 1907.

WHITTLE, Air Commodore Sir Frank, K.B.E., C.B. Developed the gas-turbine engine for jet propulsion, 1937—46. His first jet design was flown in 1941. Born 1907.

WILLIAMS, Tennessee (Thomas Lanier Williams). American playwright. Some of his most widely acclaimed plays are *A Streetcar Named Desire, Summer and Smoke* and *Cat on a Hot Tin Roof*. Born 1912.

PEOPLE AND LANGUAGE

The Development of the Alphabet. We do not know the point in man's development at which he first made sounds which could be described as 'language'. The tracing of the history of written language, however, has been possible to a high degree of accuracy, and the diagram on the following page indicates how most of our present-day letters came to be formed.

Column I shows Egyptian hieroglyphics, or picture-writing, facing to the left. Column II is of later Egyptian writing, in which the picture has become unrecognisable, and the direction has changed to the right. Column III show the progress made by the time of the Phoenicians and Column IV contains the fairly similar alphabet of early Greek civilisation. Columns V, VI and VII show further development by the Greeks; in Columns VIII, IX and X are the stages through which the Romans progressed, leaving as their legacy most of the present-day alphabet of the Western world.

Principal Languages of the World
Language

Language	Speakers (millions)	Language	Speakers (millions)
Chinese	610	Italian	55
English	265	Javanese	41
Russian	200	Bihari (India)	37
Hindustani	160	Korean	32
Spanish	150	Polish	30
Japanese	91	Telugu (India)	30
German	90	Marathi (India)	27
Arabic	75	Tamil (India)	27
Bengali (India)	75	Malay	25
French	65	Turkish	22
Portuguese	63	Punjabi (India)	21

	EGYPTIAN			GREEK				LATIN		
1				A	A		a	A	A	a a a
2					B	B	B	B	B	B b
3					Γ	Γ		<	C	c g g
4				Δ	Δ		δ	D	D	d d d
5					E	Є	Є	E	E	e e
6					YF		F	F	F	f f
7					I	Z		Z	Z	z
8				B	H	H	h η	θ	H	h h
9			⊕	⊕	⊙	θ		⊕		
10					l	l	ι	I	I	i j
11					K	K	K K	K	K	k
12					Λ	λ	λ	L	L	l l
13				M	M	M	M M	M	M	m m
14					N	N	N	Γ	N	n n
15					Ξ	ξ	ξ	⊞	+	x x
16			o	o	O	O	o	O		
17					Γ	π	π ω	P	P	P
18				M	M		λ			
19			φ	φ	φ			φ	Q	q q
20				P	P	P	P P	R	R	R r
21			W	ξ	ξ	C	C σ	ς	S	s s s
22			+	T	T	T	τ	T	T	t t

Persian	20	Kanarese (India)	14
Dutch	19	Malayam (India)	14
Siamese	19	Hungarian	13
Vietnamese	19	Oriya (India)	13
Rajasthani (India)	17	Sundanese (Indonesia)	13
Roumanian	17	Czech	9
Burmese	16	Greek	9
Gujarati (India)	16	Hausa (Africa)	9
Serbo-Croat	15		

The English Language

Our own language, English, is a mixture of words drawn from the vocabularies of the various invaders of Britain over a period of some two thousand years. That is why in English there are often several different words meaning roughly the same thing, some having Anglo-Saxon origins and others coming from Latin. Our language is also less 'regular' than French, Italian or Spanish, all of which have direct Latin origins.

Words are placed in categories according to how they are used. These categories are known as parts of speech. The English language has eight parts of speech. They are listed below.

Noun: the name of a person, place or thing. Nouns are of four Genders: Masculine, Feminine, Common and Neuter. These Genders can be illustrated by the following words: man, woman, cousin, hat. Nouns are either Singular or Plural, examples of both being: dog and dogs, penny and pence. Classes of nouns are Proper (the name of a particular person, place or thing, e. g. William, France) and Common (the name common to everything in one group, e. g. house, car).

English nouns have three Cases which they take to show their relation to the rest of a sentence. These are Nominative (denoting the person or thing taking action), Objective (the person or thing about which action is taken) and Possessive (that which belongs to a person or thing).

Adjective: a word which describes or qualifies a noun. Adjectives may be divided into three categories: those expressing Quality (bad company), those expressing Quantity (ten boys) and Demonstrative Adjectives (that window). There are three degrees of comparison in adjectives — Positive, Comparative and Superlative, examples of which are: good, better, best; young, younger, youngest.

The Articles (Definite: the; Indefinite: a, an) are also adjectives, as are the Numerals (Cardinal: one, two; Ordinal: first, second; Multiplicative: once, twice; Indefinite: many, few).

Pronoun: a word used in place of a noun. Pronouns, like nouns, have Gender, Number and Case. Pronouns may be Personal (I, she, you), Relative (that, who), Demonstrative (this, those), Indefinite (some, one), Interrogative (who? which?), Distributive (either, each) and Reflexive (yourself, themselves).

Verb: a word which states the action of a noun. Verbs are either Transitive or Intransitive. Transitive verbs describe an action which affects an object, e. g. 'I start the car.' Intransitive verbs do not affect an object, e. g. 'The car starts.' 'I start the car' is an example of a verb in Active Voice; in Passive Voice it would be, 'The car was started by me.'

Verbs have three Finite Moods: Indicative (I speak); Imperative (Speak!); Subjunctive (I may speak). There is also the Infinitive Mood (to speak).

There are two Participles, used with such verbs as to be and to have: the Present Participle (speaking) and the Past Participle (spoken). There is also a verbal noun, the Gerund (the *speaking* of English).

The Tense of a verb shows the time of its action (Past, Present, Future). The degrees of completeness of the action are: Simple (I speak, I spoke, I shall speak); Continuous (I am speaking, I was speaking, I shall be speaking); Perfect

(I have spoken, I had spoken, I shall have spoken); Perfect Continuous (I have been speaking, I had been speaking, I shall have been speaking).

Adverb: a word which modifies or qualifies a verb, an adjective or another adverb. Adverbs can be divided into the following categories: Time (often, now); Place (here, outside); Quality (well, beautifully); Quantity (enough, almost); Number (once); Cause (therefore, why); Mood (perhaps).

Preposition: a word which shows the relation between words in a sentence. Examples of prepositions are: to, on, by, of, from, for, through, about, after, except, towards.

Conjunction: a word which links words, phrases, clauses or sentences. Examples of conjunctions are: and, but, for, because, also, unless, though, therefore.

Interjection: a word standing alone in a sentence, expressing strong emotion. Examples are: Indeed! Goodness! Bother! Oh! Alas!

Foreign Words and Phrases

There are many foreign expressions used in English, a number of which are quite convenient in that there is no exact equivalent in our language. Here are some in common use (Abbreviations — F: French; G: German; Gk: Greek; I: Italian; L: Latin: P: Portuguese; S: Spanish):

ad hoc (L). For this special object.
ad infinitum (L). For ever; to infinity.
ad interim (L). In the meanwhile.
ad libitum (ad lib.) (L). To any extent; at pleasure.
ad nauseam (L). To the point of disgust.
adsum (L). I am here.
ad valorem (L). According to value.
affaire d'honneur (F). Affair of honour; duel.
a fortiori (L). With stronger reason.
à la bonne heure (F). Well done; that's good.

127

à la carte (F). From the full menu.

à la mode (F). In the fashion.

alter ego (L). Other self.

amour-propre (F). Self-esteem.

a posteriori (L). From the effect to the cause.

a priori (L). From the cause to the effect.

à propos (F). To the point.

arrière-pensée (F). Mental reservation.

au contraire (F). On the contrary.

au courant (F). Fully acquainted (with).

auf Wiedersehen (G). Till we meet again.

au naturel (F). In a natural state.

au pair (F). On an exchange basis.

au revoir (F). Till we meet again.

auto da fé (P). Act of faith.

à votre santé! (F). Your good health!

bête noire (F). Pet hate.

billet doux (F). Love letter.

bona fide (L). In good faith; genuine.

bon marché (F). A bargain; cheap.

bon vivant (F). Gourmet; one who enjoys life.

bon voyage (F). Have a good journey.

canaille (F). Common mob (term of contempt).

carpe diem (L). Enjoy today.

carte blanche (F). Full powers.

casus belli (L). Cause of war.

caveat emptor (L). Let the buyer beware.

chacun à son goût. (F) Everyone to his own taste.

chef-d'oeuvre (F). Masterpiece.

cherchez la femme (F). Look for the woman (in the case).

ci-devant (F). Former.

comme il faut (F). In good taste.

compos mentis (L.) In full possession of sanity.

corps de ballet (F). The team of dancers in a ballet.

corps diplomatique (F). The group of diplomats in a capital city.

cui bono (L). Who will get any benefit?

cum grano salis (L). With a grain of salt.

d'accord (F). Agreed.

de facto (L). In fact.

de jure (L). By right (in law).

de luxe (F). Of especially high quality.

de rigueur (F). Necessary.

dernier cri (F). The latest fashion.

de trop (F). Superfluous; not wanted.

deus ex machina (L). Providential interposition; nick-of-time solution by a superhuman agency.

Dieu et mon droit (F). God and my right (motto of the British Crown).

double entente (F). Double meaning (sometimes *double entendre*).

embarras de richesse (F). Difficulty caused by having too much.

en deshabillé (F). Dressed in clothes suitable only for lounging.

en famille (F). In the family; informal.

en fête (F). Celebrating.

en passant (F). In passing; by the way.

en rapport (F). In sympathy; in harmony.

entre nous (F). Between ourselves.

esprit de corps (F). Group spirit.

ex cathedra (L). From the chair of office; with authority.

ex libris (L). From the books (of).

fait accompli (F). An accomplished fact.

faux pas (F). False step; mistake.

femme de chambre (F). Chambermaid.

129

fête champêtre (F). Gala occasion in the open air.
fiat lux (L). Let there be light.
fin de siècle (F). Decadent.

gitano (S). Gipsy.
gourmet (F). Lover of good food.

Hausfrau (G). Housewife.
hic jacet (L). Here lies.
hoi polloi (Gk). The people.
honi soit qui mal y pense (F). Shamed be he who thinks evil of it.
hors de combat (F). No longer able to fight.

ibidem (ibid.) (L). In the same place.
ich dien (G). I serve.
idée fixe (F). Obsession.
in extremis (L). At the point of death.
infra dignitatem (infra dig.) (L). Beneath one's dignity.
in loco parentis (L). In the place of a parent.
in memoriam (L). In memory (of).
in perpetuum (L). For ever.
in re (L). In the matter of.
in situ (L). In its original position.
inter alia (L). Among other things.
in toto (L). Completely.
ipso facto (L). (Obvious) from the facts.
ipso jure (L). By the law itself.

je ne sais quoi (F). I know not what.
jeu d'esprit (F). Witticism.

laissez faire (F). Leave matters alone: a policy of non-interference.
lares et penates (L). Household gods.
lèse-majesté (F). High treason.

locum tenens (L). A substitute or deputy.

magnum opus (L). A great work; an author's principal book.

maître d'hôtel (F). Hotel-keeper; head waiter.

mal de mer (F). Sea-sickness.

mañana (S). Tomorrow (will do as well as today).

mariage de convenance (F). A marriage arranged for money or other material considerations.

mea culpa (L). It is my fault.

modus operandi (L). Method of working.

multum in parvo (L). Much in little.

mutatis mutandis (L). The necessary changes having been made.

ne plus ultra (L). Nothing further; the summit of achievement.

nil desperandum (L). Despair of nothing.

noblesse oblige (F). Noble birth imposes obligations.

nom de guerre (F). Assumed name.

nom de plume. F). Assumed name of an author.

non compos mentis (L). Of unsound mind.

non sequitur (L). It does not follow.

nota bene (N. B.) (L). Note well.

nouveau riche (F). Newly rich.

opus (L). Work (of art, music or literature).

outré (F). Eccentric; outside the bounds of propriety.

pace (L). By leave of.

par excellence (F). Pre-eminently.

par exemple (F). For example.

passim (L). Everywhere.

pax vobiscum (L). Peace be with you.

per annum (L). By the year.

per capita (L). By the head.

per centum (per cent) (L). By the hundred.
per diem (L). By the day.
per mensem (L). By the month.
persona grata (L). An acceptable person.
persona non grata (L). An unacceptable person.
pièce de résistance (F). Chief dish of a meal; main item.
pied-à-terre (F). Lodging for occasional visits.
poste restante (F). To await collection (from a post office).
prima ballerina (I). Principal female dancer in a ballet.
prima donna (I). Principal female singer in an opera.
prima facie (L). At first sight.
pro forma (L). As a matter of form.
pro rata (L). In proportion.
prosit! (G). Good health!
pro tempore (L). For the time being.

quid pro quo (L). Something offered for another of the same value.
quien sabe? (S). Who knows?
quo vadis (L). Whither goest thou?

raison d'être (F). Reason for existence.
rara avis (L). A rare bird; unusual person or thing.
reductio ad absurdum (L). A reducing to the absurd.
rendez-vous (F). Meeting-place.
requiescat in pace (L). Rest in peace.
résumé (F). Summary.

sans souci (F). Without care.
sauve qui peut (F). Save himself who can.
savoir-faire (F). Tact.
semper fidelis (L). Always faithful.
sine die (L). Indefinitely.
sine qua non (L). An indispensable condition.
sobriquet (F). Nickname.
soi-disant (F). Self-styled.

sotto voce (I). In a whisper or undertone.
status quo (L). The existing state of affairs.
stet (L). Let it stand (ignore correction marks).
sub judice (L). Before a judge (and not yet decided).
sub rosa (L). Under the rose; secretly.
sui generis (L). Of its own kind; unique.

table d'hôte (F). A set meal at a fixed price.
tempus fugit (L). Time flies.
terra firma (L). Solid earth.
tête-à-tête (F). Private talk between two people.
tour de force (F). Feat of skill or strength.
tout de suite (F). Immediately.
tout ensemble (F). Taken all together.

ubique (L). Everywhere.
ultima Thule (L). The utmost boundary.

vade mecum (L). A constant companion; manual of reference.
versus (L). Against.
vice versa (L). Conversely.
vis-à-vis (F). Opposite; face to face.

wagon-lit (F). Railway sleeping-car.
Weltschmerz (G). World weariness.

Zeitgeist (G). Spirit of the times.

Some Words with the Same Sound but Different Meanings

altar. Place for offerings to a deity; Communion table   *and*   **alter.** To change

ascent. Upwards climb   *and*   **assent.** Agreement

aught. Anything   *and*   **ought.** Should

bridal. Concerning a wedding	*and*	**bridle.** Part of a harness
calendar. The days of the year	*and*	**calender.** Roller used in paper-making
canvas. Rough fabric	*and*	**canvass.** To solicit votes
ceiling. Top of a room	*and*	**sealing.** Putting on a seal
cereal. Grain foodstuff	*and*	**serial.** Concerning a series
choir. Group of singers	*and*	**quire.** Quantity of paper (24 sheets)
coarse. Rough	*and*	**course.** Path; route
compliment. Polite remark	*and*	**complement.** That which completes
council. Assembly	*and*	**counsel.** Advice
currant. Dried grape	*and*	**current.** Stream; of the present time
draft. Rough copy (of a document)	*and*	**draught.** Current of air; drink
fare. Price of a journey	*and*	**fair.** Beautiful; honest
gamble. To play for money	*and*	**gambol.** To frolic
grate. To grind; place where a fire is laid	*and*	**great.** Famous; large
hoard. Secret store	*and*	**horde.** Gang or troop
load. Burden	*and*	**lode.** Vein of ore
miner. Person who works underground removing minerals	*and*	**minor.** Person under age
muscle. Fibre in animals producing movement	*and*	**mussel.** Type of shellfish
principal. Chief; first in rank	*and*	**principle.** Code; law
right. Correct	*and*	**rite.** Ceremony, *or* **write.** To inscribe
sight. The faculty of seeing	*and*	**site.** Place, *or* **cite.** To quote

signet. Seal	*and*	**cygnet.** Young swan
stationary. Motionless	*and*	**stationery.** Writing paper
stile. Steps over fence or wall	*and*	**style.** Manner of doing something
storey. Horizontal division of a building	*and*	**story.** Narrative
straight. Without curves or bends	*and*	**strait.** Narrow
sweet. Resembling sugar or honey in taste	*and*	**suite.** Several things constituting a set
symbol. Sign which stands for something	*and*	**cymbal.** Musical percussion instrument
weather. State of the atmosphere	*and*	**whether.** Which of two

Collective Names

We talk about 'a pack of wolves' or 'a pride of lions', and there are dozens of other special terms used for a group of animals, birds, people or things. Here are some of them:

drove of cattle
flock of sheep or goats
herd of buffalo or giraffes
litter of puppies
nest of rabbits
pack of hounds or wolves
pride of lions
swarm of ants, bees, wasps or flies
covey of partridges
flight of doves
flock of geese
stand of plovers

school of whales
shoal of fish
bench of magistrates
gang of thieves
horde of savages
posse of sheriffs, marshals or police
troop of horsemen
troupe of dancers, actors or acrobats
batch of bread
bunch of grapes or bananas
clump of trees

135

Abbreviations in General Use

More and more abbreviations are used in everyday speech as new organisations come into being; the following check list will help to identify many of them.

A1. First class.

A.A. Automobile Association.

A.A.A. Amateur Athletic Association.

A.B. Able-bodied seaman.

A.B.A. Amateur Boxing Association.

A.C. Alternating current.

A.C.A. Associate of the Institute of Chartered Accountants.

A.C.I.I. Associate of the Chartered Insurance Institute.

A.C.I.S. Associate of the Chartered Institute of Secretaries.

A.D. *Anno Domini* (in the year of Our Lord).

A.D.C. Aide-de-camp; Amateur Dramatic Club.

A.F.A. Amateur Football Association.

A.F.A.S. Associate of the Faculty of Architects and Surveyors.

A.F.C. Air Force Cross.

A.F.M. Air Force Medal.

A.I.B.P. Associate of the Institute of British Photographers.

A.M. *Ante meridiem.* (before noon).

A.M.I.C.E. Associate Member of the Institution of Civil Engineers.

A.M.I.Chem.E. Associate Member of the Institution of Chemical Engineers.

A.M.I.E.E. Associate Member of the Institution of Electrical Engineers.

A.M.I.Mech.E. Associate Member of the Institution of Mechanical Engineers.

A.N.Z.A.C. Australian and New Zealand Army Corps.

A.P. Associated Press.

A.P.M. Assistant Provost Marshal.

A.P.S. Associate of the Pharmaceutical Society.

A.R.A. Associate of the Royal Academy.

A.R.A.M. Associate of the Royal Academy of Music.

Railton-Mobil-Special, in which John Cobb reached 403.135 m. p. h.

Bluebird, Donald Campbell's record-breaking jet speed-boat

Lockheed Starfighter—type flown
by Capt. Irwin at 1,404.19 m. p. h.

Bristol Britannia

Boeing 707

De Havilland Comet 4

Handley Page Dart Herald

Vickers Vanguard

English Electric Lightning

Handley Page Victor B1

Blackburn NA. 39

De Havilland Sea Vixen

A.R.C.A. Associate of the Royal College of Art.

A.R.C.M. Associate of the Royal College of Music.

A.R.C.O. Associate of the Royal College of Organists.

A.R.C.S. Associate of the Royal College of Science.

A.R.I.B.A. Associate of the Royal Institute of British Architects.

A.R.I.C. Associate of the Royal Institute of Chemistry.

A.R.P.S. Associate of the Royal Photographic Society.

A.R.S.A. Associate of the Royal Society of Arts.

A.R.W.S. Associate of the Royal Society of Painters in Water Colours.

A.S.A. Amateur Swimming Association.

A.S.D.I.C. Anti-Submarine Detector Indicator Committee.

A.T.A. Air Transport Auxiliary.

A.T C. Air Training Corps.

B.A. Bachelor of Arts; British Association.

B.Agr. Bachelor of Agriculture.

Bart. Baronet.

B.B.C. British Broadcasting Corporation.

B.C. Before Christ; British Columbia.

B.Ch. Bachelor of Surgery.

B.C.L. Bachelor of Civil Law.

B.D. Bachelor of Divinity.

B.D.S. Bachelor of Dental Surgery.

B.E.A. British European Airways.

B.Ed. Bachelor of Education.

B. Eng. Bachelor of Engineering.

B. Litt. Bachelor of Letters.

B.M. Bachelor of Medicine.

B.M.A. British Medical Association.

B.Mus. Bachelor of Music.

B.O.A.C. British Overseas Airways Corporation.

B.O.T. Board of Trade.

B.P. British pharmacopoeia.

B.R. British Railways.

B.R.C.S. British Red Cross Society.

B.Sc. Bachelor of Science.

B.S.I. British Standards Institution.

B.S.T. British Summer Time.

Bt. Baronet.

B.Th.U. British thermal unit.

B.W.I. British West Indies.

C. Conservative; Centigrade; century.

C.A. Chartered Accountant.

Cap.; Caps. Capital letter(s).

C.B. Companion of the Bath.

C.B.E. Commander of the Order of the British Empire.

C.C. County Council.

c.c. Cubic centimetres.

C.D. Civil Defence.

C.E. Civil Engineer.

C.E. Church of England.

C.F. Chaplain to the Forces.

C.G.M. Conspicuous Gallantry Medal.

C.G.T. *Confédération Générale du Travail* (the French Trade Union Congress).

C.H. Companion of Honour.

C.I.D. Criminal Investigation Department.

C.I.E. Companion of the Order of the Indian Empire.

C.I.G.S. Chief of the Imperial General Staff.

C.J. Chief Justice.

C.L.B. Church Lads Brigade.

C.M.G. Companion of the Order of St Michael and St George.

C.M.S. Church Missionary Society.

C.O. Commanding officer.

C.O. Conscientious objector.

Co. County; company.

c/o. Care of.

C.O.D. Cash on delivery.

C. of E. Church of England.

C.O.I. Central Office of Information.

Col. Colonel.

C.P.O. Chief Petty Officer.

C.P.R. Canadian Pacific Railway.

C.S.C. Conspicuous Service Cross.

C.S.I. Companion of the Order of the Star of India.

C.T.C. Cyclists' Touring Club.

C.V.O. Commander of the Royal Victorian Order.

C.W.S. Co-operative Wholesale Society.

cwt. Hundredweight.

d. penny; day(s); date; died.

D.A. District Attorney.

D.B.E. Dame Commander of the Order of the British Empire.

D.C. Direct current; District of Columbia (United States).

D.C.L. Doctor of Civil Law.

D.C.M. Distinguished Conduct Medal.

D.D. Doctor of Divinity.

D.D.S. Doctor of Dental Surgery.

D.D.T. Dichlor-diphenyl-trichlorethane (insecticide).

deg. Degree.

D.F.C. Distinguished Flying Cross.

D.G. *Dei gratia* (By the grace of God).

D. Lit. Doctor of Literature.

D.Mus. Doctor of Music.

do. Ditto.

D.P. Displaced person.

D. Phil. Doctor of Philosophy.

Dr. Doctor; debtor.

dr. Drachm.

D.S.C. Distinguished Service Cross.

D. Sc. Doctor of Science.

D.S.M. Distinguished Service Medal.

D.S.O. Distinguished Service Order.

D.V. *Deo volente* (God willing).

dwt. Pennyweight.

E. East.

E. & O.E. Errors and omissions excepted.

e.g. *Exempli gratia* (for example).

e.m.f. Electromotive force.

E.P.N.S. Electroplated nickel silver.

E.R.P. European Recovery Programme.

Esq. Esquire.

Etc. Et cetera (and others; and so forth).

F. Fahrenheit.

f. Feminine; feet; francs.

F.A. Football Association.

F.A.N.Y. First Aid Nursing Yeomanry.

F.A.O. Food and Agriculture Organisation.

F.B.A. Fellow of the British Academy.

F.B.I. Federal Bureau of Investigation (United States); Federation of British Industries.

F.G.S. Fellow of the Geological Society.

F. Inst. P. Fellow of the Institute of Physics.

F.M. Field Marshal; frequency modulation.

F.O. Foreign Office.

F.R.Ae.S. Fellow of the Royal Aeronautical Society.

F.R.A.S. Fellow of the Royal Astronomical Society.

139

F.R.C.M. Fellow of the Royal College of Music.

F.R.C.O. Fellow of the Royal College of Organists.

F.R.C.P. Fellow of the Royal College of Physicians.

F.R.G.S. Fellow of the Royal Geographical Society.

F.R.I.B.A. Fellow of the Royal Institute of British Architects.

F.R.Met.S. Fellow of the Royal Meteorological Society.

F.R.P.S. Fellow of the Royal Photographic Society.

F.R.S. Fellow of the Royal Society.

F.R.S.L. Fellow of the Royal Society of Literature.

F.Z.S. Fellow of the Zoological Society.

G.A.T.T. General Agreement of Tariffs and Trade.

G.B. Great Britain.

G.B.E. (Knight or Dame) Grand Cross of the Order of the British Empire.

G.C. George Cross.

G.C.B. (Knight) Grand Cross of the Bath.

G.C.E. General Certificate of Education.

G.H.Q. General Headquarters.

G.I. Government issue; American enlisted man.

G.M. George Medal.

G.M.C. General Medical Council.

G.M.T. Greenwich Mean Time.

G.O.C. General Officer Commanding.

G.O.M. Grand Old Man.

G.P. General practitioner.

G.P.O. General Post Office.

G.S.O. General Staff Officer.

G.T.C. Girls' Training Corps.

H.A.C. Honourable Artillery Company.

H.C.F. Highest common factor.

H.E. His Excellency; high explosive.

H.H. His (Her) Highness.

H.M. Her (His) Majesty.

H.M.S. Her (His) Majesty's Ship; Her (His) Majesty's Service.

H.M.S.O. Her (His) Majesty's Stationery Office.

Hon. Honourable; Honorary.

h.p. Horsepower.

H.Q. Headquarters.

H.R.H. His (Her) Royal Highness.

H.W.M. High-water mark.

I.C.E. Institution of Civil Engineers.

I.C.I. Imperial Chemical Industries.

I.D.B. Illicit diamond buying.

i.e. *Id est* (that is).

I.L.O. International Labour Organisation.

Inc. Incorporated.

Incog. Incognito.

I.N.R.I. *Iesus Nazarenus Rex Iudaeorum* (Jesus of Nazareth, King of the Jews).

inst. Instant (the current month).

I.O.U. I owe you.

I.Q. Intelligence quotient.

I.R. Inland Revenue.

I.R.A. Irish Republican Army.

I.R.O. International Refugee Organisation.

I.S.O. Imperial Service Order.

it. ital. italics.

I.T.A. Independent Television Authority.

I.T.O. International Trade Organisation.

I.T.U. International Telecommunication Union.

I.T.V. Independent Television.

J.D. *Jurum Doctor* (Doctor of Laws).

J.P. Justice of the Peace.

jun.; jr. Junior.

K.B. King's Bench; Knight of the Bath.

K.B.E. Knight Commander of the Order of the British Empire.

K.C.B. Knight Commander of the Order of the Bath.

K.C.I.E. Knight Commander of the Order of the Indian Empire.

K.C.M.G. Knight Commander of the order of St Michael and St George.

K.C.S.I. Knight Commander of the Star of India.

K.C.V.O. Knight Commander of the Royal Victorian Order.

K.G. Knight of the Order of the Garter.

K.K.K. Ku-Klux Klan (United States).

K.P. Knight of the Order of St Patrick.

K.T. Knight of the Order of the Thistle; Knight Templar.

Kt. Knight.

L. Liberal.

Lab. Labour.

L.A.C. London Athletic Club.

Lat. Latin.

lb. Pound(s) in weight.

l.b.w. leg before wicket (cricket).

L.C.C. London County Council.

L.C.J. Lord Chief Justice.

L.D.S. Licentiate in Dental Surgery.

Lib. Liberal.

L.J. Lord Justice.

L.R.C.P. Licentiate of the Royal College of Physicians.

L.R.C.S. Licentiate of the Royal College of Surgeons.

l.s.d. *Librae, solidi, denarii* (pounds, shillings, pence).

L.S.E. London School of Economics.

L.T.A. Lawn Tennis Association.

Ltd. Limited.

L.W.M. Low-water mark.

M. *Monsieur;* Majesty.

M.A. Master of Arts.

M.B. Bachelor of Medicine.

M.B.E. Member of the Order of the British Empire.

M.C. Military Cross; Master of Ceremonies.

M.C.C. Marylebone Cricket Club.

M.Ch. Master of Surgery.

M.Ch.D. Master of Dental Surgery.

M.D. Doctor of Medicine.

M.F.H. Master of Foxhounds.

Mgr. *Monseigneur; Monsignor.*

M.I. Military Intelligence.

M.I.C.E. Member of the Institution of Civil Engineers.

M.I.Chem.E. Member of the Institution of Chemical Engineers.

M.I.E.E. Member of the Institution of Electrical Engineers.

M.I.M.E. Member of the Institution of Mining Engineers.

M.I.Mech.E. Member of the Institution of Mechanical Engineers.

M.I.N.A. Member of the Institution of Naval Architects.

Mlle. *Mademoiselle.*

M.M. Military Medal.

Mme. *Madame.*

M.O.H. Medical Officer of Health.

M.P. Member of Parliament; Military Police.

m.p.h. Miles per hour.

M.R.A.S. Member of the Royal Academy of Science.

M.R.C.P. Member of the Royal College of Physicians.

M.R.G.S. Member of the Royal Geographical Society.

M.R.I. Member of the Royal Institution.

M.R.I.B.A. Member of the Royal Institute of British Architects.

MS. Manuscript.

M.Sc. Master of Science.

M.T.B. Motor torpedo boat.

Mus.B. Bachelor of Music.

Mus.D. Doctor of Music.

M.V.O. Member of the Royal Victorian Order.

M.W.B. Metropolitan Water Board.

n. Neuter; noun.

N.A.A.F.I. Navy, Army and Air Force Institutes.

N.A.T.O. North Atlantic Treaty Organisation.

N.B. *nota bene* (note well).

N.C.B. National Coal Board.

N.C.O. Non-commissioned officer.

N.C.U. National Cyclists' Union.

N.F.U. National Farmers' Union.

N.H.S. National Health Service.

N.P. Notary Public.

N.R.A. National Rifle Association.

N.S. Nova Scotia.

N.S.P.C.C. National Society for the Prevention of Cruelty to Children.

N.S.W. New South Wales.

N.T. New Testament.

N.U.R. National Union of Railwaymen.

N.U.S. National Union of Students.

N.U.T. National Union of Teachers.

N.Y. New York.

N.Z. New Zealand.

O.B.E. Officer of the (Most Excellent) Order of the British Empire.

O.C. Officer Commanding.

O.C.T.U. Officer Cadets Training Unit.

O.E.D. Oxford English Dictionary.

O.E.E.C. Organisation for European Economic Co-operation.

O.H.M.S. On Her (His) Majesty's Service.

O.K. All correct.

143

O.M. Order of Merit.
o.p. Out of print.
O.T. Old Testament.
O.T.C. Officers' Training Corps.

P.A. Press Association.
P.& O. Peninsular and Oriental Steamship Company.
par. Paragraph.
P.A.Y.E. 'Pay as you earn' system of Income Tax collection.
P.C. Privy Councillor; Police Constable.
p.c. Postcard.
P.E.N. (International Association of) Poets, Playwrights, Editors, Essayists and Novelists.
Ph.D. Doctor of Philosophy.
pl. Plural.
P.L.A. Port of London Authority.
P.M. *Post meridiem* (afternoon); Prime Minister; Provost Marshal.
P.M.G. Postmaster-General.
P.M.O. Principal Medical Officer.
P.N.E.U. Parents' National Educational Union.
P.O. Post Office; Postal Order; Petty Officer.
pop. Population.
P.O.W. Prisoner of war.

P.P.S. Further postscript.
P.R. Proportional representation.
P.S. Postscript.
P.T. Physical training.
P.T.O. Please turn over.

Q. Queen.
Q.C. Queen's Counsel.
q.e.d. *Quod erat demostrandum* (which was to be demonstrated).
Q.M. Quartermaster.
Q.S. Quarter Sessions.
q.v. *Quod vide* (which see).

R. River; *Rex*.
R.A. Royal Academy; Royal Academician; Royal Artillery.
R.A.C. Royal Automobile Club; Royal Armoured Corps.
R.A.D.A. Royal Academy of Dramatic Art.
R.A.E.C. Royal Army Educational Corps.
R.Ae.S. Royal Aeronautical Society.
R.A.F. Royal Air Force.
R.A.M. Royal Academy of Music.
R.A.M.C. Royal Army Medical Corps.
R.A.N. Royal Australian Navy.

R.A.O.C. Royal Army Ordnance Corps.

R.A.P.C. Royal Army Pay Corps.

R.A.S. Royal Astronomical Society; Royal Asiatic Society.

R.A.S.C. Royal Army Service Corps.

R.A.V.C. Royal Army Veterinary Corps.

R.B.A. Royal Society of British Artists.

R.B.S. Royal Society of British Sculptors.

R.C. Red Cross; Roman Catholic.

R.C.A.F. Royal Canadian Air Force.

R.C.M.P. Royal Canadian Mounted Police.

R.C.N. Royal Canadian Navy; Royal College of Nursing.

R.D. Refer to drawer (bank mark for cheque returned unpaid).

R.D.C. Rural District Council.

R.E. Royal Engineers.

R.E.M.E. Royal Electrical and Mechanical Engineers.

Rev. Reverend.

R.G.S. Royal Geographical Society.

R.H.A. Royal Horse Artillery.

R.H.S. Royal Humane Society.

R.I.B.A. Royal Institute of British Architects.

R.I.P. *Requiescat in pace* (May he rest in peace).

R.M.A. Royal Military Academy.

R.M.S. Royal Mail Steamer; Royal Microscopical Society.

R.N. Royal Navy.

R.N.L.I. Royal National Lifeboat Institution.

R.N.R. Royal Naval Reserve.

R.N.V.R. Royal Naval Volunteer Reserve.

R.S.A.A.F. Royal South African Air Force.

R.S.M. Regimental Sergeant-Major.

R.S.P.C.A. Royal Society for the Prevention of Cruelty to Animals.

R.S.V.P. *Répondez s'il vous plaît* (please answer).

R.T.O. Railway Transport Officer.

R.U. Rugby Union.

R.V. Revised Version (of the Bible).

S. Saint.

s. Shilling; singular.

S.A. South Africa; Salvation Army.

S.C.M. Student Christian Movement.

S.E.A.T.O. South-East Asia Treaty Organisation.

S.H.A.P.E. Supreme Headquarters Allied Powers in Europe.

S.J. Society of Jesus.

S.M. Sergeant-Major.

S.O.S. 'Save Our Souls', distress signal.

S.P.C.K. Society for Promoting Christian Knowledge.

S.P.Q.R. The Senate and people of Rome; small profits, quick returns.

sq. Square.

S.R.N. State Registered Nurse.

S.S. Steamship.

Supt. Superintendent.

S.W.G. Standard wire gauge.

T.B. Tuberculosis.

T.F. Territorial Force.

T.G.W.U. Transport and General Workers' Union.

T.N.T. Trinitrotoluene (high explosive).

T.T. Tuberculin tested; teetotaller.

T.U.C. Trades Union Congress.

T.V.A. Tennessee Valley Authority (United States).

T.W.A. Trans World Airlines.

U.D.C. Urban District Council.

U.K. United Kingdom.

ult. Ultimo (last month).

U.N. United Nations.

U.N.A. United Nations Association.

U.N.E.S.C.O. United Nations Educational, Scientific and Cultural Organisation.

U.N.I.C.E.F. United Nations International Children's Emergency Fund.

U.N.O. United Nations Organisation.

U.P.U. Universal Postal Union.

U.S.A. United States of America.

U.S.S.R. Union of Soviet Socialist Republics.

v. *Versus* (against).

V.A.D. Voluntary Aid Detachment.

V.C. Victoria Cross.

V.H.F. Very high frequency.

V.I.P. Very important person.
V.S. Veterinary Surgeon.

W.A. Western Australia.
W.E.A. Workers' Educational Association.
W.F.T.U. World Federation of Trade Unions.
W.H.O. World Health Organisation.
W.I. Women's Institute.
W.O. Warrant Officer.
W.R.A.C. Women's Royal Army Corps.

W.R.A.F. Women's Royal Air Force.
W.R.N.S. Women's Royal Naval Service.
wt. Weight.
W.V.S. Women's Voluntary Services.

X. Christ.

Y.H.A. Youth Hostels Association.
Y.M.C.A. Young Men's Christian Association.
Y.W.C.A. Young Women's Christian Association.

147

PEOPLE AND SCIENCE

Nowadays a higher proportion of people than ever before live in well-built houses, have enough to eat, are well clothed and have at birth an expectation of life of some sixty to seventy years. Two centuries ago this expectation of life was not much more than half the present figure, for lack of medical knowledge together with poor living conditions resulted in much ill health and in epidemics which wiped out huge sections of the population at a single stroke.

Science has changed all this—through researches in medicine and agriculture, by finding ways to make the things we need more rapidly and more cheaply and by discovering new substances out of which we can construct the complicated machinery of the modern world.

Here are some of the techniques developed by science in the past two centuries:

Brick-making by Machine

Most countries have clay suitable for brick-making. This is dug out of the ground by mechanical shovels, then fed into a system of huge rollers which crush it into a fine, powdery substance. Moisture is added, and a band of clay is forced through a hole and then cut into individual bricks by wires. The wet bricks are slowly dried, then put in a kiln and baked at a high temperature.

Cement Manufacture

Modern building technique is very largely dependent on cement. Clay, chalk and limestone are crushed, then fed into a machine which mixes them with water into a thick cream.

This cream, known as 'slurry', is conveyed to a high-temperature kiln which reduces it to clinker. The clinker passes between a series of rollers which grind it up, and the pale grey powder which results is cement. For building purposes this is mixed in a revolving drum with sand and water, using proportions of from three to five shovels of sand to each shovel of cement. For concrete, up to six shovels of 'aggregate' (a mixture of sand and small stones) is used with each shovel of cement.

Electric Power

This is produced by using water power, some form of fuel, or atomic energy (see section on **Nuclear Power**). The pressure of water from a dam, or, alternatively, steam created by burning fuel, turns a dynamo. The rotation of this spins a rotor. The rotor is an electro-magnet, which, surrounded by a coil of wire, sets up an electric current in the wire.

Gas Production

Still the principal source of heat for household cooking, gas is made by baking coal in a container or 'retort'. The gas given off is stored in gasometers until required. By-products of the process include petrol, acids, drugs, perfumes, dyes, tar and coke.

Glass-making

The method of glass manufacture has changed little over the centuries, but the speed and mechanisation have been greatly increased. Specially selected sand is mixed with limestone and soda ash and melted until liquid. It is then rolled out to make plate glass, moulded to make the cheaper kinds of jars, tumblers and bottles or blown into shape for high quality articles. Glass-blowing is still done by hand; the blower dips a long tube into the molten glass, then blows through the tube as if inflating a balloon.

Paper Manufacture

The tremendous output of books and newspapers today means that many thousands of tons of paper have to be made every year. What was once a laborious process carried out by hand is now a highly mechanised industry. Paper is made of esparto grass, rag, wood-pulp or various mixtures of these materials. These are reduced to a fibrous pulp, boiled, and bleached. The pulp then travels along a moving belt over a suction chamber which removes excess moisture. The sheet which is formed through this process goes between rollers and drying cylinders until it emerges as a roll of white paper.

Printing

Until a hundred years ago printers had to set every letter of a book or newspaper by hand, even though a steam-driven rotary press had already come into use to speed up the actual process of printing a page. The invention of the linotype and monotype machines made it possible to set type as rapidly as a normal typewriter is operated. When a linotype machine is used, the operator presses down a letter on a keyboard, and this automatically selects a mould for that letter which is fed into place; each line in turn receives a flow of molten type-metal which cools into a complete line of type. In mono-type, perforations in a paper roll control the operation of the casting machine.

Rapid printing of newspapers and magazines is carried out by a rotary process. The complete page, when set, is used to print an indentation on a special sheet of soft material resembling cardboard. From this matrix it is possible to cast a curved metal plate containing a clear reproduction of all the type as originally set. This curved plate is bolted on to the cylinder of a rotary press, on one side of which is the ink roller and on the other side a pressure roller. Paper is fed between the cylinder and the pressure roller and emerges printed. Many great daily newspapers now have rotary presses which can turn out fifty thousand copies an hour.

Spinning

Two hundred years of progress in spinning have speeded up the process rather than changed the method. The original spinning-wheel produced one thread at a time. The wool, after washing, carding to remove lumps and combing to place the hairs in one direction, was twisted and rolled into yarn. The modern spinning machine does this to hundreds of threads at the same time.

Steel Manufacture

To make steel from cast iron it is necessary to remove certain substances which exist in it as impurities, the chief of which is carbon. The method of removal is generally by means of an open-hearth furnace, in which pigs, or bars of cast iron, are raised to a great heat by burning gas and air fed into the hearth at high pressure. The molten steel is poured into moulds, and the ingots thus made pass between rollers which press them into girders.

Water Supply and Drainage

Water as it comes from most rivers is not pure enough to drink. Also, we cannot depend on a river for supplies at all times of the year. The solutions to these two problems are purification and the use of reservoirs. River water, pumped into a reservoir, is taken out as required and placed in tanks containing purifying chemicals. From these, it flows to open tanks in which there are layers of gravel that filter away impurities. The final stage involves the addition of still more chemicals, and the water is then kept in covered tanks and reservoirs until pumped through the mains to individual houses.

Hot water is produced in the modern house by one of three methods: gas, electricity or solid fuel. In the first method, water is led over powerful burners, usually by means of a spiral tube, so that while the outlet tap is running the water is receiving heat from the burners. Water is warmed electrically by means of an immersion heater, which is an electric heating element, protected by a tube, placed inside a water tank. Heating water by a solid fuel stove requires an enclosed fire containing a water-jacket or an open fire with a back-boiler device. From the cold-water tank in the loft water runs down to the hot-water tank (often in a cupboard), and from there down a pipe to the bottom of the water-jacket. As the fire heats the water it rises up a second pipe to the hot-water tank. It is replaced automatically by colder water coming down the first pipe, and the circulation provides a constant supply of hot water in the tank-from which yet another pipe leads out, at the top, to supply the hot taps in the kitchen and bathroom.

Our modern drainage system is just as important as our water supply. In the past, refuse was thrown into open drains in the streets. Insects and germs breeding in these drains spread disease. Modern sewers all run below ground. The 'U' tube under the sink, bath and W.C., in which water always remains, prevents gases and unpleasant smells from coming up from the sewers into which the waste pipes lead. When the sewage reaches the sewage farm it is mechanically sieved to remove grit, which is later used for concrete and road-works. Then the solids are separated from the liquids in settling tanks. The liquids are agitated by a jet of compressed air, which makes the bacteria multiply rapidly and breaks down any remaining solids into small particles. The final products are a harmless liquid which can be released into a river or the sea, and mud which, when fermented, gives off a gas that supplies the main source of power for the sewage farm.

The following inventions have also done much to change the world in recent times.

Camera

Light entering a darkened box through a small hole will project an image inside the box of the scene outside—but in reverse and upside-down. In practice a lens with a shutter is used instead of a small hole, in order to admit more light. A sensitised plate or film at the back of the camera receives the impression. The film or plate is then removed in a dark room, where it is immersed in chemical solutions. This process produces a negative, with its black objects white and *vice versa*. A positive, or print, is made by placing the negative on sensitised paper and exposing it to the light, whereupon the white portions of the negative admit light. The sensitised paper is then treated with chemicals, and the original image appears.

Diesel Engine

This is a very high compression internal combustion engine. Air is drawn into a cylinder and compressed to about five hundred pounds per square inch. This raises its temperature to a point where, when fuel oil is pumped in, it immediately ignites and creates the explosion necessary to force the piston down.

Internal Combustion Engine

This is the name for the petrol engine used in cars, motorcycles and light lorries. A carburettor converts petrol into a fine vapour, and also draws in air which mixes with it. The mixture travels through a valve system into the top of a cylinder and is there exploded under pressure by means of an electric sparking plug. The explosion forces down the piston, from which a connecting rod runs to a crankshaft. On its return stroke the piston pushes out the burned gases through the valve system; its next journey down draws in a fresh supply of fuel, and its upward journey compresses the fuel in readiness for the next explosion.

Jet Engine

Turbojet. Modern aircraft are frequently fitted with turbojet engines, as they develop far greater power than piston engines. They run on paraffin, which is burned with compressed air to produce expanding gases which drive the blades of a turbine. On the same axle another turbine forces air into the firing chamber. The turbojet propels by forcing out a jet of hot air at its rear. The turboprop, a later development, uses its turbine to turn an air-screw.

Ramjet. This is an engine intended to 'take over' an aircraft once it has reached a speed of roughly two hundred miles an hour. Air is forced in at the nose of the engine, fuel is burned in it, and the resultant high pressure produces a propellant exhaust. The ramjet becomes more efficient as it gains speed, for speed adds to the intake of air and therefore to the potential thrust.

Plastics

There are two types — thermosetting and thermoplastic. The latter can be reshaped by the application of heat, but the former are subjected to heat during manufacture, and once moulded cannot be altered in shape. Thermoplastics include acrylic, vinyl and polystyrene—all in common use for household purposes and in toy-making. Many plastics are formed by treating coal derivatives such as phenol.

Steam Locomotion

Basically, the modern steam locomotive uses the same system as George Stephenson's original *Rocket*. Coal or oil is burned to produce fierce heat and create super-heated steam. This passes in controlled quantities to the cylinders, in turn pushing the pistons back and forth by being admitted to each cylinder first at one end and then at the other. This backwards and forwards movement is converted into a circular movement by connecting rods joined off-centre to the main driving wheels of the locomotive, and is passed from one main wheel to the next by coupling rods.

Submarine

The main sea-weapon in any future war would probably be the submarine, because of its proved worth in disrupting supply lines by sinking merchant ships and also because it is an ideal launching platform for short-range guided missiles. The principle of the submarine is that of double-shell construction. The crew's quarters and the engine rooms are in an air-tight shell, and between this and the outer shell are diving tanks. To submerge the submarine, these tanks are flooded by opening a series of valves. To return to the surface, powerful pumps are used to clear the tanks.
Propulsion is by diesel engine, battery-driven electric motors and, recently, nuclear power.

Great Inventions and Discoveries

Discovery or Invention	Person Responsible	Country	Year
Aeroplane	Wilbur and Orville Wright	United States	1903
Airship	Henri Giffard	France	1852
Atomic Structure	Lord Rutherford	Britain	1910—13
Balloon	Joseph Jacques Montgolfier	France	1783
Barometer	Evangelista Torricelli	Italy	1643
Bicycle	Kirkpatrick MacMillan	Britain	1839
Clock, Pendulum	Christiaan Huygens	Netherlands	1656
Diesel Engine	Rudolf Diesel	Germany	1897
Dynamite	Alfred Nobel	Sweden	1867
Dynamo	Michael Faraday	Britain	1831
Electric Arc Lamp	Sir Humphrey Davy	Britain	1809
Electric Battery	Alessandro Volta	Italy	1800
Food Preservation (in tins)	François Appert	France	1810
Gas Lighting	William Murdock	Britain	1792
Gramophone	Thomas A. Edison	United States	1877
Helicopter	Louis G. Bréguet	France	1909
Locomotive, Steam	Richard Trevithick	Britain	1801
Match, Friction	John Walker	Britain	1827
Match, Safety	J. E. Lundstrom	Sweden	1855
Microscope, Compound	Zacharias Janssen	Netherlands	1590
Motion-picture Camera	William Friese-Greene	Britain	1888

Motor-car	Gottlieb Daimler	Germany	1887
Nylon	E. I. du Pont de Nemours & Co.	United States	1938
Parachute	J. P. Blanchard	France	1785
Penicillin	Sir Alexander Fleming	Britain	1929
Photography	J. Nicéphore Niepce	France	1822
Pianoforte	Bartolommeo Cristofori	Italy	1709
Postage Stamp	Sir Rowland Hill	Britain	1840
Power Loom	Edmund Cartwright	Britain	1786
Printing, Movable Type	Johann Gutenberg	Germany	c. 1440
Radium	Pierre and Marie Curie	France	1898
Safety Lamp, Miner's	Sir Humphrey Davy	Britain	1816
Sewing Machine	Walter Hunt	United States	1832
Sextant	John Hadley	Britain	1731
Smallpox Vaccination	Edward Jenner	Britain	1796
Steam Engine	James Watt	Britain	1769
Steam Turbine	Sir Charles A. Parsons	Britain	1884
Tank	Sir Ernest Swinton	Britain	1914
Telegraph, Electro-magnetic	Samuel F. B. Morse	United States	1838
Telephone	Alexander Graham Bell	United States	1876
Thermometer, Mercury-in-glass	Gabriel Daniel Fahrenheit	Germany	1714
Torpedo (Modern)	Robert Whitehead	Britain	1868

Tungsten-fila-ment Lamp	Irving Langmuir	United States	1913
Typewriter	Christopher Sholes	United States	1868
Wireless	Guglielmo Marconi	Italy	1895
X-rays	Wilhelm Roentgen	Germany	1895

Journeys into Space

We live in the age of man's fastest progress. More scientific advances take place nowadays in an average year than were made in the first thousand years A.D. Man's curiosity takes him to the Poles, to the deepest parts of the ocean and many miles high into the sky.

What is the sum total so far in the exploration of space—and what may lie ahead within your own lifetime?

The first space 'probes' were the two Russian satellites, *Sputnik I*, and *Sputnik II*, in 1957, which were propelled by multiple-stage rockets to a distance of several hundred miles above the earth's surface and then directed into orbit so that they circled the earth on a definite course at a speed of about 18,000 miles per hour.

The Americans launched their first satellites in the early part of 1958, and then, in October, fired a multiple-stage rocket designed to explore the moon. It was equipped with television gear and it was hoped that it would send back a picture of the far side of the moon—the side which has never been seen by man.

This was a failure; at some 80,000 feet the flight ended and the object returned to the earth's atmosphere, where it rapidly overheated and was destroyed—the fate of all satellites re-entering the atmosphere, until a way can be devised of cutting down their speed of re-entry.

In January 1959, the Russians successfully launched an artificial planet, and in the summer of 1959 animals were sent up in rockets by both Americans and Russians and were returned safely to earth.

In September 1959, the Russian rocket *Lunik II* reached the moon and photographed its far side.

What will the next stage be? Possibly the setting up of space stations round the earth, with crews aboard. The pattern proposed would be that of a wheel which would rotate on its axis.

With the aid of space stations and the new sources of power which are being rapidly developed, many scientists believe trips to the nearer planets such as Venus and Mars will become possible. Mars would probably be the most rewarding, for observations by British, American and Russian astronomers in recent years have revealed the possibility of the existence of some form of life, apparently in the vegetable category, on that planet. Speculation about what are known as the 'canals' of Mars has gone one for half a century; astronomers have now observed that these follow straight paths, as if artificially created.

The answer to this and countless other questions lies in the future, but if progress continues at its present pace, uninterrupted by war, man may well make the first space journey within your lifetime.

Nuclear Power and its Peaceful Uses

Nuclear power—born of the research which made the first atomic bomb—is now being harnessed to peaceful uses and will change man's whole pattern of living within the next half century. But what is nuclear power, and how do we make it work for us?

It was a New Zealand scientist working in Britain, Lord Rutherford, who did much of the pioneer research which revealed the enormous power dormant in the nucleus of the atom—power enough to provide the world with unlimited resources, power which could heat every house and factory in the world, pump water to every desert on the globe and turn every machine-wheel man can create. His problem was how to release that power and how to do so safely.

What is an atom? The nuclear theory of the atom, which was put forward by Rutherford and his colleague Sir Joseph Thomson, was published as long ago as 1911. The atom consists of a minutely small but very heavy nucleus containing a positive electric charge; round this circulate much lighter electrons having a total negative electric charge which exactly equals the positive charge of the nucleus. In 1932, Sir James Chadwick discovered that the nucleus consists of protons, which are electrically positive, and neutrons, which are neutral.

How does power come into all this? All matter is made up of atoms of elements, and certain elements have atoms which are known as 'unstable'—meaning that the nucleus can be upset, giving off a tremendous amount of power. Once started, this process can be continued in what is known as a controlled chain reaction, providing a steady supply of power in the form of heat.

An atomic pile, or power unit, is made up of carbon blocks in which are placed rods of the unstable element uranium. Control of the heat is maintained by means of other rods, of boron or cadmium, either of which has the effect of slowing down nuclear reaction. These rods can be raised or lowered in the pile to regulate its output as the temperature drops or increases.

Putting the heat to practical use is done by forcing carbon dioxide through the pile by means of pumps. The gas emerges at high temperature and operates steam turbine generators which supply electricity to the National Grid.

The world's first economically practical atomic generator was put into use in Britain at Calder Hall, in 1956, and since then generators of various patterns but operating on the same basic principles have been working in the United States and Russia. Countries with less money and smaller industrial resources have formed groups such as the European Organisation for Nuclear Research, to provide themselves with the equipment to carry out their own experiments towards more advanced systems of developing atomic power.

But the story of nuclear power does not end with the setting up of hundreds of generators throughout the world to make us independent of coal and oil. Generators which depend on uranium to provide the active heart of the pile are expensive, as uranium is a rare metal. The next step is cheap nuclear power, and this seems likely to come from a hydrogen reactor. As the atomic reactor depends on the principle of the atomic bomb—fission—the hydrogen reactor depends on that of the hydrogen bomb, which is fusion. It is actually the fusion of light elements into heavier ones which produces the power in this case. The principle is the one which provides the sun's energy. Scientists hope to produce hydrogen reactors costing little to run and yielding electric power direct, without turbines and generators.

If they succeed, man will truly have achieved a limitless source of useful power. With it he can end poverty, end many of the diseases brought about by undernourishment, end the ill-effects of cold and damp and end hundreds of evils which seem remote from the fact of producing cheap electric power—such as road casualties. Thousands of people are killed and injured every year on the roads, mainly because we have too few resources to improve them as rapidly as the number of cars increases. Cheap power could run far more efficient road-making machines to produce high-speed safety roads, and it could also make possible far safer and more efficient cars to travel upon them. This is but one example. Stop for a moment to think of any other major problem facing mankind, and see if you can find a way in which cheap power would solve it.

Much of this change will take place in your lifetime if we take the opportunity which lies before us.

Anatomy

Like big buildings the body is constructed round a frame-work of girders. To this frame or skeleton all the muscles and important organs are attached.

The backbone or spine is made up of ring-like bones, and down the middle runs the spinal cord. At the top of the spine is the head, which is like a bone box, protecting the brain.

Attached to the spine is a cage of bones, the ribs, which protect the heart, lungs and liver. These ribs are joined at the front to the breast-bone.

To this breast-bone are joined the two collar-bones, and to these the two shoulder-blades and to these the arms.

At the lower end of the spine is the pelvis, to which are attached the legs.

The upper arm and thighs have one bone each; the fore-arms and lower legs, two bones each. The wrists and ankles contain groups of small square bones. Longer ones are in the palms and soles of the feet, and not quite so long ones in the fingers and toes.

There are seven major organs which carry out the various functions of the body.

The brain directs the body's working by receiving mes-sages through the nervous system and by sending messages to other parts of the body along the spinal cord and nerves.

The heart pumps the blood through the body by way of the arteries, and receives it back through the veins.

The lungs take air into the body by means of the upper respiratory tract. They also expel carbon dioxide, a waste product taken from the blood.

The stomach takes in food, begins the digestive process and sends the food through the intestines to complete digestion.

The liver and the pancreas discharge juices into the small intestine which aid in the digestion of food. The liver

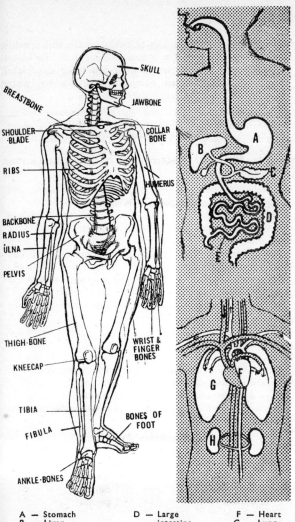

SKULL

BREASTBONE

JAWBONE

SHOULDER-BLADE

COLLAR BONE

RIBS

HUMERUS

BACKBONE

RADIUS

ULNA

PELVIS

THIGH-BONE

WRIST & FINGER BONES

KNEECAP

TIBIA

FIBULA

BONES OF FOOT

ANKLE-BONES

A — Stomach
B — Liver
C — Pancreas
D — Large intestine
E — Small intestine
F — Heart
G — Lung
H — Kidney

also stores vitamins, and aids in purifying the blood, while the pancreas regulates the amount of sugar in the blood.

The kidneys remove waste materials from the blood. These waste materials are carried to the bladder, where they are kept until evacuated from the body.

Weight and Measures

Weights. Imperial System (used in Britain and certain Commonwealth lands).

Avoirdupois Weight

27.34 grains	=	1 dram
16 drams	=	1 ounce
16 ounces	=	1 pound
14 pounds	=	1 stone
28 pounds	=	1 quarter
4 quarters	=	1 hundredweight
20 hundredweights	=	1 ton

Troy Weight (used by jewellers)

3.17 grains	=	1 carat
24 grains	=	1 pennyweight
20 pennyweights	=	1 ounce
12 ounces	=	1 pound
100 pounds	=	1 hundredweight

Apothecaries' Weight

20 grains	=	1 scruple
3 scruples	=	1 drachm
8 drachms	=	1 ounce
12 ounces	=	1 pound

Weights. Metric System (used in most other countries)

10 milligrams	=	1 centigram
10 centigrams	=	1 decigram
10 decigrams	=	1 gram
10 grams	=	1 decagram
10 decagrams	=	1 hectogram
10 hectograms	=	1 kilogram
10 kilograms	=	1 myriagram
10 myriagrams	=	1 quintal
10 quintals	=	1 metric ton

Weight Conversions

1 grain	=	0.0648 gram
1 dram	=	1.772 grams
1 ounce	=	2.835 decagrams
		(28.35 grams)
1 pound	=	0.454 kilogram
1 stone	=	6.35 kilograms
1 quarter	=	12.7 kilograms
1 hundredweight	=	50.8 kilograms

1 milligram	=	0.015 grain
1 centigram	=	0.154 grain
1 decigram	=	1.543 grains
1 gram	=	15.432 grains
1 decagram	=	5.644 drams
1 hectogram	=	3.527 ounces
1 kilogram	=	2.205 pounds
1 myriagram	=	22 pounds
1 quintal	=	1.968 hundredweights
1 metric ton	=	0.9842 ton

1 ton	=	1.016 metric tons

Measures. Imperial System

Linear Measure

12 inches	=	1 foot
3 feet	=	1 yard
5½ yards	=	1 rod, pole or perch
22 yards	=	1 chain
10 chains	=	1 furlong
8 furlongs	=	1 mile (1,760 yards; 5,280 feet)
3 miles	=	1 league

Square Measure

144 square inches	=	1 square foot
9 square feet	=	1 square yard
30¼ square yards	=	1 square rod, pole or perch
40 square rods	=	1 rood
4 roods (4,840 square yards)	=	1 acre
640 acres	=	1 square mile

Capacity Measure

4 gills	=	1 pint
2 pints	=	1 quart
4 quarts	=	1 gallon (0.833 Imperial gallon = 1 U.S. gallon)
2 gallons	=	1 peck
4 pecks	=	1 bushel
8 bushels	=	1 quarter
4½ quarters	=	1 chaldron

Cubic Measure

1,728 cubic inches	=	1 cubic foot
27 cubic feet	=	1 cubic yard

Measures. Metric System

Linear Measure

10 millimetres	=	1 centimetre
10 centimetres	=	1 decimetre
10 decimetres	=	1 metre
10 metres	=	1 decametre
10 decametres	=	1 hectometre
10 hectometres	=	1 kilometre
10 kilometres	=	1 myriametre

Square Measure

100 square millimetres	=	1 square centimetre
10,000 square centimetres	=	1 square metre
100 square metres	=	1 are
100 ares	=	1 hectare
100 hectares	=	1 square kilometre

Capacity Measure

10 millilitres	=	1 centilitre
10 centilitres	=	1 decilitre
10 decilitres	=	1 litre
10 litres	=	1 decalitre
10 decalitres	=	1 hectolitre
10 hectolitres	=	1 kilolitre

Cubic Measure

1,000 cubic millimetres =	1 cubic centimetre
1,000 cubic centimetres =	1 cubic decimetre
1,000 cubic decimetres =	1 cubic metre

Measure Conversions

Linear Measure

1 inch	=	2.54 centimetres
1 foot	=	30.48 centimetres
1 yard	=	0.9144 metre
1 rod	=	5.029 metres
1 chain	=	20.116 metres
1 furlong	=	201.16 metres
1 mile	=	1.6093 kilometres
1 millimetre	=	0.03937 inch
1 centimetre	=	0.3937 inch
1 decimetre	=	3.937 inches
1 metre	=	39.37 inches
		(1.0936 yards)
1 decametre	=	10.936 yards
1 hectometre	=	109.36 yards
1 kilometre	=	0.62137 mile

Square Measure

1 square inch	=	6.4516 square centimetres
1 square foot	=	9.29 square decimetres
1 square yard	=	0.836 square metre
1 square rod	=	25.293 square metres
1 rood	=	10.117 ares

1 acre	=	0.405 hectare
1 square mile	=	259 hectares
1 square centimetre	=	0.155 square inch
1 square metre	=	10.764 square feet
		(1.196 square yards)
1 are	=	119.6 square yards
1 hectare	=	2.47 acres

Cubic Measure

1 cubic inch	=	16.387 cubic centimetres
1 cubic foot	=	0.0283 cubic metre
1 cubic yard	=	0.7646 cubic metre
1 cubic centimetre	=	0.061 cubic inch
1 cubic decimetre	=	61.024 cubic inches
1 cubic metre	=	35.315 cubic feet
		(1.308 cubic yards)

Capacity Measure

1 gill	=	1.42 decilitres
1 pint	=	0.568 litre
1 quart	=	1.136 litres
1 gallon	=	4.546 litres
1 bushel	=	36.37 gallons
		(3.637 decalitres)
1 quarter	=	2.91 hectolitres
1 centilitre	=	0.07 gill
1 decilitre	=	0.176 pint
1 litre	=	1.7598 pints
1 decalitre	=	2.2 gallons
1 hectolitre	=	2.75 bushels
		(21.99 gallons)

Nautical Measures

6 feet	=	1 fathom
100 fathoms	=	1 cable
10 cables (6,080 feet)	=	1 nautical mile
1 knot	=	1 nautical mile *per hour*

Other Measures

1 tablespoon	=	$\frac{1}{2}$ fluid ounce
1 dessertspoon	=	$\frac{1}{4}$ fluid ounce
1 teaspoon	=	$\frac{1}{8}$ fluid ounce

Miscellaneous

1 gallon of water weighs 10 pounds.
1 horsepower is the power required to raise 550 pounds by 1 foot in 1 second.
1 kilowatt is the power required to raise 737.6 pounds by 1 foot in 1 second

Measures and Sizes for Paper and Books

Paper Sizes

Size	Inches
Foolscap	$13\frac{1}{2} \times 17$
Large Post	$16\frac{1}{2} \times 21$
Demy	$17\frac{1}{2} \times 22\frac{1}{2}$
Medium	18×23
Royal	20×25
Crown	15×20
Imperial	22×30
Elephant	20×27

Paper Measures

24 sheets	=	1 quire
20 quires (480 sheets)	=	1 ream
516 sheets	=	1 printer's ream
2 reams	=	1 bundle
5 bundles	=	1 bale

Book Sizes

Size	Inches
Foolscap Octavo	$6\frac{3}{4} \times 4\frac{1}{4}$
Crown Octavo	$7\frac{1}{2} \times 5$
Large Crown Octavo	$8 \times 5\frac{1}{4}$
Demy Octavo	$8\frac{3}{4} \times 5\frac{5}{8}$
Medium Octavo	$9\frac{1}{2} \times 6$
Royal Octavo	$10 \times 6\frac{1}{4}$
Imperial Octavo	$11 \times 7\frac{1}{2}$
Foolscap Quarto	$8\frac{1}{2} \times 6\frac{3}{4}$
Crown Quarto	$10 \times 7\frac{1}{2}$
Demy Quarto	$11\frac{1}{4} \times 8\frac{3}{4}$
Medium Quarto	$12 \times 9\frac{1}{2}$
Royal Quarto	$12\frac{1}{2} \times 10$
Imperial Quarto	15×11
Crown Folio	15×10
Demy Folio	$17\frac{1}{2} \times 11\frac{1}{4}$
Royal Folio	$20 \times 12\frac{1}{2}$

Thermometer Readings

The three systems for marking thermometers are Centigrade, Fahrenheit and Réaumur. Centigrade, which shows 0° for freezing and 100° for boiling water, is used throughout the world for scientific purposes; it is used for general purposes in Europe. Fahrenheit, in which 32° is the freezing temperature and 212° the boiling temperature, is the scale generally used in the British Commonwealth and in the United States. Réaumur, with 0° for freezing and 80° for boiling water, is nearly obsolete but is occasionally found in old books of European origin on scientific matters and cookery.

A comparison of Centigrade and Fahrenheit scales follows:

Centigrade		Fahrenheit
—40	=	—40
—30	=	—22
—25	=	—13
—20	=	— 4
—17.8	=	0
—15	=	5
—10	=	14
— 5	=	23
0	=	32
5	=	41
10	=	50
15	=	59
20	=	68
25	=	77
30	=	86
35	=	95
40	=	104
45	=	113
50	=	122
55	=	131
60	=	140
70	=	158
80	=	176
90	=	194
100	=	212

To change Centigrade to Fahrenheit, multiply by 9, divide by 5 and add 32.

To change Fahrenheit to Centigrade, subtract 32, multiply by 5 and divide by 9.

Normal blood temperature in human beings is 98.4° Fahrenheit.

Roman Numerals

I	=	1	LXXX	=	80
II	=	2	XC	=	90
III	=	3	C	=	100
IV	=	4	CC	=	200
V	=	5	CCC	=	300
VI	=	6	CD	=	400
VII	=	7	D	=	500
VIII	=	8	DC	=	600
IX	=	9	DCC	=	700
X	=	10	DCCC	=	800
XI	=	11	CM	=	900
XII	=	12	M	=	1,000
XIII	=	13	MCMLX	=	1,960
XIV	=	14	MM	=	2,000
XV	=	15	MMM	=	3,000
XVI	=	16	$M\bar{V}$	=	4,000
XVII	=	17	$\bar{V}$	=	5,000
XVIII	=	18	$\bar{X}$	=	10,000
XIX	=	19	$\bar{L}$	=	50,000
XX	=	20	$\bar{C}$	=	100,000
XXX	=	30	$\bar{D}$	=	500,000
XL	=	40	$\bar{M}$	=	1,000,000
L	=	50			
LX	=	60			
LXX	=	70			

Common Formulae

Circumference of Circle	=	$2\pi r$ ($\pi = 3.1416$; r = radius)
Area of Circle	=	πr^2
Volume of Sphere	=	$\frac{4}{3}\pi r^3$
Surface of Sphere	=	$4\pi r^2$
Volume of Cylinder	=	$\pi r^2 h$ (h = height)

173

Specific Gravity

Glass	=	2.4—2.6
Brass	=	8.1—8.6
Iron	=	8.95
Copper	=	8.95
Silver	=	10.3—10.5
Mercury	=	13.596

Coefficients of Expansion

Glass	=	0.000022
Iron	=	0.000033—0.000044
Copper	=	0.000051
Brass	=	0.000053—0.000057
Gases	=	0.00366

Boiling Points at 760 mm Pressure

Nitrous Oxide	—87.9° C
Chlorine	—33.6° C
Ammonia	—33.5° C
Ether	35.0° C
Chloroform	60.2° C
Alcohol	78.3° C
Benzene	80.4° C
Distilled Water	100.0° C
Sulphuric Acid	325.0° C
Mercury	357.25°C
Sulphur	444.7° C

Speed of Sound

Medium	Feet per Second
Through Air at 0° C	1,090
Through Water	4,758
Through Carbon Dioxide	850
Through Hydrogen	4,160
Through Glass approx.	16,500

Chemical Names of Everyday Substances

Substance	Chemical Name
Alcohol	Ethyl Alcohol
Alum	Aluminium Potassium Sulphate
Baking Powder	Sodium Bicarbonate
Boracic Acid	Boric Acid
Borax	Sodium Borate
Chalk	Calcium Carbonate
Common Salt	Sodium Chloride
Epsom Salts	Magnesium Sulphate
Fire-damp	Methane
Glauber Salts	Sodium Sulphate
Hypo	Sodium Thiosulphate
Lime	Calcium Oxide
Magnesia	Magnesium Oxide
Plaster of Paris	Calcium Sulphate
Red Lead	Triplumbic Tetroxide
Sal Ammoniac	Ammonium Chloride
Saltpetre	Potassium Nitrate
Salts of Lemon	Potassium Hydrogen Oxalate
Sal Volatile	Ammonium Carbonate
Spirits of Salts	Hydrochloric Acid
Vinegar	Dilute Acetic Acid
Washing Soda	Crystalline Sodium Carbonate
White Lead	Basic Lead Carbonate

Table of Elements

Atomic No.	Element	Symbol	Atomic Weight
1	Hydrogen	H	1.008
2	Helium	He	4.003
3	Lithium	Li	6.94
4	Beryllium	Be	9.013

5	Boron	B	10.82
6	Carbon	C	12.01
7	Nitrogen	N	14.008
8	Oxygen	O	16.00
9	Fluorine	F	19.00
10	Neon	Ne	20.183
11	Sodium	Na	22.997
12	Magnesium	Mg	24.32
13	Aluminium	Al	26.97
14	Silicon	Si	28.06
15	Phosphorus	P	30.975
16	Sulphur	S	32.066
17	Chlorine	Cl	35.457
18	Argon	A	39.944
19	Potassium	K	39.096
20	Calcium	Ca	40.08
21	Scandium	Sc	45.10
22	Titanium	Ti	47.90
23	Vanadium	V	50.95
24	Chromium	Cr	52.01
25	Manganese	Mn	54.93
26	Iron	Fe	55.85
27	Cobalt	Co	58.94
28	Nickel	Ni	58.69
29	Copper	Cu	63.57
30	Zinc	Zn	65.38
31	Gallium	Ga	69.72
32	Germanium	Ge	72.60
33	Arsenic	As	74.91
34	Selenium	Se	78.96
35	Bromine	Br	79.916
36	Krypton	Kr	83.70
37	Rubidium	Rb	85.48
38	Strontium	Sr	87.63
39	Yttrium	Y	88.92
40	Zirconium	Zr	91.22

41	Niobium	Nb	92.91
42	Molybdenum	Mo	95.95
43	Technetium	Tc	98.00
44	Ruthenium	Ru	101.70
45	Rhodium	Rh	102.91
46	Palladium	Pd	106.70
47	Silver	Ag	107.88
48	Cadmium	Cd	112.41
49	Indium	In	114.76
50	Tin	Sn	118.70
51	Antimony	Sb	121.76
52	Tellurium	Te	127.61
53	Iodine	I	126.91
54	Xenon	Xe	131.30
55	Caesium	Cs	132.91
56	Barium	Ba	137.36
57	Lanthanum	La	138.92
58	Cerium	Ce	140.13
59	Praseodymium	Pr	140.92
60	Neodymium	Nd	144.27
61	Promethium	Pm	146.00
62	Samarium	Sm	150.43
63	Europium	Eu	152.00
64	Gadolinium	Gd	156.90
65	Terbium	Tb	159.20
66	Dysprosium	Dy	162.46
67	Holmium	Ho	164.94
68	Erbium	Er	167.20
69	Thulium	Tm	169.40
70	Ytterbium	Yb	173.04
71	Lutetium	Lu	174.99
72	Hafnium	Hf	178.60
73	Tantalum	Ta	180.88
74	Tungsten	W	183.92
75	Rhenium	Re	186.31
76	Osmium	Os	190.20

77	Iridium	Ir	193.10
78	Platinum	Pt	195.23
79	Gold	Au	197.20
80	Mercury	Hg	200.61
81	Thallium	Tl	204.39
82	Lead	Pb	207.21
83	Bismuth	Bi	209.00
84	Polonium	Po	210.00
85	Astatine	At	210.00
86	Radon	Rn	222.00
87	Francium	Fr	223.00
88	Radium	Ra	226.05
89	Actinium	Ac	227.00
90	Thorium	Th	232.12
91	Protoactinium	Pa	231.00
92	Uranium	U	238.07
93	Neptunium	Np	237.00
94	Plutonium	Pl	238.00
95	Americium	Am	243.00
96	Curium	Cm	245.00
97	Berkelium	Bk	249.00
98	Californium	Cf	249.00
99	Einsteinium	E	255.00
100	Fermium	Fm	255.00
101	Mendelevium	Mv	256.00

Chemical Indicators

Indicators show whether a substance is alkaline, acid or neutral. The following list gives the effect of adding an indicator.

Indicator	Alkaline	Acid	Neutral
Litmus	turns blue	turns red	turns purple
Methyl Orange	turns yellow	turns pink	remains orange

Wind Force

When weather forecasters want to inform shipping of the exact strength of winds likely to blow in their areas, they do so by using the Beaufort Scale, referring to 'Force 2' or 'Force 5' as the case may be. The Scale is:

Force Number	Description	M. P. H.
0	Calm	0—1
1	Light air	1—3
2	Slight breeze	4—7
3	Gentle breeze	8—12
4	Moderate breeze	13—18
5	Fresh breeze	19—24
6	Strong breeze	25—31
7	High wind	32—38
8	Gale	39—46
9	Strong Gale	47—54
10	Whole gale	55—63
11	Storm	64—72
12	Hurricane	72—82
13		83—92
14		93—103
15		104—114
16		115—125
17		126—136

PEOPLE AND THE ARTS

Nowadays most of us are a little inclined to forget the importance of the arts in adding enjoyment and beauty to our lives and in shaping the world in which we live. Many people are inclined to dismiss great paintings as 'a lot of dry and dusty old pieces of canvas in museums', although the art of the great painters in the past has given us our skill in present-day industrial design, our knowledge of colours and our ability to make our own homes pleasant to look at and pleasant to live in.

Here are some of the leading artists, sculptors, musicians and writers of the past:

ADAM, *Robert (1728—1792).* Scottish architect who helped revive the handsome building styles of ancient Greece. Much of his work can still be seen in central London and in Edinburgh, where a large proportion of the 'New Town' was erected according to his designs. He was also a leading interior decorator, and rooms designed by him are very much prized today.

ADDISON, *Joseph (1672—1719).* Leading writer and politician. He is remembered today as a writer of light and amusing essays for the journal called *The Spectator,* which he founded in partnership with Sir Richard Steele. These essays are regarded as some of the finest examples of English writing.

AESCHYLUS *(525—456 B.C.).* One of the leading playwrights of ancient Greece, he is regarded as the father of Greek tragedy. His plays have been translated into English and make interesting reading.

AESOP *(620—560 B.C.).* Greek slave who compiled a large collection of moral fables, many of which are as applicable today as they were when first told.

180

ANGELICO, *Fra (1387—1455).* One of the greatest Italian Renaissance painters. Many of his finest pictures are in the galleries at Florence.

ARISTOPHANES *(450—385 B.C.).* Leading playwright of ancient Greece. Most of his plays are satirical and are still widely read and performed.

AUSTEN, *Jane (1775—1817).* English novelist. Wrote six books, *Sense and Sensibility, Pride and Prejudice, Northanger Abbey, Mansfield Park, Emma* and *Persuasion,* which are among the greatest novels in the English language. They have seldom been 'out of print' since they were first published.

BACH, *Johann Sebastian (1685—1750).* German composer and organist; was one of the founders of his country's tradition of orchestral music. Among his works are the *Mass in B Minor,* the *St Matthew Passion* and many cantatas and works for the organ.

BACON, *Francis (1561—1626).* Leading British politician during the reign of Queen Elizabeth I and King James I, but it is as an author that he is largely remembered. His best-known works are his *Novum Organum* and his *Essays.*

BALZAC, *Honoré de (1799—1850).* French novelist, famous for his penetrating studies of the society of his time. Among his best-known novels are *Le Père Goriot* and *La Cousine Bette.*

BEETHOVEN, *Ludwig van (1770—1827).* German composer, famous in particular for his symphonies. By the age of thirty he was completely deaf, though much of his great music was written after this time.

BERLIOZ, *Hector (1803—1869).* French composer of symphonies, operas and songs. His best known symphonic work is *Romeo and Juliet.*

BIZET, *Georges (1838—1875).* French composer of operas, including *The Pearl-Fishers* and *Carmen,* which is one of the world's most popular operas.

BLAKE, *William (1756—1827).* British poet and artist; author of many religious works, among them the *Prophetic Books* from which the popular hymn 'Jerusalem' is taken.

131

BOTTICELLI, *Sandro (1444—1510).* Italian Renaissance painter of the Florentine school. His greatest works are in art galleries in Florence.

BRAHMS, *Johannes (1833—1897).* German composer, whose works include several major symphonies, sonatas and much piano music popular with concert audiences.

BRONTË *Sisters: Charlotte(1816—1855), Emily(1818—1848) and Anne (1820—1849).* British novelists. Charlotte's books include *Jane Eyre, Shirley* and *Villette;* Emily wrote *Wuthering Heights;* Anne's two books were *Agnes Grey* and *The Tenant of Wildfell Hall.* Of these, *Jane Eyre* and *Wuthering Heights* are the most widely read today.

BROWNING, *Elizabeth Barrett (1806—1861).* English poet, and wife of poet Robert Browning. She is best known for her sonnets.

BROWNING, *Robert (1812—1889).* English poet. Some of his best-known works are *Paracelsus, Sordello* and *The Ring and the Book.*

BRUEGHEL, *Pieter, the Elder (1525—1569).* Flemish painter; one of the greatest of his period and founder of a school of artists.

BURNS, *Robert (1759—1796).* Scottish poet, famous for such poems as *Tam o'Shanter* and *The Cottar's Saturday Night* and for such popular songs as *Auld Lang Syne.*

BYRON, *George Gordon, Lord (1788—1824).* English poet, whose work has remained constantly 'in print' for a century and a half. He died in Greece, to which he had gone to aid the Greeks in their struggle for independence.

CÉZANNE, *Paul (1839—1906).* One of the greatest of the French Post-Impressionist painters. Like many of his contemporaries, he was not fully appreciated as an artist during his lifetime.

CHAUCER, *Geoffrey (1340—1400).* One of the greatest of English poets. His *Canterbury Tales* are widely read and enjoyed today.

CHEKHOV, *Anton (1860—1904).* Russian writer of short

stories and plays. Among his best-known works are the plays *The Cherry Orchard*, *The Three Sisters* and *Uncle Vanya*.

CHIPPENDALE, *Thomas (c. 1718—1779).* English furniture designer, who set the pattern for the furnishing of thousands of British households. Surviving examples of his work sell for many hundreds of pounds.

CHOPIN, *Frederic (1810—1849).* Polish composer and musician, famed for his piano compositions. It was a phrase of his music, broadcast over and over again by Warsaw Radio in 1939, which signalled to the world that the Polish Army was still holding out against the invading Germans.

COLERIDGE, *Samuel Taylor* (1772—1834). Poet, philosopher and critic. In the first rank of English poets. Some of his best-known works are *Kubla Khan*, *The Ancient Mariner* and *Christabel*.

COLERIDGE-TAYLOR, *Samuel (1875—1912).* British composer and violinist, best remembered for his cantata *Hiawatha*.

DANTE ALIGHIERI, *(1265—1321).* Italy's greatest poet; he was also a soldier and politician and at one time was sentenced to be burned at the stake for his political allegiance. His greatest work is the *Divina Commedia*.

DA VINCI *Leonardo (1452—1519).* Florentine painter and scientist. He produced plans for a submarine and an aeroplane, among other things, four centuries before they became practical engineering possibilities. His best-known painting is the world-famous *Mona Lisa*.

DEBUSSY, *Claude Achille (1862—1918).* French composer; wrote many well-known piano pieces, of which *Clair de Lune* is perhaps the most familiar.

DEGAS, *Hilaire Germain Edgar (1834—1917).* French Impressionist painter, famous for his studies of ballet dancers.

DICKENS, *Charles (1812—1870).* Leading English novelist, who is still widely read. His best-known works include *David Copperfield*, *Oliver Twist*, *The Pickwick Papers*, *Great Expectations* and *A Christmas Carol*.

DOSTOIEVSKY, *Fyodor (1821—1881).* Russian novelist, whose work has had much influence on subsequent writing. Among his best-known novels are *Crime and Punishment, The Idiot* and *The Brothers Karamazov.*

DUMAS, *Alexandre (1802—1870).* French novelist and dramatist. His best-remembered novels are *The Three Musketeers* and *Twenty Years After.* His son Alexandre (1824—1895) was also an author and playwright.

ELGAR, *Sir Edward (1857—1934).* British composer, wrote 'Land of Hope and Glory' as part of the *Pomp and Circumstance* march. His *Enigma Variations* is a popular concert work, and he also wrote many oratorios, among them *The Dream of Gerontius.*

EURIPIDES *(c. 484—407 B.C.).* Greek dramatist, famous for his tragedies, only a few of which survive. Among the best-known are *Alcestis, Medea* and *The Trojan Women.*

FLAUBERT, *Gustave (1821—1880).* French author, well known for his novel *Madame Bovary.*

GAUGUIN, *Paul (1848—1903).* French painter, renowned for his pictures of life in the Pacific Islands.

GIOTTO *(1267—1337).* Italian painter, considered the first painter whose work truly belonged to the Renaissance rather than the Middle Ages.

GOETHE, *Johann Wolfgang von (1749—1832).* German poet; the most famous of his works is his play *Faust.* In German writing he takes much the same position as Shakespeare in the history of English literature and drama. He was also a scientist of considerable importance.

GOGOL, *Nikolai Vasilievich (1809—1852).* Russian novelist and dramatist. His best-known works are his novel *Dead Souls* and his play *The Government Inspector.*

GORKY, *Maxim (1868—1936).* Russian novelist and dramatist. His best-known works are the novels *Mother* and *Comrades,* and the play *The Lower Depths.*

GOUNOD, *Charles François (1818—1893).* French composer, well known for his opera *Faust.*

GOYA Y LUCIENTES, *Francisco (1746—1828)*. Spanish painter and official Court artist. Although most of his works are in Spain, several paintings can be seen in the National Gallery in London.

GRECO, *El (1542—1614)*. The correct name of this Spanish artist was Domenico Theotocopuli, but his associations with the island of Crete led to the name 'El Greco'. His paintings and sculpture were religious in character.

HANDEL, *George Frederick (1685—1759)*. Composer; German-born, but became a British subject. He wrote nearly fifty operas and many oratorios, including *The Messiah*.

HARDY, *Thomas (1840—1928)*. English poet and novelist. Among his best-known novels are *Tess of the d'Urbervilles*, *Far from the Madding Crowd*, *The Mayor of Casterbridge*, *The Return of the Native* and *Jude the Obscure*.

HAYDN, *Franz Joseph (1732—1809)*. Austrian composer of many symphonies, operas, oratorios and anthems. His oratorios *The Creation* and *The Seasons* are performed frequently.

HOGARTH, *William (1697—1764)*. British painter, best remembered for his satirical cartoons of eighteenth-century life and manners in England.

HOLBEIN, *Hans, the Younger (1497—1543)*. German portrait painter, several of whose pictures are in the National Gallery in London. His painting of the family of King Henry VIII was lost in the Great Fire of London, but much of his work remains.

HOMER *(c. 850 B. C. ?)*. Probably born in Greece, he was the author of two great works, *The Iliad* and *The Odyssey*.

JOHNSON, *Samuel (1709—1784)*. British poet, essayist and lexicographer. Much information regarding him comes to us by way of his biographer, James Boswell.

JONSON, *Ben (1572—1637)*. English dramatist, famous for such comedies as *Volpone* and *The Alchemist*.

JOYCE, *James (1882—1941)*. Irish author; spent most of his life in Italy, Switzerland and France. His best-known works are *A Portrait of the Artist as a Young Man, Ulysses* and *Finnegan's Wake.*

KEATS, *John (1795—1821).* English poet; wrote for only about five years, but his outstanding work had a tremendous influence on later poets. Among his best-remembered writings are *Endymion, The Eve of St. Agnes, Ode on a Grecian Urn* and *Ode to a Nightingale.*

LAWRENCE, *David Herbert (1885—1930).* English novelist and poet; also wrote a number of penetrating travel essays. His leading novels include *Sons and Lovers, Aaron's Rod, The Rainbow* and *Women in Love.*

LISZT, *Franz (1811—1886).* Hungarian pianist and composer. His piano music, including the *Hungarian Rhapsodies,* is often heard at concerts.

MANET, *Édouard (1832—1883).* French Impressionist painter; was one of the first painters to use colour to express light and shadow.

MARLOWE, *Christopher (1564—1593).* English dramatist and poet, whose work undoubtedly influenced Shakespeare's early plays. His best-known plays are *Dr Faustus, Tamburlaine* and *The Jew of Malta.*

MATISSE, *Henri (1869—1954).* French painter. One of the leading artists of the modern schools, he was known especially for his use of pure colour and for his intricate compositions.

MAUPASSANT, *Guy de (1850—1893).* French writer, famous for his short stories.

MELVILLE, *Herman (1819—1891).* American novelist, many of whose writings dealt with the sea. His best-known books are *Moby Dick, Billy Budd* and *Typee.*

MENDELSSOHN - BARTHOLDY, *Jakob Ludwig Felix (1809—1847).* German composer, whose works are often played. Among his best-loved compositions are the oratorio *Elijah,* the '*Scotch*' *Symphony,* the '*Italian*' *Symphony* and the overture *Fingal's Cave.*

MICHELANGELO BUONARROTI, *(1475—1564).* Italian sculptor, architect and painter. The most famous of the

Florentine artists, he painted the frescoes in the Sistine Chapel in Rome.

MILTON, *John (1608—1674)*. One of the greatest English poets. Among his best-known works are *Paradise Lost*, *Samson Agonistes* and *Areopagitica*.

MOLIÈRE *(Jean Baptiste Poquelin) (1622—1673)*. Leading French dramatist. His most popular plays include *Tartuffe*, *Le Bourgeois Gentilhomme* and *L'École des Maris*.

MOZART, *Wolfgang Amadeus (1756—1791)*. Austrian composer. His most popular works include the operas *The Magic Flute* and *The Marriage of Figaro*, and many symphonies, concerti and string quartets.

OFFENBACH, *Jacques (1819—1880)*. German composer of light operas. These include the often-performed *Tales of Hoffmann*.

OVID *(43 B. C. — 17 A. D.)*. Roman poet; author of the *Heroides*, the *Amores*, the *Metamorphoses* and many other works which are read both in Latin and in translation.

PROUST, *Marcel (1871—1922)*. French novelist, famed for his series of novels *A la Recherche du Temps Perdu*.

PUCCINI, *Giacomo (1858—1924)*. Italian composer of many popular operas, including *La Bohème* and *Madame Butterfly*.

PURCELL, *Henry (1658—1695)*. English composer. He wrote much fine church music, including chants for the psalms, while organist at London's Westminster Abbey.

PUSHKIN, *Alexander (1799—1837)*. Russian poet and writer of stories. One of his most famous short stories is *The Queen of Spades*.

RACHMANINOFF, *Sergei Vassilievitch (1873—1943)*. Russian composer and pianist; wrote many popular concert works and also several operas.

RACINE, *Jean (1639—1699)*. Leading French tragic dramatist. His best-known plays include *Phèdre* and *Andromaque*.

RAPHAEL SANZIO *(1483—1520)*. One of the greatest

Italian painters of the Renaissance. His works are found in art galleries throughout the world.

REMBRANDT HARMENSZ VAN RIJN *(1606—1669)*. Dutch artist; one of the world's greatest portrait painters. Some of his work can be seen in London's National Gallery.

RENOIR, *Pierre Auguste (1841—1919)*. French Impressionist painter, famous in particular for his studies of women. His works appear in galleries all over the world.

REYNOLDS, *Sir Joshua (1723—1792)*. The first President of the Royal Academy and the greatest British portrait painter of his day.

ROSSINI, *Gioacchino Antonio(1792—1868)*. Italian operatic composer, best known for *The Barber of Seville* and *William Tell.*

ROUSSEAU, *Jean Jacques (1712—1778)*. French writer and philosopher. His best-known writings include *Confessions, Émile* and *Le Contrat Social.*

RUBENS, *Peter Paul (1577—1640)*. One of the best-known and appreciated of the Flemish school of painters; he had much influence on later artists. His paintings are found in major art galleries all over the world.

SCHUBERT, *Franz Peter (1797—1828)*. Austrian composer; died at the age of thirty-one. His many songs and his chamber music are very popular, as is his *Unfinished Symphony.*

SCHUMANN, *Robert (1810—1856)*. German composer, renowned for his symphonies, chamber music and many major piano works.

SHAKESPEARE, *William (1564—1616)*. English dramatist and poet, generally regarded as the world's greatest playwright. His wide range of tragedies, historical dramas and comedies has been performed more than the work of any other dramatist in history.

SHAW, *George Bernard (1856—1950)*. Irish playwright and critic. Among his best-known plays are *Pygmalion, Caesar and Cleopatra, Man and Superman* and *Saint Joan.*

SHELLEY, *Percy Bysshe (1792—1822)*. English poet. In his day he was considered revolutionary; today he is regarded as a poetic genius. Among his best-known writings are *Adonais*, *Prometheus Unbound* and *To a Skylark*.

SIBELIUS, *Jean (1865—1957)*. Finnish composer, renowned for his tone-poems, particularly *Finlandia*.

STENDHAL *(Henri Beyle) (1783—1842)*. French novelist; author of *Le Rouge et le Noir* and *La Chartreuse de Parme*.

STEVENSON, *Robert Louis (1850—1894)*. British novelist and poet, author of *Treasure Island, Kidnapped, The Strange Case of Dr Jekyll and Mr Hyde* and many other widely-read books.

STRAUSS, *Johann, the Younger (1825—1899)*. Austrian composer. His best-known works include the *Blue Danube Waltz* and *Tales from the Vienna Woods*, and the opera *Die Fledermaus*.

STRAUSS, *Richard (1864—1949)*. German composer, best known for such operas as *Der Rosenkavalier* and *Elektra* and such compositions as *Till Eulenspiegel*.

SWIFT, *Jonathan (1667—1745)*. British satirist, author of *Gulliver's Travels*.

TCHAIKOWSKY, *Peter Ilyich (1840—1893)*. Russian composer of symphonic, operatic and ballet music, including *Swan Lake, Nutcracker Suite* and *The Sleeping Beauty*. Others of his most popular works are the *1812 Overture* and the Fifth and Sixth symphonies.

TENNYSON, *Alfred, Lord (1809—1892)*. English poet. He was made Poet Laureate for his consistently high standard of work over many years. His greatest verses, such as *The Idylls of the King*, had medieval England as their subject.

TITIAN *(c. 1477—1576)*. The greatest painter of the Venetian school; many of his works can be found in the art galleries of Britain, France, Germany, Italy and the United States, as well as other countries.

TOLSTOY, *Leo Nikolayewich, Count (1828—1910)*. Russian novelist, two of whose works, *War and Peace* and *Anna Karenina*, are considered among the greatest novels of all time.

TURNER, *Joseph Mallord William (1775—1851).* English painter, famous for his seascapes and landscapes in which he devoted himself to the study of light, using brilliant, luminous colour.

TWAIN, *Mark (Samuel Langhorne Clemens) (1835—1910).* American novelist; author of *Tom Sawyer, Huckleberry Finn, The Prince and the Pauper* and *Pudd'nhead Wilson.*

VAN DYCK, *Sir Anthony (1599—1641).* Flemish portrait painter, appointed Court painter to King Charles I of England.

VAN GOGH, *Vincent (1853—1890).* Dutch painter, who in a short period of seven years as an artist produced vividly coloured canvases which are known and loved throughout the world.

VELASQUEZ, *Diego Rodriguez de Silva y (1599—1660).* Spanish portrait painter, famous in particular for his Court paintings such as *Las Meninas* (the *Maids of Honour*). His work influenced the development of modern painting.

VERDI, *Guiseppe (1813—1901).* Italian composer of church and operatic music. He wrote a number of operas which are widely performed, such as *Aida, Rigoletto* and *La Traviata.*

VERMEER *van Delft, Jan (1632—1675).* Dutch painter of portraits and landscapes, famed for his beautiful studies of light and its effects.

VERONESE, *Paolo (1528—1588).* Italian painter of the Veronese and Venetian Schools. His pictures are remarkable for their colouring.

VIRGIL *(70—19 B. C.).* Considered the greatest of all the Roman poets. His major work is the unfinished *Aeneid*, based on the story of the settlement of Aeneas in Italy after the destruction of Troy.

VOLTAIRE *(François Marie Arouet) (1694—1778).* French writer and satirist. Among his leading works are *Candide* and the *Dictionnaire Philosophique.*

WAGNER, *Richard (1813—1883).* German composer, whose operas, revolutionary in style in their day, include *Die*

Walküre, Lohengrin, Die Meistersinger and *Tristan und Isolde.*

WOOLF, *Virginia (1882—1941).* English novelist and critic. Among her best-known novels are *Mrs Dalloway, To the Lighthouse* and *The Waves.*

WORDSWORTH, *William (1770—1850).* English poet, noted for his supreme mastery of language. Was made Poet Laureate in 1843.

WREN, *Sir Christopher (1632—1723).* English architect and scientist. Was called upon by Charles II to plan repairs to old St Paul's Cathedral, but before these could be carried out the Cathedral was gutted in the Great Fire of London, and his work became that of designing the present Cathedral. He also designed more than fifty other churches.

YEATS, *William Butler (1865—1939).* Irish poet. One of the great poets of recent times, he was awarded the Nobel Prize for Literature in 1923.

PEOPLE AND SPORT

What is the purpose of sport? Is it records, results or simply the most enjoyable method of keeping healthy? Nobody can give the complete answer, but it is probably a combination of all three.

Every sport has its own story—usually a fascinating history and an origin far back in time. In the following pages you will find brief histories of some of the most popular sports, with their principal facts and figures.

Athletics

The first great athletes were the Greeks, who held Olympic Games more than two thousand seven hundred years ago. These Games were a regular feature of Greek life for more than a thousand years, but when the Romans abolished them, in 394 A. D., athletics became almost a forgotten art for many centuries. It was not until about two hundred years ago that cross-country running for wagers renewed interest in the sport. By the eighteen-fifties most schools had athletic teams and the universities held their own championships. The standards were low, however, compared with those of the present day. It took seventy years to push the high-jump record from six feet to seven feet, and long-distance runners have clipped many minutes off the best times ever recorded by their grandfathers.

It was the revival of the Olympic Games in 1896 that made athletics a sport for the millions, for the appeal of international competition is greater than any other.

Here are some of the world's athletics records:

Running

Event	Holder	Nation	Record	Year
100 yd.	M. E. Patton*	U. S. A.	9.3 s.	1948
220 yd.	D. W. Sime	U. S. A.	20 s.	1956
440 yd.	G. A. Davis	U. S. A.	45.7 s.	1958
880 yd.	T. W. Courtney	U. S. A.	1 m. 46.8 s.	1957
1 mile	H. J. Elliott	Australia	3 m. 54.5 s.	1958
2 miles	A. G. Thomas	Australia	8 m. 32 s.	1958
3 miles	A. G. Thomas	Australia	13 m. 10.8 s.	1958
6 miles	S. Iharos	Hungary	27 m. 43.8 s.	1956
10 miles	E. Zátopek	Czechoslo-vakia	48 m. 12 s.	1951
15 miles	E. Zátopek	Czechoslo-vakia	1 h. 14 m. 1 s.	1955
1 hour	E. Zátopek	Czechoslo-vakia	12 mi. 809 yd.	1951

Field Events

Event	Holder	Nation	Record	Year
High Jump	Y. N. Stepanov	U.S.S.R.	7 ft. 1 in.	1957
Long Jump	J. C. Owens	U. S. A.	26 ft. 8¼ in.	1935
Hop, Step and Jump	O. Fyedo-seyev	U.S.S.R.	54 ft. 9¼ in.	1959
Pole Vault	R. A. Gutowski	U. S. A.	15 ft. 8½ in.	1957
Putting the Shot	W. H. Nieder	U. S. A.	65 ft. 7 in.	1960
Hammer	H. V. Connolly	U. S. A.	225 ft. 4 in.	1958
Discus	E. Piatkowski	Poland	196 ft. 6½ in.	1959
Javelin	A. Cantello	U.S.A.	282 ft. 3½ in.	1959

* *First holder of record.*

Hurdles

Event	Holder	Nation	Record	Year
120 yd.	J. Davis	U. S. A.	13.4 s.	1956
220 yd.	E. Gilbert	U. S. A.	22.1 s.	1958
440 yd.	G. C. Potgieter	South Africa	49.7 s.	1958

193

Cycling

Since the bicycle craze of the eighteen-eighties, cycle racing speeds have steadily improved. Unfortunately, the value of world records has been reduced by the complexity of the ways in which they can be set up—such as *unpaced*, *standing start*, *flying start*, *human paced* and *motorcycle paced*. Not all performances come under the recognition of the *Union Cycliste Internationale*, and there is some doubt in certain cases about the accuracy of the timings to fractions of a second. The following is a selection of the more outstanding records:

Event	Class	Holder	Record	Country and Year
¼ mile	unpaced, standing start	L. Faucheux	27.8 s.	France, 1936
½ mile	unpaced, standing start	L. Michard	56.2 s.	France, 1931
1 mile	unpaced, standing start	G. Renaudin	2 m. 0.6 s.	France, 1938
1 hour	motorcycle paced	L. Vanderstuyft	76 mi. 504 yd.	France, 1928

Football

The history of football may date as far back as Roman times, when men of the army probably played *harpastum*, a Roman game remarkably like modern Rugby Football. In the sixteenth century the game was played in England by whole villages, often with as many as a hundred men on each side. Injuries were numerous and severe, and the game was extremely dangerous until the early part of the last century when many schools in England improved the game and set up codes of rules. These became standardised in the eighteen-sixties, when those who favoured 'the handling game' formed the Rugby Union and those who preferred non-handling established the Football Association. There are now seven distinct forms of football, but the three most widely played are Association (eleven players; world wide), Rugby Union (fifteen players; Britain, France, Australia, New Zealand, South Africa) and Rugby League (thirteen players; Britain, France, Australia, New Zealand).

Association Football

The world record crowd at an Association Football match was 200,000, at the World Cup Final of 1950, between Brazil and Uruguay in Rio de Janeiro. The highest score in a match recognised as official was Arbroath 36, Bon Accord 0, in a Scottish Cup match in 1885. The highest score in an international match was England 17, Australia 0, at Sydney in 1951.

World Cup Winners

1930 Uruguay	1950 Uruguay
1934 Italy	1954 West Germany
1938 Italy	1958 Brazil

F. A. Cup Winners

1871—2	Wanderers	1881—2	Old Etonians
1872—3	Wanderers	1882—3	Blackburn
1873—4	Oxford		Olympic
	University	1883—4	Blackburn
1874—5	Royal Engineers		Rovers
1875—6	Wanderers	1884—5	Blackburn
1876—7	Wanderers		Rovers
1877—8	Wanderers	1885—6	Blackburn
1878—9	Old Etonians		Rovers
1879—80	Clapham Rovers	1886—7	Aston Villa
1880—1	Old Carthusians		

1887—8	West Bromwich Albion		1910—11	Bradford City
1888—9	Preston North End		1911—12	Barnsley
			1912—13	Aston Villa
			1913—14	Burnley
1889—90	Blackburn Rovers		1914—15	Sheffield United
			1915—19	No competition
1890—1	Blackburn Rovers		1919—20	Aston Villa
1891—2	West Bromwich Albion		1920—1	Tottenham Hotspur
1892—3	Wolverhampton Wanderers		1921—2	Huddersfield Town
1893—4	Notts County		1922—3	Bolton Wanderers
1894—5	Aston Villa		1923—4	Newcastle United
1895—6	Sheffield Wednesday		1924—5	Sheffield United
1896—7	Aston Villa		1925—6	Bolton Wanderers
1897—8	Nottingham Forest		1926—7	Cardiff City
1898—9	Sheffield United		1927—8	Blackburn Rovers
1899—1900	Bury		1928—9	Bolton Wanderers
1900—1	Tottenham Hotspur		1929—30	Arsenal
1901—2	Sheffield United		1930—1	West Bromwich Albion
1902—3	Bury		1931—2	Newcastle United
1903—4	Manchester City		1932—3	Everton
1904—5	Aston Villa		1933—4	Manchester City
1905—6	Everton		1934—5	Sheffield Wednesday
1906—7	Sheffield Wednesday		1935—6	Arsenal
1907—8	Wolverhampton Wanderers		1936—7	Sunderland
1908—9	Manchester United		1937—8	Preston North End
1909—10	Newcastle United		1938—9	Portsmouth
			1939—45	No competition

1945—6	Derby County	1953—4	West Bromwich Albion
1946—7	Charlton Athletic	1954—5	Newcastle United
1947—8	Manchester United	1955—6	Manchester City
		1956—7	Aston Villa
1948—9	Wolverhampton Wanderers	1957—8	Bolton Wanderers
1949—50	Arsenal	1958—9	Nottingham Forest
1950—1	Newcastle United	1959—60	Burnley
1951—2	Newcastle United		
1952—3	Blackpool		

1. Football League Champions (1st Division)

1888—9	Preston North End	1905—6	Liverpool
1889—90	Preston North End	1906—7	Newcastle United
		1907—8	Manchester United
1890—1	Everton	1908—9	Newcastle United
1891—2	Sunderland	1909—10	Aston Villa
1892—3	Sunderland	1910—11	Manchester United
1893—4	Aston Villa		
1894—5	Sunderland	1911—12	Blackburn Rovers
1895—6	Aston Villa	1912—13	Sunderland
1896—7	Aston Villa	1913—14	Blackburn Rovers
1897—8	Sheffield United	1914—15	Everton
1898—9	Aston Villa	1915—19	No competition
1899—1900	Aston Villa	1919—20	West Bromwich Albion
1900—1	Liverpool	1920—1	Burnley
1901—2	Sunderland	1921—2	Liverpool
1902—3	Sheffield Wednesday	1922—3	Liverpool
		1923—4	Huddersfield Town
1903—4	Sheffield Wednesday	1924—5	Huddersfield Town
1904—5	Newcastle United		

1925—6	Huddersfield Town	1948—9	Portsmouth
1926—7	Newcastle United	1949—50	Portsmouth
1927—8	Everton	1950—1	Tottenham Hotspur
1928—9	Sheffield Wednesday	1951—2	Manchester United
1929—30	Sheffield Wednesday	1952—3	Arsenal
1930—1	Arsenal	1953—4	Wolverhampton Wanderers
1931—2	Everton	1954—5	Chelsea
1932—3	Arsenal	1955—6	Manchester United
1933—4	Arsenal		
1934—5	Arsenal	1956—7	Manchester United
1935—6	Sunderland		
1936—7	Manchester City	1957—8	Wolverhampton Wanderers
1937—8	Arsenal		
1938—9	Everton	1958—9	Wolverhampton Wanderers
1939—46	No competition		
1946—7	Liverpool	1959—60	Wolverhampton Wanderers
1947—8	Arsenal		

2. Scottish Cup Winners

1873—4	Queen's Park	1887—8	Renton
1874—5	Queen's Park	1888—9	Third Lanark
1875—6	Queen's Park	1889—90	Queen's Park
1876—7	Vale of Leven	1890—1	Hearts
1877—8	Vale of Leven	1891—2	Celtic
1878—9	Vale of Leven	1892—3	Queen's Park
1879—80	Queen's Park	1893—4	Rangers
1880—1	Queen's Park	1894—5	St Bernard's
1881—2	Queen's Park	1895—6	Hearts
1882—3	Dumbarton	1896—7	Rangers
1883—4	Queen's Park	1897—8	Rangers
1884—5	Renton	1898—9	Celtic
1885—6	Queen's Park	1899—	
1886—7	Hibernian	1900	Celtic

1900—1	Hearts	1929—30	Rangers
1901—2	Hibernian	1930—1	Celtic
1902—3	Rangers	1931—2	Rangers
1903—4	Celtic	1932—3	Celtic
1904—5	Third Lanark	1933—4	Rangers
1905—6	Hearts	1934—5	Rangers
1906—7	Celtic	1935—6	Rangers
1907—8	Celtic	1936—7	Celtic
1908—9	Cup withheld	1937—8	East Fife
	after riot	1938—9	Clyde
1909—10	Dundee	1939—46	No competition
1910—11	Celtic	1946—7	Aberdeen
1911—12	Celtic	1947—8	Rangers
1912—13	Falkirk	1948—9	Rangers
1913—14	Celtic	1949—50	Rangers
1914—19	No competition	1950—1	Celtic
1919—20	Kilmarnock	1951—2	Motherwell
1920—1	Partick Thistle	1952—3	Rangers
1921—2	Morton	1953—4	Celtic
1922—3	Celtic	1954—5	Clyde
1923—4	Airdrieonians	1955—6	Hearts
1924—5	Celtic	1956—7	Falkirk
1925—6	St Mirren	1957—8	Clyde
1926—7	Celtic	1958—9	St. Mirren
1927—8	Rangers	1959–60	Rangers
1928—9	Kilmarnock		

3. Scottish League Champions

1890—1	Dumbarton and	1896—7	Hearts
	Rangers	1897—8	Celtic
1891—2	Dumbarton	1898—9	Rangers
1892—3	Celtic	1899—	
1893—4	Celtic	1900	Rangers
1894—5	Hearts	1900—1	Rangers
1895—6	Celtic	1901—2	Rangers

1902—3	Hibernian	1929—30	Rangers
1903—4	Third Lanark	1930—1	Rangers
1904—5	Celtic	1931—2	Motherwell
1905—6	Celtic	1932—3	Rangers
1906—7	Celtic	1933—4	Rangers
1907—8	Celtic	1934—5	Rangers
1908—9	Celtic	1935—6	Celtic
1909—10	Celtic	1936—7	Rangers
1910—11	Rangers	1937—8	Celtic
1911—12	Rangers	1938—9	Rangers
1912—13	Rangers	1939—46	No competition
1913—14	Celtic	1946—7	Rangers
1914—15	Celtic	1947—8	Hibernian
1915—16	Celtic	1948—9	Rangers
1916—17	Celtic	1949—50	Rangers
1917—18	Rangers	1950—1	Hibernian
1918—19	Celtic	1951—2	Hibernian
1919—20	Rangers	1952—3	Rangers
1920—1	Rangers	1953—4	Celtic
1921—2	Celtic	1954—5	Aberdeen
1922—3	Rangers	1955—6	Rangers
1923—4	Rangers	1956—7	Rangers
1924—5	Rangers	1957—8	Hearts
1925—6	Celtic	1958—9	Rangers
1926—7	Rangers	1959—60	Heart of
1927—8	Rangers		Midlothian
1928—9	Rangers		

4. Home International Championship (since 1946)

1946—7	England	1952—3	England and
1947—8	England		Scotland
1948—9	Scotland	1953—4	England
1949—50	England	1954—5	England
1950—1	Scotland	1955—6	England,
1951—2	Wales and		Scotland, Wales
	England		and Ireland

| 1956—7 | England | 1958—9 | England and Ireland |
| 1957—8 | England and Ireland | 1959—60 | England, Wales and Scotland |

5. Rugby Union

International Championship (since 1946)

1946—7	Wales and England	1953—4	England, France and Wales
1947—8	Ireland	1954—5	Wales and France
1948—9	Ireland	1955—6	Wales
1949—50	Wales	1956—7	England
1950—1	Ireland	1957—8	England
1951—2	Wales	1958—9	France
1952—3	England	1959—60	England and France

6. Rugby League

Championship (since 1946)

1946—7	Wigan	1953—4	Warrington
1947—8	Warrington	1954—5	Warrington
1948—9	Huddersfield	1955—6	Hull
1949—50	Wigan	1956—7	Oldham
1950—1	Workington Town	1957—8	Hull
1951—2	Wigan	1958—9	St Helens
1952—3	St Helens	1959—60	Wigan

7. Challenge Cup Winners (since 1946)

1946—7	Bradford Northern	1952—3	Huddersfield
1947—8	Wigan	1953—4	Warrington
1948—9	Bradford Northern	1954—5	Barrow
1949—50	Warrington	1955—6	St Helens
1950—1	Wigan	1956—7	Leeds
1951—2	Workington Town	1957—8	Wigan
		1958—9	Wigan
		1959—60	Wakefield

Golf

Golf was begun in Scotland about five hundred years ago and shares with Association Football the distinction of being a truly international game, for there are golf courses today in almost every country in the world.

British Open Championship Winners (since 1946)

1946 S. Snead (U.S.A.)
1947 F. Daly (Great Britain)
1948 T. H. Cotton (Great Britain)
1949 A. D. Locke (South Africa)
1950 A. D. Locke
1951 M. Faulkner (unattached)
1952 A. D. Locke

1953 B. Hogan (U.S.A.)
1954 P. W. Thomson (Australia)
1955 P. W. Thomson
1956 P. W. Thomson
1957 A. D. Locke
1958 P. W. Thomson
1959 G. J. Player (South Africa)
1960 K. Nagle (Australia)

Ryder Cup Competition (Professional) (since 1947)

1947 U. S. A. 11 matches — Great Britain 1 match
1949 U. S. A. 7 matches — Great Britain 5 matches
1951 U. S. A. 9½ matches — Great Britain 2½ matches
1953 U. S. A. 6½ matches — Great Britain 5½ matches
1955 U. S. A. 8 matches — Great Britain 4 matches
1957 Great Britain 7½ matches — U. S. A. 4½ matches
1959 U. S. A. 8½ matches — Great Britain 3½ matches

Walker Cup Competition (Amateur) (since 1947)

1947 U. S. A. 8 matches — Great Britain 4 matches
1949 U. S. A. 10 matches — Great Britain 2 matches
1951 U. S. A. 6 matches — Great Britain 3 matches
(3 matches halved)

1953 U. S. A. 9 matches — Great Britain 3 matches
1955 U. S. A. 10 matches — Great Britain 2 matches
1957 U. S. A. 8½ matches — Great Britain 3½ matches
1959 U. S. A. 9 matches — Great Britain 3 matches

Lawn Tennis

This is a modern game, born of one much older. Real, or Royal, Tennis was played centuries ago and is still played to a limited extent today, but as it requires a walled court it is an expensive game. In the eighteen-seventies lawn tennis was invented in Britain, and the Wimbledon Championship —the unofficial championship of the world—was instituted almost immediately.

Wimbledon Champions (Men's Singles)

1877	S. W. Gore	1919	G. L. Patterson
1878	P. F. Hadow	1920—1	W. L. Tilden
1879—80	J. T. Hartley	1922	G. L. Patterson
1881—6	W. Renshaw	1923	W. M. Johnston
1887	H. F. Lawford	1924	J. Borotra
1888	E. Renshaw	1925	R. Lacoste
1889	W. Renshaw	1926	J. Borotra
1890	W. J. Hamilton	1927	H. Cochet
1891—2	W. Baddeley	1928	R. Lacoste
1893—4	J. Pim	1929	H. Cochet
1895	W. Baddeley	1930	W. T. Tilden
1896	H. S. Mahony	1931	S. B. Wood
1897—1900	R. F. Doherty	1932	H. E. Vines, Jr
1901	A. W. Gore	1933	J. H. Crawford
1902—6	H. L. Doherty	1934—6	F. J. Perry
1907	N. E. Brookes	1937—8	J. D. Budge
1908—9	A. W. Gore	1939	R. L. Riggs
1910—13	A. F. Wilding	1940—5	No competition
1914	N. E. Brookes	1946	Y. Petra
1915—18	No competition	1947	J. A. Kramer

1948	R. Falkenburg	1954	J. Drobný
1949	F. R. Schroeder, Jr.	1955	M. A. Trabert
		1956—7	L. A. Hoad
1950	J. E. Patty	1958	A. J. Cooper
1951	R. Savitt	1959	A. Olmedo
1952	F. A. Sedgman	1960	N. A. Fraser
1953	E. V. Seixas		

Davis Cup (International Lawn Tennis Championship) (since 1946)

1946	U. S. A. 5, Australia 0
1947	U. S. A. 4, Australia 1
1948	U. S. A. 5, Australia 0
1949	U. S. A. 4, Australia 1
1950	Australia 4, U. S. A. 1
1951	Australia 3, U. S. A. 2
1952	Australia 4, U. S. A. 1
1953	Australia 3, U. S. A. 2
1954	U. S. A. 3, Australia 2
1955	Australia 5, U. S. A. 0
1956	Australia 5, U. S. A. 0
1957	Australia 3, U. S. A. 2
1958	U. S. A. 3, Australia 2
1959	Australia 3, U. S. A. 2

Yachting

Probably the world's most famous yachting event is the series of races for the America's Cup. This was first competed for in 1851, and until 1958 it was a condition that the challenger had to sail across the Atlantic to qualify to compete. America has so far won every contest. The results since 1920 are:

1920 *Resolute* beat *Shamrock IV*
1930 *Enterprise* beat *Shamrock V*
1934 *Rainbow* beat *Endeavour*
1937 *Ranger* beat *Endeavour II*
1958 *Columbia* beat *Sceptre*

Cricket

Cricket became widespread in England in the seventeenth and eighteenth centuries, then became popular abroad as English settlers went to Australia, New Zealand, South Africa, India, Pakistan and the West Indies, all of which today take part in the Test Match series. Other countries where cricket is played are Holland, the United States, Canada, South America and most British Colonies, though in none of these does the standard approach what is recognised as 'first class'—the standard of the main national competitions in the Test-playing countries.

The first major overseas tour by an English team was a visit to Australia in 1861—2. It was in Melbourne, in 1877, that Australia won the first of all Test Matches.

Records in Cricket

Some of the most interesting cricket records are the following:

Highest score in first-class cricket—499 not out (Hanif Mohammed, in Pakistan, 1959)

Highest score in Test cricket—365 not out (G. Sobers, West Indies, for England against Pakistan, in Kingston, 1958)

Highest known score in School cricket—628 not out (A. E. Collins, in a match at Clifton College, Bristol, 1899)

Greatest number of runs in first-class cricket—61,237 between 1905 and 1934 (Sir J. B. Hobbs)

Most runs scored off a six-ball over—34 (E. Alletson of Nottinghamshire, off E. Killick of Sussex, at Hove, 1911)

Highest batting partnership—577 (V. S. Hazare and Gul Mahomed, in Indian cricket, 1947)

Highest score in a season—3,816 (D. C. S. Compton, in 1947, with an average of 90.85)

Greatest number of wickets by a bowler in one match—19 (J. C. Laker, for England against Australia, at Old Trafford, 1956, for 90 runs)

Greatest number of wickets in first-class cricket—4,187
between 1898 and 1930 (W. R. Rhodes)

Greatest total—1,107 (by Victoria against New South
Wales, 1926)

Test Match Results — England and Australia (The Ashes)

1876—7   Australia 1, England 1
1878—9   Australia 1
1880   England 1
1881—2   Australia 2, drawn 2
1882   Australia 1
1882—3   Australia 2, England 2
1884   England 1, drawn 2
1884—5   England 3, Australia 2
1886   England 3,
1886—7   England 2
1887—8   England 1
1888   England 2, Australia 1
1890   England 2, abandoned 1
1891—2   Australia 2, England 1
1893   England 1, drawn 2
1894—5   England 3, Australia 2
1896   England 2, Australia 1
1897—8   Australia 4, England 1
1899   Australia 1, drawn 4
1901—2   Australia 4, England 1
1902   Australia 2, England 1, drawn 2
1903—4   England 3, Australia 2
1905   England 2, drawn 3
1907—8   Australia 4, England 1
1909   Australia 2, England 1, drawn 2
1911—12   England 4, Australia 1
1912   England 1, drawn 2
1920—1   Australia 5

1921	Australia 3, drawn 2
1924—5	Australia 4, England 1
1926	England 1, drawn 4
1928—9	England 4, Australia 1
1930	Australia 2, England 1, drawn 2
1932—3	England 4, Australia 1
1934	Australia 2, England 1, drawn 2
1936—7	Australia 3, England 2
1938	England 1, Australia 1, drawn 2, abandoned 1
1946—7	Australia 3, drawn 2
1948	Australia 4, drawn 1
1950—1	Australia 4, England 1
1953	England 1, drawn 4
1954—5	England 3, Australia 1, drawn 1
1956	England 2, Australia 1, drawn 2
1958—9	Australia 4, drawn 1

English County Championship

1873	Gloucestershire and Nottinghamshire	1884	Nottinghamshire
1874	Derbyshire	1885	Nottinghamshire
1875	Nottinghamshire, Lancashire and Sussex	1886	Nottinghamshire
1876	Gloucestershire	1887	Surrey
1877	Gloucestershire	1888	Surrey
1878	Middlesex	1889	Surrey, Lancashire and Nottinghamshire
1879	Nottinghamshire and Lancashire	1890	Surrey
1880	Nottinghamshire	1891	Surrey
1881	Lancashire	1892	Surrey
1882	Nottinghamshire and Lancashire	1893	Yorkshire
1883	Nottinghamshire	1894	Surrey
		1895	Surrey
		1896	Yorkshire
		1897	Lancashire
		1898	Yorkshire

1899	Surrey	1930	Lancashire
1900	Yorkshire	1931	Yorkshire
1901	Yorkshire	1932	Yorkshire
1902	Yorkshire	1933	Yorkshire
1903	Middlesex	1934	Lancashire
1904	Lancashire	1935	Yorkshire
1905	Yorkshire	1936	Derbyshire
1906	Kent	1937	Yorkshire
1907	Nottinghamshire	1938	Yorkshire
1908	Yorkshire	1939	Yorkshire
1909	Kent	1940—5	No competition
1910	Kent	1946	Yorkshire
1911	Warwickshire	1947	Middlesex
1912	Yorkshire	1948	Glamorgan
1913	Kent	1949	Middlesex and Yorkshire
1914	Surrey		
1915—18	No competition	1950	Lancashire and Surrey
1919	Yorkshire		
1920	Middlesex	1951	Warwickshire
1921	Middlesex	1952	Surrey
1922	Yorkshire	1953	Surrey
1923	Yorkshire	1954	Surrey
1924	Yorkshire	1955	Surrey
1925	Yorkshire	1956	Surrey
1926	Lancashire	1957	Surrey
1927	Lancashire	1958	Surrey
1928	Lancashire	1959	Yorkshire
1929	Nottinghamshire		

Australian Championship for the Sheffield Shield

1892—3	Victoria	1898—9	Victoria
1893—4	South Australia	1899—1900	New South Wales
1894—5	Victoria		
1895—6	New South Wales	1900—1	Victoria
1896—7	New South Wales	1901—2	New South Wales
1897—8	Victoria	1902—3	New South Wales

1903—4	New South Wales	1930—1	Victoria
1904—5	New South Wales	1931—2	New South Wales
1905—6	New South Wales	1932—3	New South Wales
1906—7	New South Wales	1933—4	Victoria
1907—8	Victoria	1934—5	Victoria
1908—9	New South Wales	1935—6	South Australia
1909—10	South Australia	1936—7	Victoria
1910—11	New South Wales	1937—8	New South Wales
1911—12	New South Wales	1938—9	South Australia
1912—13	South Australia	1939—40	New South Wales
1913—14	New South Wales	1940—6	No competition
1914—15	Victoria	1946—7	Victoria
1915—19	No competition	1947—8	Western Australia
1919—20	New South Wales	1948—9	New South Wales
1920—1	New South Wales	1949—50	New South Wales
1921—2	Victoria	1950—1	Victoria
1922—3	New South Wales	1951—2	New South Wales
1923—4	Victoria	1952—3	South Australia
1924—5	Victoria	1953—4	New South Wales
1925—6	New South Wales	1954—5	New South Wales
1926—7	South Australia	1955—6	New South Wales
1927—8	Victoria	1956—7	New South Wales
1928—9	New South Wales	1957—8	New South Wales
1929—30	Victoria	1958—9	New South Wales

New Zealand Championship for the Plunket Shield

In the New Zealand Championship for the Plunket Shield, Auckland have won 15 times, Canterbury 13, Wellington 10, Otago 6 and Central Districts 1.

Rowing

There is no official world championship, but the events at the Henley Royal Regatta in Britain are generally recognised as indicating the champions. The two events which attract most interest are the Grand Challenge Cup and the Diamond Challenge Sculls.

209

Grand Challenge Cup (for Eights) (since 1946)

Year	Winner	Time
1946	Leander Club	7 m. 1 s.
1947	Jesus College Cambridge	7 m. 14 s.
1948	Thames R. C.	7 m. 2 s.
1949	Leander Club	6 m. 54 s.
1950	Harvard University (U. S. A.)	7 m. 23 s.
1951	Lady Margaret B. C. Cambridge	7 m. 16 s.
1952	Leander Club	6 m. 38 s.
1953	Leander Club	6 m. 49 s.
1954	Krylia Sovetov Club (U. S. S. R.)	7 m. 16 s.
1955	University of Pennsylvania (U. S. A.)	6 m. 56 s.
1956	French Army (France)	7 m. 6 s.
1957	Cornell University (U. S. A.)	6 m. 53 s.
1958	Trud Club (U. S. S. R.)	6 m. 40 s.
1959	Harvard University (U. S. A.)	6 m. 57 s.
1960	Molesey R. C.	6 m. 35 s.

Diamond Challenge Sculls (for Single Oarsmen) (since 1946)

Year	Winner	Time
1946	J. Séphériadés (France)	8 m. 21 s.
1947	J. B. Kelly (U. S. A.)	8 m. 49 s.
1948	M. T. Wood (Australia)	8 m. 24 s.
1949	J. B. Kelly (U. S. A.)	8 m. 12 s.
1950	A. D. Rowe (Leander Club)	9 m. 11 s.
1951	T. A. Fox (Pembroke College Cambridge)	8 m. 59 s.
1952	M. T. Wood (Australia)	8 m. 12 s.
1953	T. A. Fox (London R. C.)	8 m. 12 s.
1954	P. Vlasic (Yugoslavia)	8 m. 42 s.
1955	T. Kocerka (Poland)	8 m. 33 s.
1956	T. Kocerka (Poland)	8 m. 37 s.
1957	S. A. Mackenzie (Australia)	8 m. 25 s.
1958	S. A. Mackenzie (Australia)	8 m. 6 s.
1959	S. A, Mackenzie (Australia)	8 m. 29 s.
1960	S. A.. Mackenzie (Australia)	8 m. 3 s.

Oxford and Cambridge Boat Race

The Oxford and Cambridge Boat Race, from Putney to Mortlake, is another outstanding event in rowing. Winners since 1829 are:

1829	Oxford	1874	Cambridge
1836	Cambridge	1875	Oxford
1839	Cambridge	1876	Cambridge
1840	Cambridge	1877	Drawn
1841	Cambridge	1878	Oxford
1842	Oxford	1879	Cambridge
1845	Cambridge	1880	Oxford
1846	Cambridge	1881	Oxford
1849	Cambridge	1882	Oxford
1849	Oxford	1883	Oxford
1852	Oxford	1884	Cambridge
1854	Oxford	1885	Oxford
1856	Cambridge	1886	Cambridge
1857	Oxford	1887	Cambridge
1858	Cambridge	1888	Cambridge
1859	Oxford	1889	Cambridge
1860	Cambridge	1890	Oxford
1861	Oxford	1891	Oxford
1862	Oxford	1892	Oxford
1863	Oxford	1893	Oxford
1864	Oxford	1894	Oxford
1865	Oxford	1895	Oxford
1866	Oxford	1896	Oxford
1867	Oxford	1897	Oxford
1868	Oxford	1898	Oxford
1869	Oxford	1899	Cambridge
1870	Cambridge	1900	Cambridge
1871	Cambridge	1901	Oxford
1872	Cambridge	1902	Cambridge
1873	Cambridge	1903	Cambridge

1904 Cambridge	1932 Cambridge
1905 Oxford	1933 Cambridge
1906 Cambridge	1934 Cambridge
1907 Cambridge	1935 Cambridge
1908 Cambridge	1936 Cambridge
1909 Oxford	1937 Oxford
1910 Oxford	1938 Oxford
1911 Oxford	1939 Cambridge
1912 Oxford	1940—
1913 Oxford	1945-No competition
1914 Cambridge	1946 Oxford
1915—	1947 Cambridge
1919 No competition	1948 Cambridge
1920 Cambridge	1949 Cambridge
1921 Cambridge	1950 Cambridge
1922 Cambridge	1951 Cambridge
1923 Oxford	1952 Oxford
1924 Cambridge	1953 Cambridge
1925 Cambridge	1954 Oxford
1926 Cambridge	1955 Cambridge
1927 Cambridge	1956 Cambridge
1928 Cambridge	1957 Cambridge
1929 Cambridge	1958 Cambridge
1930 Cambridge	1959 Oxford
1931 Cambridge	1960 Oxford

Cross Country

International Championship (since 1946)

1946 France	1953 England
1947 France	1954 England
1948 Belgium	1955 England
1949 France	1956 France
1950 France	1957 Belgium
1951 England	1958 England
1952 France	1959 England

Swimming

Standards of swimming have improved very rapidly during the last hundred years as new strokes have been discovered. The 'marathon' in swimming is the Channel swim. This was first achieved in 1874 by Captain M. Webb (Britain), in 21 hours and 45 minutes; the fastest time so far has been 10 hours and 50 minutes, made by Hassan Abd el Rehim (Egypt), in 1950.

World Records (Free-style)

Distance	Holder	Nation	Time	Year
110 yards	J. Devitt	Australia	55.1 s.	1959
220 yards	J. Konrads	Australia	2 m. 2.2 s.	1959
440 yards	J. Konrads	Australia	4 m. 19 s.	1960
880 yards	J. Konrads	Australia	8 m. 59.6 s.	1959
1,650 yards	J. Konrads	Australia	17 m. 28.7 s.	1960

Walking

World Records

Distance	Holder	Nation	Time	Year
2 miles	G. H. W. Hardmo	Sweden	12 m. 45 s.	1945
5 miles	J. Doležal	Czechoslovakia	34 m. 32.8 s.	1955
7 miles	G. H. W. Hardmo	Sweden	48 m. 15.2 s.	1945
10 miles	J. Doležal	Czechoslovakia	1 h. 10 m. 45.8 s.	1954
20 miles	A. Vedjakov	U. S. S. R.	2 h. 3 m. 33 s.	1958

Skating

World Speed Champions (Men) (since 1947)

1947 L. Parkkinen (Finland)
1948 O. Lundberg (Norway)
1949 K. Pajor (Hungary)
1950 H. Andersen (Norway)
1951 H. Andersen
1952 H. Andersen
1953 O. Goncharenko (U.S.S.R.)

1954 B Schilkov (U.S.S.R.)
1955 S. Ericsson (Sweden)
1956 O. Goncharenko
1957 K. Johannesen (Norway)
1958 O. Goncharenko
1959 J. Jaervinen (Finland)
1960 B. Stenin (U.S.S.R.)

Top Sportsmen

Here are some of the leading personalities in soccer, cricket, rugger, athletics, swimming, diving and other sports which make the headlines.

A'COURT, Alan. England International wing-forward; signed for Liverpool in 1952 and the following year toured America with them, at outside-left.

ALLCHURCH, Ivor. Welsh International inside-left since 1950. One of Swansea Town's highest scorers for many seasons and now with Newcastle United, he has played in more than a dozen Internationals.

ALLCHURCH, Len. Welsh International in the Swansea forward line; won his first Cap in 1955, and by 1958 was a regular choice for Wales.

ALLDAY, Peter. British Olympic hammer-thrower at the 1956 Games in Melbourne; set up an English Native Record of 191 feet 3 inches for the hammer. Has won the A. A. A. Championship.

ALLEN, Ronnie. England soccer International since 1951; has several times been top scorer of the season in the West Bromwich League side.

214

ALLISS, Peter. Played golf as an amateur for England against Scotland in Boys' Internationals; later, as a professional, competed for Britain in the Ryder Cup, and won numerous tournaments.

BAILEY, Trevor. First played cricket for Essex in 1946; was a Cambridge Blue in the next two seasons. Has played for England in over fifty Tests as right-hand batsman and right-arm medium-pace bowler.

BAKER, Douglas. Oxford Rugger Blue in 1951—2; later became outside-half or full-back for Middlesex. Has been an England International since 1955.

BARRETT, John. Cambridge Lawn Tennis Blue in 1952—1953; captained the Lawn Tennis Association team in America in 1953, and played in the 1956 Davis Cup.

BARRINGTON, Ken. A leading Surrey batsman, he played for England for the first time in the 1959 Test series against India, and established himself for the West Indies tour the next winter and the 1960 series against South Africa.

BEAVAN, John. Breast-stroke swimmer; began swimming for Wales in 1955. Swam for Britain in 1956, in which year he was second in the National Championships.

BECKER, Roger. British Davis Cup lawn tennis player; reached Junior Championship class in 1951, and went on to win many senior tournaments. Was Inter-Services and R.A.F. Champion in 1952.

BEDSER, Alec. Has played cricket for Surrey for more than twenty years. He is one of only four England bowlers who have taken more than a hundred wickets in Tests against Australia.

BEDSER, Eric. Twin brother of Alec; joined Surrey at the same time. An all-rounder who, though just missing Test honours, played a big part in Surrey's successes.

BEHARRELL, John. Played golf for English Boys against Scottish in 1955, and was semi-finalist in the Boys' Championship. Won the British Amateur Championship in the following year.

BEVAN, Brian. Rugby League right-winger with Warrington; holds two Cup Final Winners' Medals, also three Championship Medals. Has scored over six hundred tries.

BINGHAM, Billy. Outside-right for Ireland in many Internationals, he moved from the Irish club Glentoran to Sunderland in 1950, and on to Luton Town in 1959.

BLANCHFLOWER, Danny. Irish International Captain; was right-half for Aston Villa until 1954, and then moved to Tottenham Hotspur.

BLICK, Ray. Won the British Senior Championship for Single Kayak Canoes in 1955, and reached the finals at the Melbourne Olympic Games of 1956.

BLUNSTONE, Frank. England International outside-left; moved from Crewe Alexandra to Chelsea in 1953, and won his first England Cap the following season.

BONALLACK, Michael. Won the Boys' Golf Championship in 1952, and has since had many successes in senior golf championships and tournaments, including membership of the British Team against the Rest of Europe.

BOOKER, Michael. Began skating at eleven, and a year later won the Boys' Open Free Skating Championship. Won the British Amateur Championship in 1952, and became a British International Skater.

BOSTON, Billy. At nineteen, was the youngest Rugby League player ever to be picked for an Australian tour, and has since been one of Wigan's highest scorers.

BOUSFIELD, Ken. Ryder Cup golfer; has won many tournaments and championships in Britain and on tours abroad, including the P. G. A. Close Championship, the German Open and the *News of the World* Tournament.

BRADSHAW, Harry. Ryder Cup golfer; has been Irish Professional Champion nine times. Was runner-up in the British Open Championship in 1949, and won the P. G. A. Close Championship in 1958.

BROWN, Eric. Became a professional golfer after winning the Scottish Amateur Championship in 1946. Has since won

Roger Bannister breaking
the 4-minute mile record

Emil Zátopek

Jesse Owens—Long Jump

G. C. Potgieter—440 Yards Hurdles

Throwing the Javelin

Hop, Step and Jump

Pole Vault

H. V. Connolly—
Throwing the Hammer

Putting the Shot

Throwing the Discus

Lew Hoad

Peter May

Billy Wright

Alex Olmedo

many Open Championships, and has played for the British Ryder Cup team.

BUTTERFIELD, Jeffrey. England Rugby Union International; toured South Africa with the British Lions team in 1955 and was highest scorer in the Tests.

CANN, Raymond. Began diving at the age of twelve, and won the Boys' National Championship in 1953. Was in the 1956 Olympic diving team.

CARR, Donald. Oxford Cricket Blue and Captain in 1950; played for Derbyshire from 1951, and became Captain in 1955. Was Vice-Captain of the M. C. C. team in India and Pakistan in 1951—2. Holds the Derbyshire batting record 2,292 in a season.

CHARLTON, Bobby. Leading goal-scorer for Manchester United in 1959; was first capped for England in the previous season and has since held a regular place in the National side.

CHARNLEY, Dave. Leading British lightweight boxer; has been a serious contender for the World Title for several years. He is a former Youth and A. B. A. Champion.

CLAPTON, Danny. One of the up-and-coming players in English soccer; joined Arsenal from amateur football in 1953 as a fast-scoring outside-right, and was capped for England in 1959.

CLARK, Ron. Began athletics in 1950, and progressed from half-mile and one-mile events to cross-country and long-distance running. Has won many marathons, and raced in the 1956 Olympic Marathon.

COLYER, Geoffrey. British canoe racer; won the 10,000 Metres Singles Championship three years running. Canoed for Britain in the 1952 Olympics and the 1954 World Championships.

COTTON, Henry. Three times British Open Golf Champion in the nineteen-thirties; was seventh in the 1958 Championship, more than twenty years later. Holds many course and championship records.

COWDREY, Colin. Scored 93 in school cricket at the age of seven. Played for Kent from 1950, and has appeared for England in most Tests since 1954.

CRANMER, Steffen. Was English Junior Small-bore Rifle Shooting Champion from 1950 to 1952. Competed in the 1954 World Championships and the Olympic Games of 1952 and 1956.

DALY, Fred. Irish golfer; was British Open Champion in 1947 and Match Play Champion in the same year. Played in his first Ryder Cup 1947.

DANIEL, Ray. Welsh International soccer player since 1951. Was an amateur for Swansea, then a professional with Arsenal and Sunderland, as centre-half.

DAVIES, Michael. Was Welsh Junior Lawn Tennis Champion for three years, and played in the Davis Cup at the age of nineteen. Has since beaten many leading players.

DAVIS, Joe. World Professional Snooker Champion from 1927 to 1946, and United Kingdom Billiards Champion from 1926 to 1946. Holds the world record snooker break of 147.

EASON, Leo. Began skating in 1948, and after winning many area championships gained International honours and represented Great Britain in the 1956 World Championships.

EVANS, Godfrey. Began County cricket for Kent in 1939, after playing since childhood. Played in over eighty Tests for England. Holds world record of Test dismissals by a wicket-keeper.

FAULKNER, Max. Was British Open Golf Champion in 1951. A Ryder Cup player from 1947, he has also won the Spanish Open, The Match Play Championship and many tournaments in Britain and overseas.

FINNEY, Tom. Has played as England's outside-right in about seventy soccer Internationals, and was chosen as Footballer of the Year in 1954. In January, 1960, completed his twentieth year of League football with Preston North End.

218

FLOWERS, Ron. Joined Wolverhampton Wanderers in 1952 as left-half, and after playing in representative matches became an England International in 1954—5.

GRAVENEY, Tom. Gloucestershire cricketer; played his first match for the County in 1948, and has since been high in England's batting order in more than twenty Tests.

HAYNES, Johnny. England soccer inside-left since 1954; earlier he played in Schoolboy and Youth Internationals. Has been a heavy scorer in Fulham's League team.

HEWSON, Brian. Won the A.A.A. Half-mile Championship in 1953 and 1954, and the Mile in 1955. Ran at Melbourne in the 1956 Olympic Games.

HILDRETH, Peter. Many times A.A.A. 120 Yards Hurdles Champion, and several times 220 Yards Champion. Competed in the Melbourne Olympic Games in 1956.

HUNT, Bernard. Leading British professional golfer; made rapid progress after winning the Assistants' Championship. Has since won numerous titles and has played for Britain in the Ryder Cup.

IBBOTSON, Derek. Started athletics in 1948, and after winning many area events won the A. A. A. Three Miles in 1956. Became a four-minute miler in 1956, ran in the 1956 Olympics, and later set up a short-lived World Mile record.

ILLINGWORTH, Ray. An all-round cricketer who played a major part in Yorkshire's 1959 County Championship victory. He gained his first England Cap against New Zealand in 1958, and has since played in many Tests. Achieved the cricketers' 'double' in 1957 and 1959.

INSOLE, Doug. Essex all-round cricketer; has played in a number of Tests for England from 1950. In 1955 scored 2,427 runs—the highest in England.

KELSEY, Jack. Became Arsenal's goal-keeper in 1949 on the retirement of Swindin; played his first International for Wales in 1953.

KNIGHT, Billy. British Davis Cup lawn tennis player; has been playing since the age of twelve. Toured Australia twice. Has beaten many leading players in first-class tournaments.

LAKER, Jim. England off-break bowler; has played against every Test-match nation. Some of his greatest bowling successes have been in these matches, but it was for Surrey, against the Australians, in 1956, that he achieved 10 wickets for 88. Now retired.

LOADER, Peter. Right-arm medium-fast bowler; played his first cricket for Surrey in 1951, and his first Test for England in 1954.

LOCK, Tony. Slow left-arm bowler for England; began playing for Surrey in 1946. Took part in a bowling partnership with Laker which gained the Ashes at the Oval in 1953.

McPARLAND, Peter. Irish International outside-left; joined Aston Villa from football in Ireland in 1952. He is a fast-moving wing-forward with a good scoring record.

MATTHEWS, Reg. Won his England Cap as goal-keeper in 1956. In League football, moved from Coventry City to Chelsea in the same year for a fee of £20,000—a record for a goal-keeper.

MATTHEWS, Stanley. Chosen as Footballer of the Year in 1948, he is regarded by many as the greatest wing-forward in soccer history. Has played in over eighty Internationals for England.

MAY, Peter. England cricket Captain in many tests from 1956 onwards. A right-hand batsman, he was a Cambridge Blue in 1950 and began playing for Surrey in the same season. He made 138 in his first Test in 1951.

MEDWIN, Terry. After becoming Swansea Town's leading scorer in 1955—56, he was transferred to Tottenham Hotspur. Plays at centre-forward or outside-right; has been capped many times for Wales.

MERRICK, Gil. Has been Birmingham City's goal-keeper for many years. Took part in the World Cup series. He has won more than twenty England Caps.

MICKLEM, Gerald. One of Britain's leading amateur

golfers; won the English Championship in 1947 and 1953. Played in the Walker Cup matches against the United States from 1951, and was for some years England's Captain for all Internationals.

MILTON, Arthur. An opening or middle-order batsman, he has played cricket for Gloucestershire since 1949. He was formerly a soccer player, with one England Cap and a long record of service with Arsenal.

MOSS, Stirling. Has been champion British racing driver in many seasons. He has twice won the Empire Trophy and the Rheims Sports Car Race. Other successes include the New Zealand, British, Italian and Buenos Aires Grands Prix.

NORRIS, Fred. Long-distance runner; set up British records for the Ten Miles and the One Hour, as well as several English Native records. Raced in the 1956 Olympic Marathon in Australia.

NORRIS, Ken. Long-distance runner; won the National Cross-Country Championship in 1956, and holds several English Native records for five to ten miles. Ran in the Olympic 10,000 Metres in 1956.

PIGGOTT, Lester. Became a leading jockey while still an apprentice, and now rides in both flat and National Hunt racing. Has ridden winners in five countries; won the Derby in 1954.

PIRIE, Gordon. Set up world records for the 3,000 and 5,000 Metres; has also been a leading British mile runner for many years. Competed in the 1956 Olympics and was second in the 5,000 Metres.

POWELL, John. One of the leading young small-bore rifle-shooting experts; has shot in the Dewar and Wakefield Trophy teams. Won the Scottish Junior Championship in 1951, and many senior events since then.

PULLAR, Geoff. Lancashire and England left-handed batsman; achieved 2,000 runs in 1959. Has been capped for England, first against India, and then in more recent Test series.

QUIXALL, Albert. Joined Sheffield Wednesday as an inside-forward at the age of seventeen, and played for England two years later. A heavy scorer, Quixall has been picked by England for tours abroad.

REES, Dai. British Ryder Cup golfer; has twice been joint second in the Open Championship. He has won many championships and tournaments, including the Match Play' the New South Wales and New Zealand Open Championships and the Dunlop Masters' Tournament.

RICHARDSON, Dick. Left-handed batsman for Worcestershire; began with Worcestershire's Minor Counties side at the age of fourteen. Has since become a high scorer in County matches.

RICHARDSON, Peter. Older brother of Dick; left-handed batsman, with a number of Test appearances for England. Now with Kent; was Worcestershire's County Captain.

SILLETT, Peter. England soccer International, full-back; began League career with Southampton, where his father had played previously, but moved to Chelsea in 1953.

SLATER, Bill. Formerly a forward, he has had his greatest success since his conversion to right-half. Played as an amateur in Blackpool's 1951 Cup Final side; now with Wolves, and an England International.

SMITH, Douglas. Became a jockey at thirteen, and has won over two thousand races, as well as the Jockeys' Championship three years running.

SMITH, Michael. Warwickshire cricket captain; originally played for Leicestershire. Won his England Cap in 1958. He has consistently topped the thousand for the season.

STATHAM, Brian. Played his first cricket for Lancashire in 1950. Was promptly picked for England as a right-arm fast bowler, a place he has held in most Test series ever since.

SURTEES, John. Motorcyclist; began road-racing at seventeen and reached prominence in 1956 when he first won the Isle of Man Senior T.T. and the 500 c.c. World Championship.

TAPSCOTT, Derek. Inside-forward with Arsenal and, since 1959, Cardiff City. Has been a regular choice for Wales in Internationals since 1954.

TRUEMAN, Freddie. England fast bowler; has played for Yorkshire since 1949 and taken part in most Test series since then. He is also a hard-hitting end-of-the-order batsman.

TYSON, Frank. English fast bowler; has played for Northamptonshire since 1952, and, in partnership with Statham, formed England's opening attack in the 1954 Test series against Pakistan. Has since held a fairly regular place in the Test side.

WILSON, Bobby. British lawn tennis player; has made several Davis Cup appearances and has been a regular winner of major tournaments since 1950.

WRIGHT, Billy. England's soccer Captain who retired in 1959, at which time he had won more than a hundred Caps. Joined Wolverhampton Wanderers when fifteen, and was their regular centre-half throughout his football career.

PEOPLE AND LEISURE

Here are some of the dozens of spare-time activities which may appeal to you—ranging from camping to stamp collecting, from model-making to keeping tortoises.

Use of the Road

The open road is yours—on your bicycle or on foot—but your right to use it involves responsibilities on your part in return.

Cyclists, though they don't have to pass a driving test, must be fully aware of the Highway Code for their own safety as well as that of others. They are also obliged *by law* to have efficient brakes on *both* wheels, and a means of warning (either a bell or a horn). After dark they *must* have a head-lamp and red tail-lamp. Cyclists are also advised to wear light-coloured clothes at night—and this is a safety measure for those on foot as well, particularly in country districts where because of the absence of a pavement it is necessary to walk along the edge of the road. Whenever walking on the road, whether by day or by night, you should *face* the oncoming traffic.

Cyclists should give clear hand-signals before making left or right turns, by raising the appropriate arm shoulder-high. On slowing down or stopping, the correct signal is an up-and-down movement of the right arm.

What the Highway Code tells you can be roughly summarised as follows:

For Pedestrians

1. Where there is no footpath, walk *facing* oncoming traffic.
2. Before crossing the road, look right, look left, then look

right again. Cross at right-angles, use zebra crossings, central refuges or other pedestrian aids whenever possible, and take extra care if your view is limited or blocked in any way.

3. Before stepping on to a zebra crossing, allow approaching traffic ample time to stop. Remember that when a zebra crossing has a central refuge each half of the crossing must be treated separately.

4. At junctions, always watch for vehicles turning the corner.

5. If there is a police officer controlling traffic, be guided by his signals.

6. Do not get on or off any moving vehicle.

For Cyclists

1. When moving off, make the signal for a right turn before pulling out from the kerb.

2. Keep well to the left, except when overtaking or turning right.

3. Always, in riding at night, make sure you could pull up within the range of your lights. If dazzled by oncoming lights, slow down or stop.

4. Slow down before bends and sharp corners.

5. Give way to pedestrians on zebra crossings. They have the legal right of way. At crossings controlled by lights or police, give way to pedestrians already on the crossings when the signal to move is given.

6. When making a turn at a junction, remember that pedestrians who are crossing have the right of way.

7. Look out for pedestrians on country roads, and give them ample room, particularly at left-hand bends.

8. Go slow when passing animals, and give them plenty of room.

9. Do not overtake near corners, road junctions or pedestrian crossings, or when approaching the brow of a hill, a humpback bridge or a narrower section of road. Be extremely careful about overtaking at dusk or in fog.

225

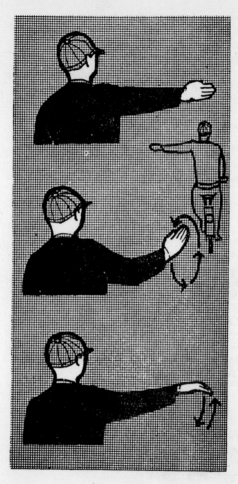

I am
about to
turn right.

I am
about
to turn
left. (for
cyclists)

I am
about to
turn left.
(for
motorists)

I am about
to slow
down or
stop.

10. Overtake on the right, except when the driver or rider in front has signalled that he intends to turn right.

11. Never cross a continuous white line along the middle of the road unless you can see a clear road ahead.

12. When approaching a road junction where there is a 'Slow' sign, slow down and be prepared to stop if necessary. At a 'Halt' sign you *must* stop at the major road, even if it is clear.

13. To turn right, signal in good time and take up a position just left of the middle of the road. For left turns keep over to the left, signal well in advance and avoid swinging out to the right.

14. When you draw up, pull in close to the near side of the road.

15. When riding, glance behind before you signal, move off, change course, overtake or turn.

16. Slow down, look both ways and listen carefully before going through a railway level crossing that has no gates. When there are unattended gates, open both gates before crossing, then close them after you. *Do not stop on the lines.* Never cross the lines when a warning signal is flashing or when the barriers have not lifted after the passing of a train—another train may be on the way.

17. If there is a track for cycles, use it.

18. *Never* ride more than two abreast, carry anything which could interfere with your control of your bicycle, hold on to another vehicle or cyclist, or ride close behind a moving vehicle.

19. It is against the law to stop a bicycle within the limits of a pedestrian crossing, except in circumstances beyond your control or to avoid an accident.

20. It is illegal to ride on the footpath or to carry a passenger on a bicycle not built or adapted for more than one.

21. It is illegal to ride recklessly, to interrupt the free passage of another road user or to leave your cycle on the road in such a way that it could cause danger to others.

Here are some road signs which must be observed.

Country Code

1. Avoid dangers of fire. Be sure any cooking fires are extinguished before you move on.
2. Fasten all gates after use.
3. Keep dogs under control.
4. When crossing farm land keep to the path.
5. Do not damage fences, hedges or walls.
6. Leave no litter. You can be heavily fined for leaving rubbish behind.
7. Do nothing which could pollute water supplies.
8. Protect wild life, plants and trees.
9. Respect the countryside.

Map-making and Map-reading

Start by making a map of your own district. The first thing you must do is decide what scale it is going to be. The most common scale is one inch to a mile (that is, one inch of map represents one mile of actual ground), and this is the one you will find on official maps such as the Ordnance Survey sheets. But for maps that only cover a small area you may prefer a scale of two inches to the mile, which will provide room for more details.

When you have the streets drawn and named, put in the most important landmarks, such as the police station, hospital, post office and doctor's house, after which you can go on and put in your friends' houses, the shop you use most frequently, your school and so on, until in the end you have the map completely filled.

You can also trace out in different colours the shortest routes from your home to important places, with the time it takes written beside each place. In this way you can tell at a glance the quickest way to any given place and know before you start how long it will take to get there.

Once you've mapped your own district, why not go out exploring and make maps of your trips? Take a printed map with you at first (preferably an Ordnance Survey map, as these are by far the best), and learn to read it so that you can see how it is made. You will see that the map is covered with all sorts of lines and signs which are a picture of what the ground actually looks like. These may look rather confusing at first, but understanding them is really quite easy.

Contour Lines

Contour lines tell you the height and slope of the ground. They measure off each increase in height of fifty feet and indicate the shape of the hills. The figures give the height above sea level and, of course, the closer they are together,

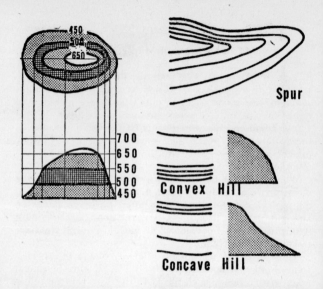

the steeper the slope is. If your map shows any coastline you will see similar lines for the depth of the sea.

Conventional Symbols

Certain symbols are used to show houses, churches, post offices, telegraph lines, viaducts, railway lines, trees—anything, in fact, that isn't just fields. Most of these look like the things they represent, so they are easy to remember. Here are some of them, and you'll find others printed for you at the bottom of the Ordnance Survey maps.

Map References

If you're planning to meet a friend in the country it's obviously no good saying 'I'll meet you on the hill with trees

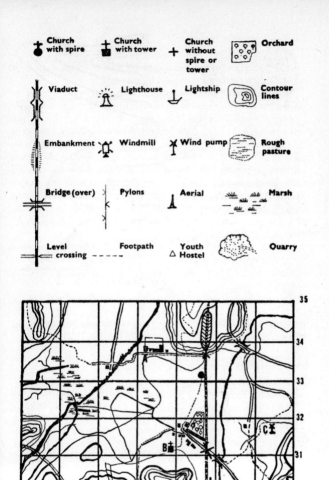

Symbol	Description	Symbol	Description	Symbol	Description	Symbol	Description
	Church with spire		Church with tower	+	Church without spire or tower		Orchard
	Viaduct		Lighthouse		Lightship		Contour lines
	Embankment		Windmill		Wind pump		Rough pasture
	Bridge (over)		Pylons		Aerial		Marsh
	Level crossing	- - - -	Footpath	△	Youth Hostel		Quarry

Map References   A—122338   B—129311   C—154317

on the top', because there might be half a dozen such hills. So, to make quite sure, you refer to your map.

If you look at the map you'll find that it is crossed by a number of horizontal and vertical lines. At the ends of each line is a two-figure number. Find the number of the last horizontal line below your intended meeting-place, and note the figure down. Now your meeting-place will rarely be exactly on a line, so to make your map reference absolutely accurate imagine that the square is crossed by ten smaller lines. Decide which line your meeting-place is on or nearest, and add its number to the two you've already got. If it is exactly between lines 32 and 33, your final figure will be 325. (If the place actually does fall on a line, put a nought after the grid number.)

Now do the same thing with your vertical lines; then write the six figures out one after the other, placing the horizontal reading first. You now have your final six-figure map reference.

Camping

Camping can be one of the most pleasant and rewarding of summer recreations, but a camping trip may be spoiled if some necessary item has been omitted from the gear, or, on the other hand, if you overload yourself by carrying things you don't need. The following checklist should prove helpful when you plan your camping trip.

Personal Equipment:

Rucksack
Change of clothing
Change of underclothing
2 spare pairs of socks
Spare pair of shoes

Spare shoelaces
Pair of pyjamas
Handkerchiefs
Mackintosh
Warm pullover
Swimming costume
Towel (possibly 2)
Flannel
Soap
Toothbrush and paste
Brush and comb
Nail brush
Maps
Metal mirror
Compass
Pocket-knife
Water-bottle
Money

Equipment Shared among the Party:

Tent
Tent-pegs
Cord
Small spade or trowel
Axe
Groundsheets
Sleeping bags (or blankets)
Spare blankets (if desired)
Inflatable mattresses and pillows
Torch, with spare batteries
Cooking stove
Fuel and matches
Stewing-pot, frying-pan and kettle
Plastic, aluminium or paper plates and
    mugs

233

Cutlery
Teacloth
Can and bottle opener
Food box (for perishable items)
Canvas bucket for washing
Small First Aid kit

Tents

If you are buying a tent for your trip, you will find illustrated below, some of the many varieties from which to make a choice.

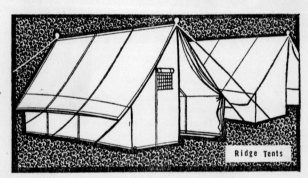

Ridge Tents

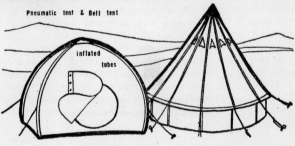

Pneumatic tent & Bell tent

inflated tubes

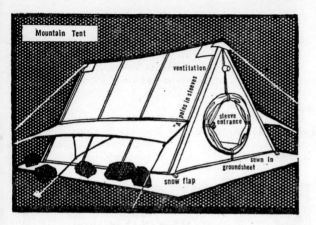

Youth Hostels

Hikers and cyclists using Youth Hostels can get full details of membership from their National Headquarters.

The rules vary slightly from country to country. In Britain you can join the Youth Hostels Association from the age of five onwards. Up to the age of nine you must be accompanied by a parent or legal guardian when using Youth Hostels, and up to twelve by any adult member. From twelve onwards members may use the Hostels without being accompanied.

Youth Hostels are for travellers on foot, by bicycle or by canoe; members touring by any power-assisted vehicle are barred. You may stay up to three consecutive nights at any one Hostel. The standard charge for junior members is 2/- per night. Most Hostels provide meals at low charges; alternatively, cooking facilities are available.

National headquarters are:

England and Wales: Y. H. A., National Office, Trevelyan House, St Albans, Herts.

Scotland: S. Y. H. A., 7 Bruntsfield Crescent, Edinburgh 10.

Northern Ireland: Y. H. A. N. I., 28 Bedford Street, Belfast.

Republic of Ireland: I. Y. H. A., 39 Mountjoy Square, Dublin.

Australia: Y. H. A., 161 Flinders Lane, Melbourne, Victoria.

New Zealand: Y. H. A., c/o Mr. J. L. McKie, P. O. Box 436, Christchurch, C. l.

South Africa: Y. H. A., P. O. Box 4640, Johannesburg.

Canada: C. Y. H. A., 581 Spadina Avenue, Toronto 4, Ontario.

United States: A. Y. H. A., 14 West 8th Street, New York 11, N. Y.

First Aid When Out and About

When giving First Aid remember that unless you've had training through the Red Cross or some similar organisation you may do more harm by doing too much than too little. Your attempts to treat serious burns or to straighten a fracture may make it more difficult for the doctor who later has to cure the patient.

The *first* object of First Aid is to save life, that is, to prevent the casualty from dying before medical aid can be obtained. Therefore, look immediately for signs of asphyxia or severe bleeding and, if necessary, stop bleeding and begin artificial respiration. *Every second counts.*

The *second* object is to prevent any deterioration in the condition of the casualty and to avoid the development of shock. This is done by covering the wound with a dressing, fixing the injured part, in particular immobilising any fractured bones, and carefully placing the casualty in a suitable position. *Never attempt to give liquids to an unconscious person.*

The *third* object is to ease pain, both physical and mental, by gentle handling and by reassurance.

After attention has been given to the above points, a severely injured casualty must be removed to hospital as soon as possible.

Asphyxia or Suffocation

Do not lose an instant; act quickly and methodically.

1. Lay casualty face down with head to one side, arms bent and forehead resting on his hands so that nose and mouth are unobstructed and the neck is extended.

2. See that the airway is clear and not blocked by a foreign body or by the tongue falling back, or by any swelling of the throat. With your finger hook out any foreign body (food or false teeth) and draw the tongue forward.

3. If breathing is still stopped, immediately perform artificial respiration (see below).

4. Loosen all clothing round the neck and waist.

5. Keep casualty warm and treat to prevent or lessen shock (see page 249).

Artificial Respiration

Do not lose an instant; act quickly and methodically.

1. Turn the casualty face downwards with head to one side; if there is a slope, place head lowermost.

2. Quickly clear the mouth of any false teeth or weeds.

3. Loosen any clothing around the neck and waist.

4. Apply Holger Nielsen's method of artificial respiration (see pages 238-241), which ensures good expansion of the lungs and helps to oxygenate the blood.

5. If there is a fracture of arms or of the ribs, apply Schafer's method instead (see pages 241-2).

6. Keep casualty warm and treat to prevent or lessen shock (see page 249).

7. *Do not let casualty sit up,* even after apparent recovery, otherwise there may be collapse.

8. Transfer to care of a doctor or hospital as soon as possible.

Holger Nielsen Method

The illustrations referred to will be found on the next two pages.

1. Lay casualty with face downwards and turned to one side, arms bent and forehead resting on his hands, so that nose and mouth are unobstructed and the neck is extended.

2. Kneel at his head, placing one knee near casualty's head and one foot alongside his elbow (see Fig. 5).

3. Place your hands over casualty's shoulder blades, with thumbs touching in the mid-line and fingers spread out, the arms being kept straight (see Fig. 5).

4. Rock forward gently with arms straight and apply light pressure by weight of upper part of body only (see Fig. 1); *count in seconds 'One, Two'*. This causes expiration.

5. Rock back with arms straight, release pressure gradually, and slide your hands to elbows of casualty, *counting 'Three' for one second* (see Fig. 2).

6. Raise and pull casualty's arms until tension is felt for two seconds (see Fig. 3), *counting 'Four, Five'*, to cause inspiration.

7. Then lay casualty's arms down and place your hands on his back as in Fig. 1, *counting 'Six' for one second*.

8. Repeat above movements with rhythmic rocking at the rate of ten times a minute until breathing has been re-established, counting as follows:

'One, Two' (for two seconds); apply light pressure to back (Fig. 1).

'Three' (for one second); slide hands to elbow (Fig. 2).

'Four, Five' (for two seconds); raise and pull on the arms (Fig. 3).

'Six' (for one second); slide hands to back to repeat cycle of operation (Fig. 1).

9. *If the arms are injured*, place them by the sides of the body; then do the complete procedure but insert your hands under the casualty's shoulders and raise them for inspiration.

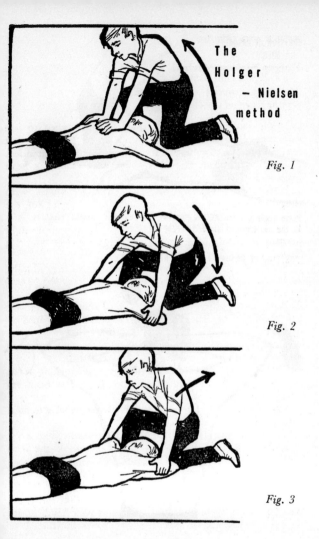

The
Holger
— Nielsen
method

Fig. 1

Fig. 2

Fig. 3

239

The Holger–Nielsen method

Fig. 4

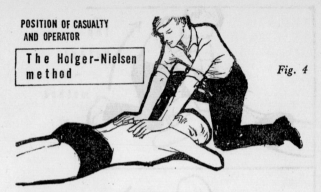

Place hands over casualty's shoulder — blades with thumbs touching in the mid-line and arms straight

POSITION OF CASUALTY AND OPERATOR

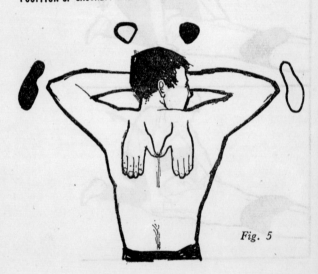

Fig. 5

10. *If arms and chest are both injured,* doarm raising and lowering by inserting your hands under the casualty's shoulders only.

11. *Apply pressure depending on sex and age,* just sufficient to lightly compress the chest; the smaller the individual, the less the pressure required.

    24—30 lb. for adults.

    12—14 lb. for half-grown children and slender
      women.

    2—4 lb. for infants.

It is advisable to practise these pressures on a spring weighing machine placed about twelve inches from the floor.

Schafer's Method

1. Lay casualty face downwards with head turned to one side, arms bent and forehead resting on his hands (see Fig. 1) with neck extended.

2. Kneel to one side of casualty's hips, facing his head (see Fig. 1).

3. Place your hands flat on the small of casualty's back, just above the top of the pelvic bones, your thumbs almost touching each other in the mid-line, your fingers being spread over the loins and pointing towards the ground (see Fig. 1).

4. Sit on your heels and swing your body slowly forward from the knees, keeping your arms straight and hands in place all the time, but apply only gentle pressure by the weight of your body. This forces air out of the lungs *(expiration)* (see Fig. 2). *Maintain this position for two seconds, counting 'One, Two'.*

5. Relax the pressure by swinging gently and gradually backwards on to your heels, to allow of *inspiration* as in Fig. 3, *counting 'Three, Four, Five' in three seconds* before swinging forward again to first movement—*keeping the arms straight and hands in place all the time.*

6. Repeat these swaying to-and-fro movements regularly at a rate of twelve to a minute, until breathing has been re-established.

241

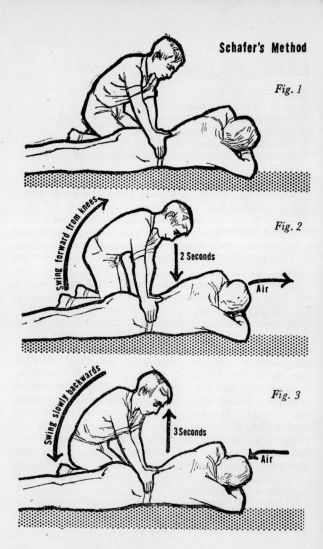

Schafer's Method

Fig. 1

Swing forward from knees

2 Seconds

Air

Fig. 2

Swing slowly backwards

3 Seconds

Air

Fig. 3

242

Bleeding or Haemorrhage

External

Act immediately.
1. Lay casualty flat and keep warm.
2. Raise bleeding part if there is no fracture.
3. Expose the wound but remove as little clothing as possible.
4. Do not disturb any blood clot.
5. Remove any foreign bodies which can be easily picked out or wiped off.
6. Apply direct pressure to bleeding area, as follows:
   a. If there is no foreign body or broken bone, press a clean dressing and pad firmly down into wound and maintain in position by firm bandaging.
   b. If there is a foreign body or broken bone, cover the wound with a dressing and pad around the wound so that general pressure can be applied without pressure on the foreign body or broken bone.
7. If blood soaks through the bandage, apply more padding and bandage firmly on top of the previous bandage.
8. If bleeding continues, apply firm finger pressure to appropriate arterial pressure point on the heart side of wound (see illustration overleaf).
9. In the case of severe bleeding from either an arm or leg, it may be necessary to apply a constrictive bandage (narrow-fold triangular bandage, elastic braces or belt, or a two to two-and-a-half inches wide elastic bandage) to the middle of the upper arm or to the upper third of the thigh.
10. Cautiously loosen the constrictive bandage *for one minute after every fifteen minutes' application* until bleeding stops, but leave it in position where it can be seen and tightened should bleeding recur.
11. Immobilise the injured part, and treat for shock (see page 249).
12. *Get a doctor or send to hospital as soon as possible.*

243

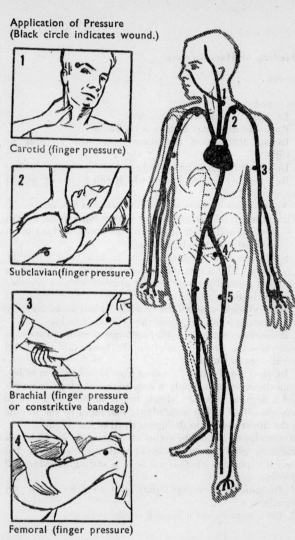

Application of Pressure
(Black circle indicates wound.)

Carotid (finger pressure)

Subclavian (finger pressure)

Brachial (finger pressure
or constriktive bandage)

Femoral (finger pressure)

244

Internal

Act immediately.

1. Lay casualty down with legs raised and keep him quiet and warm.
2. Treat for shock (see page 249).
3. Do not give anything to eat or drink.
4. *Get casualty to hospital as quickly as possible.*

Burns and Scalds

Never handle a burned area and do not apply any lotions or ointment.

If the burn is severe or extensive, wrap up casualty to maintain warmth and transport to hospital as quickly as possible. Do not give food or drink, as an anaesthetic may have to be given at hospital. Otherwise:

1. Treat to lessen shock:
   a. Lay casualty down
   b. Wrap him well to keep warm
   c. Give him drinks—sweetened tea or coffee
   d. Handle casualty as gently and as little as possible
   e. Never remove clothing, unless soaked with petrol or corrosive.
2. Exclude air and germs by applying dry sterile dressings or lint or clean linen.
3. Get a doctor or transport to hospital as soon as possible.
4. *Never open a burn blister.*

Dislocations

Treat as for simple fractures (see page 247) or sprains (see page 250).

1. Immobilise part in position of greatest comfort, but *never attempt to reduce a dislocation.*
2. Apply cold compresses.
3. Guard against shock (see page 249).
4. In case of the lower jaw, remove any dentures and support the jaw by a bandage tied over the top of the head.
5. Send to or for a doctor.

Drowning (apparent)

Do not lose an instant; act quickly and methodically.

1. While carrying casualty out of water raise body by hands placed round the casualty's abdomen to encourage water to run out of the air passages.

2. Lay casualty face down with head to one side, arms bent and forehead on hands as in Fig. 4 on page 240. If clothed, loosen at neck and waist.

3. Quickly clear mouth of any false teeth or weeds.

4. Apply Holger Nielsen's method of artificial respiration (see pages 238-241).

5. Wrap casualty in blankets or coats but never stop artificial respiration until breathing has been re-established or until life is pronounced by a doctor to be extinct.

6. When consciousness returns, give hot drink and treat generally for shock (see page 249).

7. *Do not let casualty sit up.*

8. Transfer, lying down, to care of a doctor or hospital.

Electric Shock

Act promptly, taking care not to electrocute yourself.

1. Remove casualty from contact with electric current but *do not touch casualty with your bare hands.* Protect your hands with dry gloves, coat or newspaper.

    a. Switch off current, if possible, or unplug cable.

    b. If this is not possible, stand on an insulating material (a dry, folded mackintosh, book or newspaper), and

    c. pull casualty away by means of a rope or walking-stick (not an umbrella which has metal ribs).

2. Apply artificial respiration (see pages 238-241) if breathing has stopped.

3. Treat for shock (see page 249).

4. Treat burns (see page 245).

5. Transfer to hospital when fit to be moved.

Fainting

1. If casualty is conscious, sit him down and lower his head between the knees.
2. If unconscious, lay casualty down with head turned to one side and lower than feet. Do not leave unattended.
3. Loosen clothing at neck and waist.
4. Allow plenty of fresh air, but protect from cold.
5. Hold smelling salts to nostrils.
6. When casualty regains consciousness gradually raise him and give sips of water, tea or coffee, or half a teaspoonful of sal volatile in a cupful of water.

Fractures

Do not remove casualty until injured part is immobilised.

Simple (closed)

1. Place casualty in comfortable position with injured part well supported, but *do not remove clothing*.
2. Keep warm, handle gently and generally guard against shock (see page 249).
3. Immobilise injured part by means of bandages and slings. The chest wall or the sound leg serve as good splints. In certain circumstances well padded splints may be required.
   - *a.* In the case of an arm, apply padding; bandage and support arm in a sling with the elbow bent and hand pointing to uninjured shoulder (illustrated overleaf).
   - *b.* If a leg, pad well between the knees and ankles; bandage the sound leg to the injured.
4. *Never try to set the bones*.
5. Do not give food or drink, as an anaesthetic may require to be given shortly. At most, give a few sips of hot tea or coffee.
6. Get a doctor or send to hospital quickly.

Compound (open).

Treat as for a simple fracture but, in addition:
1. Expose and cover the wound with a dry dressing.
2. Stop any bleeding (see page 243).
3. Especially take care to counteract shock (see page 249).
4. *Do not try to push protruding bone back into place.*

Examples

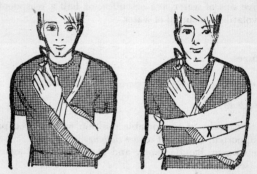

Fracture of arm

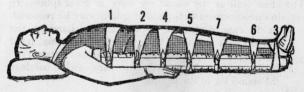

Fracture of thigh

248

Shock

1. Lay casualty on his back with head to one side and legs slightly raised, unless they are fractured in which case wait till fracture is immobilised.
2. Stop any bleeding.
3. Loosen clothing at neck and waist.
4. Keep casualty warm—therefore, do not remove clothing; wrap round with blankets, rugs or coats. Do not apply hot water bottles.
5. Handle as gently as possible and avoid any unnecessary movements.
6. See there is plenty of fresh air, and protect against any inclemency of weather.
7. Give sips of hot tea or coffee, if there is no abdominal injury or unconsciousness.
8. Be cheerful and support morale.
9. *Get a doctor as soon as possible.*

Snake Bite

1. If a limb is bitten, apply a constrictive bandage on the heart side of the bite just tight enough to congest the veins and stop flow of poison to the general circulation but not to block the arterial flow; you should be able to feel the pulse at the wrist or ankle. Hang the limb downwards. *Relax bandage for a half minute every half hour.*
2. Encourage bleeding.
3. Hold bite under a fast-running water tap, if available.
4. Bathe wound with water made dark red with potassium permanganate to neutralise any poison on the surface of the wound.
5. Give hot coffee or tea and protect casualty from cold in order to avoid shock.
6. Send for doctor or take casualty to the doctor or nearest hospital.

7. Should breathing fail, apply artificial respiration (see pages 237—242).

Sprains and Strains

1. Treat all cases as possible simple (closed) fractures.
2. Immobilise injured part.
3. Do not remove shoe or boot, unless swelling of the foot is great.
4. Apply cold compress firmly, where possible.
5. Send to a doctor—the part being supported as comfortably as possible.

Sketching and Painting

This is a hobby that can give anyone a great deal of enjoyment and satisfaction — even if he has always felt that he 'can't draw a straight line'. In fact, it is often those having the greatest doubts as to their ability who eventually produce the best results. Painting and drawing are wonderful ways of increasing your powers of observation, and they can provide a far more personal record of the things you see than the camera can ever hope to achieve.

For pencil sketching a beginner needs a range of soft and hard pencils, some sticks of soft charcoal, a block or book of cartridge paper, a soft india-rubber and a charcoal eraser. A small bottle of charcoal fixative, together with a blower, will be needed to 'fix' charcoal drawings.

Art classes at school may have taught the chief rule of perspective; briefly, it is that distant objects appear smaller. If you stand in the middle of a railway track and look along it, the two rails appear to draw closer together in the distance. This applies to all objects; the wall of a house, viewed at an angle, appears taller at the end nearest the point at which you are standing. Easy practice in perspective can be had by sketching open country with fields. Trees, hedges and fences will give you a challenge in perspective which will stand you in good stead when you tackle something more difficult.

Light and shade in pencil sketching are achieved by depth of pencil shading. There is no need to pay too much attention to the way in which this shading is applied, or to try to put in a great many details. The best way to begin is to look for the main masses of light and dark in front of you and to try to represent their shapes, as well as their sizes and tones in relation to one another. The more outstanding details that you see can be put in later. You should, however, bear in mind that a sketch of a scene is always a simplification of that scene.

Drawing in perspective

level view

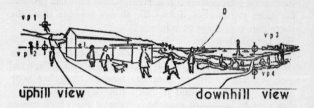

uphill view　　　　downhill view

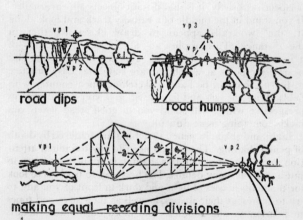

road dips　　　road humps

making equal receding divisions

V.P. = vanishing point
e.l. = eye level - of viewer
1,2,3,4,5,6,7. = order of construction lines

252

Should you wish to sketch in pen and ink—a more limiting medium for a beginner—you will need a harder-surfaced paper, a small range of nibs and a bottle of black India ink. You can also buy India ink in a variety of colours.

If you would like to try painting, you may choose to start with oil paints, water-colours, poster colours or even pastels. If you are beginning in oils, you will find prepared hardboard a satisfactory surface to use and inexpensive compared with canvas. It is best to equip yourself with large brushes, to use a good-sized surface, and to treat the subject matter broadly, looking for areas of colours and tones, and for their relations to one another. Try some exercises which will help you to see how one colour affects another; place patches of different colours, or of different shades of one colour, next to each other and study the effect. Some colours are heavier than others; some come forward while others seem to recede; some combinations of colours are harmonious while some are discordant. All of these discoveries can be applied to your painting. Many other colour exercises can be found in the various books on painting which are in your public library.

You may find it useful to keep to a fairly small selection of colours at first. The following is a suggested basic palette for oil painting:

> Cadmium Yellow
> Cadmium Red
> Alizarin Crimson
> Monastral Blue
> Ultramarine (blue)
> Viridian (green)
> Flake, Titanium or Zinc White
> Ivory Black

Useful colours to add to this are Yellow Ochre, Light Red, Cobalt Blue and Terre Verte (earth green).

Film Sizes

Standard film sizes in general use for ordinary photography are the following:

Film Size (millimetres)	Pictures per Film	Size of Picture (inches)
35	36	$1 \times 1\frac{1}{2}$
127	16	$1\frac{1}{8} \times 1\frac{3}{4}$
127	12	$1\frac{3}{4} \times 1\frac{3}{4}$
127	8	$2\frac{1}{4} \times 1\frac{3}{4}$
120 and 620	16	$2\frac{1}{4} \times 1\frac{5}{8}$
120 and 620	12	$2\frac{1}{4} \times 2\frac{1}{4}$
120 and 620	8	$2\frac{1}{4} \times 3\frac{1}{4}$

Standard sizes of cine-film in general use are: 8, 9.5, 16 and 35 millimetres.

Film Scripting

The economical sizes of cine-film for amateurs are 8 and 9.5 millimetres. Silent film in both cases is exposed at 16 'frames' or pictures per second and projected at the same speed. Spoken commentaries for silent film should be based on a calculation of 3 words per second. Preparation of a running commentary is done by means of a table made on the following lines:

Scene	Seconds	Aggregate Seconds	Commentary
G/V Fishing village	3	3	Throughout Cornwall we found small fishing villages, most with only three
M/S Moored boats	2	5	or four boats.
C/U Elderly fisherman	3	8	Each boat is a family concern. This seventy-

M/CU Dad talks to him	2	10	year-old skipper told my father that he'd been at sea since he was only
C/U Hands Dad fish	6	16	eight—and gave Dad an odd-looking fish like an octopus!
T/S Deck of boat	2	18	They were unloading; most of the fish is sent up
L/V Wagons at dock-side	4	22	to London by rail straight away.
C/U Curious fish	3	25	But we didn't send *our* odd fish! When the skip-
M/S Fish into hole; Mother holding her nose	4	29	per wasn't looking, we dug a hole and buried it!

This family adventure, running half a minute approximately, takes just over a third of a 'roll' of 9.5 millimetre film, and a much smaller proportion in the case of 8 millimetre.

Key to Standard Abbreviations used in Film Scripting

G/V   = General view
L/V   = Long view
M/S   = Medium shot
T/S   = Top shot
M/CU = Medium close-up
C/U   = Close-up
B/V   = Back view
PAN   = Shot in which camera is swung sideways from one object to another or following a moving object
TILT = Shot in which camera is swung vertically from one object to another or following a moving object

Handicrafts

Not only is it far more fun and more satisfying to make things yourself, but it saves your pocket-money for the things which you *cannot* make. Here is the 'know-how' for some interesting 'make-it-yourself' projects, none of which need special tools or equipment.

Making Model Railway Scenery

There's all the difference in the world between playing with toy trains and being a model railway enthusiast— and you can bridge that gap without digging deeply into your pocket. Scenery and buildings are expensive to buy; make them yourself at a fraction of the cost.

Scenery—hills, valleys, embankments, cliffs and so on— is best made from papier mâché. This doesn't involve fine modellers' papier mâché, which takes many hours to prepare. For tunnels, hills, etc., a rough, lumpy surface is realistic, so lumpy papier mâché will do perfectly well. Fill a bucket with newspaper torn into small scraps, add a tablespoonful of size or a small square of carpenter's glue, then pour on boiling water and stir. Keep adding water and stirring until the mixture is like thick, lumpy porridge; let it cool enough to handle, and then use it to model your scenery. Painted in greens, browns and greys, it is far more realistic than any of the expensive scenery sold in modelling shops.

Railway buildings, houses, churches and factories are also easy to build, as long as you are satisfied with approximate scale. To reduce a building on your own local station to the standard '00' scale, count the number of bricks on an end wall, first vertically, then horizontally, and then allow seven bricks to the inch horizontally and twenty-two to the inch vertically.

Sturdy buildings can be made from card as long as the base is wooden. The method is very easy, and the sketch below shows an example which is simple to adapt for other purposes. Once you understand how it's done, it requires only a little thought to apply it to any building of your own design.

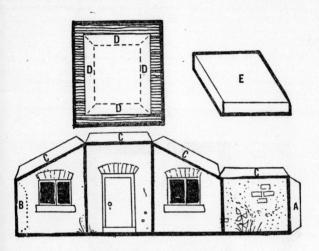

In this example of a plate-layer's hut, the roof could be painted grey or black and the walls covered with 'red-brick' paper—which costs only a few coppers to buy. The chimney is a round wooden lollipop stick painted black. Before gluing A to B and C to D, fasten squares of cellophane on to the inside of each window. Finally, glue the completed building on to the base block E, which should fit snugly inside.

In this way stations, factories, houses and shops can be made cheaply and to designs which fit in with the layout of the track and the restrictions of space available.

257

Bookbinding

Whole works have been written on the *proper* way to set about binding books at home, but the methods described require a heavy press. This simple way of putting sturdy covers on paper-backed books needs nothing except scraps of material, cardboard, scissors, glue and common sense.

First find a piece of stiff material big enough to cover the book with an inch to spare all round. If no stiff material is handy, use a piece of an old sheet, well starched. Cut out three pieces of cardboard, the sizes of the front, back and spine of the book. Glue these to the material as in the diagram.

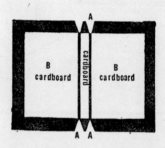

Now cut slots at A, bend the material down and glue on to the card. Next glue B to the front and back of the book. Fold down and glue the edges of the material, being careful to make neat, flat folds at the corners. Finally, paste white paper on the inside of each cover, to hide the folds of the material. If you want the title of the book on the spine, neat lettering on a strip of white paper glued into place will finish off a thoroughly professional-looking job.

Printing from Linocuts

You can make black-and-white pictures or full-colour illustrations for Christmas cards and other purposes by linocut printing. A piece of high-quality thick lino is needed. This can be bought ready cut from an art materials shop in sizes from 3 × 3 inches upwards, or can be trimmed from scraps after laying household lino. Thin lino isn't suitable, as the design for printing has to be cut into its surface. The lino should have a plain surface without any glossy design on it.

On the lino, draw the outlines of the picture which is to be made, remembering that the final result will be the exact reverse of your drawing. Avoid excessive detail; a picture drawn with a few bold strokes of the pencil is most likely to be successful. The outline should then be gone over with black India ink so that it will not be rubbed away by your hand while cutting the outlines.

You may already have a narrow 'V'-shaped chisel suitable for gouging out the unwanted areas of lino, but if not, one can be quite easily made from the broken rib of an old umbrella, fixed into a wooden handle and then ground to a sharp cutting edge. When all the areas which are not to be printed have been chiselled away, the picture is ready for inking.

This is done by means of a small roller and a piece of glass. The roller should be made of gelatine compound, and small ones can be obtained very cheaply at any art materials shop. So can small tubes of printing ink, and suitable paper.

Squeeze a small amount of printing ink on to the sheet of glass and work it to a thin, even surface with the roller which, of course, will then be similarly coated. Roll back and forth across the linocut; then place a sheet of printing paper on the linocut and press evenly and gently over the surface. This is best done with a circle of wood such as five-ply, of about four inches in diameter. This can easily be made with a fret-saw. The under side, which is to be used for pressing and rubbing, should have its edge smoothed off to prevent it from digging into the surface of the paper. Care should be taken that the lino does not slip while on the paper.

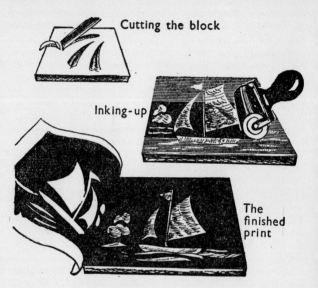

Cutting the block

Inking-up

The finished print

Linocuts in more than one colour can be made in the same way. A block is made for each colour of the full picture, and the only extra problem is that of making sure that all blocks 'register' accurately—in other words, that the colours do not overlap where this is not intended. If the picture is first drawn on to tracing paper and the appropriate outlines are then transferred on to each block of lino, this problem should not arise.

Making a Kite

Some designs of kite are hard to build, but this one takes only an hour or so and needs no complicated tools. Start with three straight sticks, one thirty inches long, the other two twenty-five inches in length. Nail the centres of the two shorter pieces to the centre of the long piece, and open out the shorter pieces so that if the long piece pointed to twelve and six on the clock the shorter pieces would be set at two, four, eight and ten. Make a small hole in the ends of each stick, and run a piece of very fine wire from hole to hole, securing it in each one with a knot. Then lay the framework on a piece of an old sheet, and cut out a section of sheet about one inch larger all round than the framework. Lap this extra inch round the wire so that the material is stretched fairly tightly and evenly over the framework, and sew it on.

Tie pieces of string about fifteen inches long to the four, six and eight o'clock struts; join the ends together and add a yard of extra string on which scraps of coloured paper have been knotted every few inches. Then, from the centre and from the ten, twelve, and two o'clock struts, run four more short lengths of string, joined at their ends. To this join is tied the end of the kite-string, which should be rolled on a stick when not in use.

Building a Rabbit Hutch

Much of the wood for this can be salvaged scraps, such as pieces of old orange crates. To keep rabbits warm and dry they should be well off the ground, so you need two posts five feet in length as legs for the front and two posts four feet in length for the back. Three feet off the ground, mount a four-foot length to join the two front legs and another four-foot length to join the two back legs, and do the same at the top of each pair of legs. You now have two frames. These are joined at the three-foot level by two pieces three feet in length, and at the top by slightly longer pieces because there is a slope from front to back to allow water to run off the roof.

Fasten boards across the framework of the floor to cover it, and also cover the back, sides and roof, allowing an overhang at the front to keep the rain off. Then, inside, mount a division two-thirds of the way along, with a hole in it about eight by six inches square to allow easy movement from the larger day-section to the sleeping-area. If two strips of wood are mounted on each side of this doorway, then a sliding door can be fitted which can be raised or lowered by a string from outside the hutch.

The front of the hutch is simply two doors, one being a wooden frame with netting attached for the day-section; the other, for the sleeping-area, is built up of boards attached to two cross-pieces on the inside, and with half a dozen holes half an inch in diameter bored through to provide ventilation.

A piece of roofing-felt, tacked on to the roof and lapped over the edges, completes the job. If you use creosote or paint to protect it from the weather, be sure to give the hutch a few days to dry out thoroughly before putting it into use.

Building a Dog Kennel

If your dog has to sleep out of doors then he needs a warm and comfortable kennel. This need not be expensive if you make it of second-hand floor-boards, of which your local wood-yard or building contractor is almost certain to have a supply. For the average-size dog, a kennel three feet by two feet in area is sufficient. The floor of this is made by cutting enough boards three feet in length and joining them underneath by nailing across two strong pieces of timber, each two feet long. The sides, three feet long and two feet

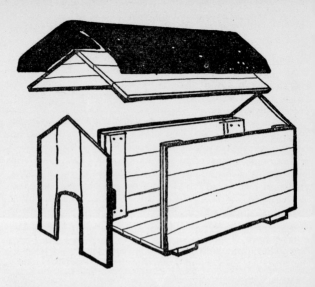

six inches in height, are built up in the same way, with the cross-pieces nailed on the inside. The back has a width of two feet two inches (if your floor-boards are each an inch thick), and is three feet three inches in height. Mark the top centre, then two points two feet six inches from the base at each side; rule lines from the side marks to the top centre, and cut away to make an inverted 'V' shape. Do the same at the front, allowing for an entrance two feet high and twelve inches wide. Across the inside of the top of this doorway you will need a cross-piece, if your timbers run vertically. If they run horizontally, you will need a vertical cross-piece at each side.

The two sections of the roof are each three feet four inches by eighteen inches, to leave an overhang at the front and sides. The roof will need a covering of roofing-felt, lapped over its edges, to keep out the damp. The whole of the sides and back can be covered in the same way to keep out draughts.

Collecting as a Hobby

Stamp Collecting

Of all the hobbies there are, probably none has such widespread popularity as stamp collecting. Millions of people in the world today are, have been, or will be stamp collectors.

The first postage stamps were issued in Britain, in 1840, to overcome the problem of standardising postal rates, which had become so high that most ordinary folk couldn't afford to send letters. The first country to follow Britain's lead was Brazil, in 1843, and by 1870 most of the principal nations had adopted the idea of stamps to pay postal charges. By that time the practice of collecting these stamps was firmly established. In those days, and indeed until twenty or thirty years ago, it was still possible to make a serious attempt to collect the stamps of all countries, but nowadays most 'philatelists' prefer to specialise. Here are a few suggestions for collections with plenty of scope yet which are reasonable enough in size to ensure that an active collector is not fighting a losing battle and collecting stamps more slowly than new ones are being issued:

> Australasia
> British Africa
> British America
> Great Britain and British
>   Possessions in Europe
> British Asia
> France and Colonies
> Spain and Portugal, with their Colonies
> North America
> South America
> The Caribbean
> China and Japan

All of these are groups for which a good start is likely to be possible using parts of a general collection which has grown out of hand. But if you are really ambitious, you might like to choose 'thematics'—the modern idea of collecting stamps by subjects rather than by countries. This way you can make a collection which will serve as an aid to your other interests and hobbies. The following are subjects on which enough stamps have been issued to make any one of them suitable for a large collection:

> The history of aviation
> The sea and shipping
> World transport
> Engineering
> Botany
> Birds, animals and fishes
> World sport
> Exploration
> Scouting, and other youth movements

But in making a choice what could be better than inventing your own theme—an original one which you can feel sure will make yours the only collection of its kind?

Stamp Identification

Stamps bearing unfamiliar inscriptions can be traced through this identification list.

Inscription on Stamp	Country using this Inscription
ACCP	Azerbaijan
Açores	Azores
Africa Occidental Española	Spanish West Africa
Africa Orientale Italiana	Italian East Africa
Afrique Occidentale Française	French West Africa

A Payer	Belgium (Postage Due)
Archipel des Comores	Grand Comoro Island
Bani	Austrian Occupation of Roumania
Bayern	Bavaria
Benadir	Somalia
Bengasi	Italian Post Offices in Tripoli
Böhmen und Mähren	Bohemia and Moravia
Bolivar	Colombia
CCCP	U.S.S.R.
C.E.F. (on German Colonials)	Cameroons Expeditionary Force
C.E.F. (on India)	China Expeditionary Force
Československo	Czechoslovakia
Chiffre Taxe	France or French Colonies (Postage Due)
Colombia (with map of Central America)	Panamá
Comunicaciones	Spain
Corée	Korea
Côte d'Ivoire	Ivory Coast
CPbNJA	Serbia
CPNCKA	Serbia
CTOTNHKN	Bulgaria
Danmark	Denmark
Dansk Vestindien	Danish West Indies
Derechos de Firma	Philippine Islands
Deutsche Demokratische Republik	East Germany
Deutsches Reich	Germany
Deutschösterreich	Austria
Diligencia	Uruguay
Doplatit	Czechoslovakia
Drzava	Yugoslavia
East India Postage	India
E.E.F.	Palestine

Eesti	Estonia
Egeo	Aegean Islands
Elsaß	German Occupation of Alsace
Elua Keneta	Hawaii
Emp. Ottoman	Turkey
EONIKH	Greece
EPMAKb	South Russia
Equateur	Ecuador
Escuelas	Venezuela
España	Spain
Estado da India	Portuguese India
Estado Español	Spain
Estados Unidos de Nueva Granada	Colombia
Ethiopie	Ethiopia
Eupen	Belgian Occupation of Germany
Fdo Poo	Fernando Poo
Filipinas	Philippine Islands
Filler	Hungary
Francobollo	Italy
БАТУМСКАЯ ПОЧТА	Batum
Grand Liban	Lebanon
Grønland	Greenland
Großdeutsches Reich	Germany
Guyane Française	French Guiana
Haute Silesie	Upper Silesia
Haute-Volta	Upper Volta
Hejaz	Saudi Arabia
Helvetia	Switzerland
Holkar	Indore
Hrvatska	Croatia
Indie	French India
Instruccion	Venezuela
Ionikon	Ionian Islands
Iran	Persia

Island	Iceland
Kamerun	Cameroons
Karolinen	Caroline Islands
K.C. Novita	Serbia
K.K. Post Stempel	Austria, or Austrian Italy
Korona	Hungary
КРАЈЬЕВСТВО	Yugoslavia
КРНТН	Crete
Kraljevstvo	Yugoslavia
Krone	Austria
K.U.K. Feldpost	Austrian Military Post, or Bosnia
K.U.K. Militärpost	Bosnia
K. Württ	Württemberg
Latvija	Latvia
Liban	Lebanon
Lietuva	Lithuania
Litwa Srodkowa	Central Lithuania
Magyar (Kir) Posta	Hungary
Magyarorszag	Hungary
Marruecos	Spanish Morocco
Mejico	Mexico
Metalik	Crete
Militärpost	Bosnia
Moyen Congo	Middle Congo
Nederland	Netherlands
Ned. Indie	Netherlands Indies
Nieuwe Guinea	Netherlands New Guinea
Norge	Norway
Nouvelle-Calédonie	New Caledonia
Nouvelles-Hébrides	New Hebrides
Nowta	Serbia
ПОЧТА	Russia
ПОЧТ.МАРКА	Azerbaijan
Nueva Granada	Colombia
Oahampka	Finland

269

Offentlig Sak	Norway
Oil Rivers	Niger Coast
OKCA	Russia
Oltre Giuba	Italian Jubaland
Österreich	Austria
PCCP	Russia
Penni	Finland
Persane	Persia
РОССИЯ	South Russia
Poczta Polska	Poland
Pohjois	Ingermanland
Porto	Austria
Portomark	Bosnia
Post Stamp	Hyderabad
Postzegel	Netherlands
Preussen	Prussia
Qarku	Albania
Qintar	Albania
Recargo	Spain
Reichspost	Germany
Republica Oriental	Uruguay
Republica Peruana	Peru
République Libanaise	Lebanon
R.F.	France and Colonies
R.H.	Haiti
Rialtar Sealadac Na hÉireann	Republic of Ireland
Saargebiet	Saar
Sachsen	Saxony
Saorstát Éireann	Republic of Ireland
Sarkari	Soruth
Saurashtra	Soruth
Segnatasse	Italy (Postage Due)
Sen	Japan
Shqipenia	Albania
Shqyptare	Albania

Slesvig	Schleswig
Slovensko	Slovakia
STOTHHKI	Bulgaria
Suidafrika	Union of South Africa
Suidwes Afrika	South West Africa
Suomi	Finland
Sverige	Sweden
S.W.A. (on South Africa)	South West Africa
TAKCA	Bulgaria
Tannu Tuva	North Mongolia
Toga	Tonga
Touva	North Mongolia (Tannu Tuva)
Ultramar	Cuba and Puerto Rico
Van Diemen's Land	Tasmania
YCCP	Ukraine
Yen	Japan

Collecting Match-box Labels

Collecting match-box labels, like stamp collecting, is a hobby dating back to the last century. You set about it by saving all you can find and making exchanges with other collectors for the ones you need. Pen pals in other countries are an ideal source of foreign labels.

Remove the labels from the boxes by soaking them for a few minutes in hot water, peeling them off, and then drying them between sheets of blotting paper. Loose-leaf albums are the best for mounting collections of match-box labels, and stamp-hinges are the safest method of fixing them to the page without damage.

British match-box labels are usually rather dull and uninteresting in design, but there are thousands of foreign ones with highly-coloured action pictures on them. You can find labels showing portraits of native warriors, ships and

planes, railways, and you can find some with exciting for-
geries printed by wartime resistance groups, bearing slogans
encouraging the guerilla fighters.

Coin Collecting

This is a hobby in which the lucky collector can still come
across rare finds of great value or tremendous historical
interest. Unlike stamps and match-box labels, coins can be
lost for centuries and still survive undamaged, and it is
not unusual, when new ground is being turned over or old
buildings are being demolished, for coins dating back even
as far as Roman times to be unearthed. Coins have been
in existance since about 700 B.C., and appeared in Britain
before the last century B.C.

Modern coins of many countries can be obtained easily
through exchange or by buying a bag of assorted foreign
coins for a few shillings.

A cabinet to house your collection needs shallow drawers
lined with baize into which holes have been cut to let the
coins lie snugly without moving. A small gummed identification label can be stuck below each coin.

Cigarette-card Collecting

Cigarette manufacturers no longer issue cards in their
packets, but for many years, until 1939, there was a card in
nearly every packet in Britain, the Commonwealth and
many other countries. Millions of these have survived, and
so it is still possible to start collecting. But the wise collector
will look beyond cigarette cards to include *all* cards of
a similar kind—which means the many issued in packets
and boxes of sweets. Sets, usually of twenty-five or fifty,
range in subject from great sportsmen to ocean fishes, from
ancient weapons to Derby winners. Many cards issued in

the ten years before World War II were accompanied by albums for mounting them.

Elder relatives may be able to add to your collection, and cards may also be purchased from dealers.

Cheese-label Collecting

The proper name for this is 'fromology', and the makers of cheese in many countries have recognised the rapid growth of the hobby in recent years by issuing many new and colourful designs. It is possible to build up a collection of more than thirty thousand different labels by exchanging with other collectors. The original source of supply is, of course, your own family kitchen. Friends travelling abroad and pen pals in foreign countries can help to enlarge your collection.

A collection of cheese labels is best mounted and stored in the same way as a stamp collection, using stamp-hinges to fasten the labels in place in a safe way so that they can be removed for exchange or remounting without damage. Removing labels which are gummed tightly to the wrapping of the cheese is best done without using water, as certain labels have colours which 'run' when moistened. Suitable methods are levering the label off the paper by cautious work with a paper knife or peeling off one corner and allowing steam from a kettle to penetrate the glue without coming into direct contact with the printed surface.

There are plenty of different pictorial subjects on cheese labels, ranging from wild animals, flowers and country scenes to aircraft, ships and sportsmen.

Collecting Old Books

This is a hobby for those who enjoy reading and who are, perhaps, interested in writing as well. And though buying new books is expensive, collecting old ones is a hobby that, if carried out carefully, need cost no more than a few coppers a week.

Your own interests and other hobbies will help you to decide the subjects which will form the basis of your collection. There are, of course, hundreds to choose from, but a few which can make absorbingly interesting collections without much cost are:

Printing—its history and development

Your favourite sport

What towns and country looked like in the past

Early cars and railways

Wild life at home and abroad

These suggestions have been made bearing in mind the available sources of old books—second hand book shops, junk shops and auction rooms. Very often at small auctions you can buy odd lots of books fifty or a hundred years old for prices as low as half a crown for a hundred. Of this hundred, ninety-five are likely to be completely useless to you, but exchanges with other collectors, or even subsequent auctions, will enable you to get rid of the ones you don't want.

Condition is important if you are collecting books for their own sake, but if you are simply hoping, for instance, to accumulate pictures and information about early railways, you will not be unduly worried if some of your books have torn covers and missing pages. Damaged books can be repaired quite easily (see '*Bookbinding*', page 258) so your bookcases need not remain untidy simply because your books, when you bought them, were in shabby condition.

Collecting Pottery

Collectors of rare china pay thousands of pounds for individual pieces of particular quality and historical interest, but you can have just as much fun for a few shillings and build up a collection with as much variety. Auction rooms and junk shops have large quantities of old china and pottery which change hands for very low prices, and though much of it is rubbish, now and again rare and attractive oddments can be found among the heaps of old teacups and pie-dishes. But if this doesn't appeal to you then the collecting of modern pottery may. In Britain, and in many other countries, there are small 'one-man' potteries producing excellent craftsmanship. If you buy their work at fashionable shops you will have to pay high prices for it, but if on holiday in Devon and Cornwall, for example, you visit some of these tiny potteries, you can buy the same articles for a considerably lower price.

Keeping Pets

Dogs

Choosing a dog for a pet needs careful thought. It isn't enough to decide, 'That's for me!' when a friendly puppy in a pet shop rolls his eyes at you and licks your hand. What you have to consider is the size he will reach, the amount of exercise he'll need, and the amount he is likely to eat. You also have to make up your mind whether the desire to have a dog is just a passing fancy or a feeling that will remain, for when you have bought or been given a dog not only does that dog belong to you, *but you belong to him*. Dogs have as intense a feeling of loyalty as do human beings, and an unwanted dog feels just as lost as an unwanted person does.

There are many breeds from which to choose a dog that suits your requirements; or you may prefer a mongrel to a pedigree pup. Your local dogs' home will be able to help you there. Remember that a large dog can be an encumbrance in a flat or a small house—and his food bills will be high. A dog bred for an active open-air life may be unhappy in a town. So think it over carefully before making your choice.

As soon as you get your dog, buy him a licence if he is over six months old. This can be obtained at any Post Office. It is against the law to keep a dog without a licence.

He will need a box or basket. Dog baskets are rather expensive, but a comfortable box can be made out of scrap wood without any difficult carpentry. Make it big enough for him to move about in and to stretch in his sleep, yet cosy enough to keep him warm. The box should be in a corner free from draughts, and should be lined with several newspapers to keep in the warmth. On top of these he should have an old rug or blanket, or, alternatively, an old eiderdown. Don't just give him a pillow; most dogs like to roll themselves up in their bedding, just as many of to roll

The bedding should be taken out of doors and shaken every day or two and the newspaper changed at frequent intervals.

If you have a garden and your dog is able to get plenty of exercise in it, then one short walk every day should be all he needs. Except in country districts, this should preferably be on a lead.

He will probably be untrained when you first get him. Training needs patience, and if it seems to take a long time, remember that the training of a human baby takes far longer. It will help your puppy if you can start off with a regular routine of meals, walks and grooming.

At first, puppies need to be let out of doors every two or three hours during the day. A few messes indoors must be expected, and the dog which learns quickly is the one which is praised for attending to his needs out of doors rather than the one which is punished for making a mess in the hall.

Teach your dog to 'come to heel' when taken out of doors without a lead. A little perseverance should make him completely obedient to your orders. A disobedient dog is less to blame than his owner, for a dog naturally regards man as his master and disobeys only when that master no longer deserves respect. To earn that respect, you have to be absolutely consistent about discipline. If your dog is punished or spoken to sharply for making a mess on the pavements then he must *always* be punished or spoken to sharply for it. If he is praised when he comes to heel promptly, then he must *always* be praised. Above all, he must never be punished without knowing why.

Grooming needs vary for different breeds of dogs. Short-haired dogs need only a brisk rub-down from time to time with a rough towel or a brush; long-haired varieties need more frequent attention, with a steel comb and stiff brush. Your dog should be taught to look forward to this as a regular habit and should be complimented on his smartness afterwards. Washing need not be frequent for most breeds and should be done either with ordinary toilet soap or with dog soap sold by your pet-shop. Don't use kitchen soap, as the soda will harm his coat as well as irritate the pores of his skin. The temperature of the water should be moderate. Immediately after his bath your dog should be very thoroughly dried, otherwise he'll undertake this himself and in doing so probably make himself dirtier than he was before.

A dog's diet should consist of about a half ounce of meat for each pound of his weight, as well as about the same amount of cereal and vegetable matter. The quantities required must be adjusted according to the amount of exercise the dog gets. It is as important not to over-feed as it is not to under-feed, as over-feeding brings about various stomach troubles which may be difficult to cure.

Meat should not be overcooked, and many dogs prefer it raw. Bones, carefully chosen in order to avoid those which may cause injury through sharp splinters, are used by most dogs more as playthings than as a source of food, and to compensate a dog for the lack of mineral from bones he should be given a small amount of ground bone-meal in his diet.

A puppy should be fed four or five times a day, but by the time a dog is fully grown he should be fed only one main meal a day and should know the exact time at which to expect his food. Your dog should always have access to a supply of fresh water.

Cats

A kitten is ready to leave its mother at eight weeks, by which time it should have learned to attend to its needs out of doors or in an ash-box placed in a corner. A cat needs the same kind of bedding as a dog and also the same chance to go out of doors for exercise. Do not attempt to help a cat keep itself clean; unlike the dog, the cat spends much of its time doing this very efficiently, and your assistance will not be appreciated.

Kittens should receive several feeds a day, but by the time they are six months old this should have been reduced to two, or even one, given at regular times of the day. A healthy adult cat should receive about half an ounce of food for every pound it weighs. Milk, meat, fish, liver, lights and most table scraps, providing they do not contain too much spice, are their basic diet. A cat should always have access to a supply of fresh water.

Mice

All varieties of tame mice need a warm temperature, and must be given a cage with plenty of room. Its floor should be littered with clean sawdust, which should be changed frequently. Grain mixture and bread is the ideal diet, with fragments of cheese and greenstuff. The water supply must be kept fresh.

Hamsters

Golden hamsters are kept in the same way as mice. As well as bread and cereal, they enjoy carrots, maize meal and milk.

Guinea-pigs

Guinea-pigs are best kept out of doors in a warm shed which is thoroughly proof against rats, cats and dogs. They should have an outdoor run on the sheltered side of their shed. The shed itself should contain plenty of litter for bedding; wood-wool or fine shavings are ideally suitable for this. The bedding should be changed frequently to avoid unpleasant smells and the danger of disease. Guinea-pigs

279

need about an ounce of cereal daily (bran and crushed oats), with a plentiful supply of garden greenstuff. Fresh water should always be available.

Rabbits

Rabbits require much the same housing as guinea-pigs, but the food may be more varied. Rabbits will thrive on many kinds of household scraps, such as bread, cooked potatoes and plenty of green food.

Tortoises

A tortoise, as he carries his own house with him, needs only a shelter to keep off heavy rain and wind. A small wooden box on its side in the garden is adequate. In a garden which contains plants of value it may be necessary to limit the tortoise's movements by boards or low fencing, for he will spend much of his time wandering about and sampling different kinds of greenstuff. In winter he will hibernate, and it is important to know *where*, as once this has happened he must not be disturbed until the warmer weather returns. If brought into a greenhouse or shed to hibernate in a box, he should be given plenty of straw and dry leaves with which to cover himself completely. If he hibernates in the garden, he will probably fail to cover himself with a thick enough layer of earth to keep out the frost, and so a thick wad of straw should be placed on top.

During the summer the moisture from greenstuff may be insufficient; a tortoise should then be given a supply of fresh water in a shallow plate or saucer.

Cage Birds

Canaries require a diet composed of canary seed, summer rape seed, cuttlefish bone and a little greenstuff. Fresh water should always be provided in the cage. Budgerigars should receive millet and canary seed, with lettuce or other greenstuff in small quantities. The secret of successful bird-keeping is attention to cleanliness; the cage must be kept spotlessly clean and the water changed as often as possible. Care must also be taken to prevent draughts.

Flowers Easy to Grow

If starting a small corner of your own in the family garden, prepare the ground by digging over thoroughly and removing weeds and grass. Work in any compost or old manure before planting. Here are some flowers which are easy to grow, some of which you might like to try in your own garden. (Remember, annuals are plants which last only a single year, biennials flower in their second year and then die; perennials live on from year to year.)

Ageratum is a half-hardy annual, with mauve, pink, blue or white flowers, 6 to 9 inches in height. It is sown under glass in early spring.

Alyssum is a useful hardy annual for sunny borders and rockeries. It can be sown in the open and has mauve or white flowers. Perennial varieties are also available. Height 3 to 6 inches.

Antirrhinum, usually known as *Snapdragon*, can be grown as an annual or kept as a perennial. It is sown under glass from January to March and planted out in May. Height ranges from 6 inches to 3 feet; all colours are available except blue.

Armeria, also called *Thrift*, is a cushiony, hardy perennial with red, pink or white flowers, ideal for borders and rockeries. Height 6 inches.

Aster, a family of half-hardy annuals available in many colours, includes the *Michaelmas Daisy*—a hardy perennial which ranges from blue and mauve to pale pink and white. China Asters, sown in May, are ideal as cut flowers.

281

Aubrietia is a trailing rock-plant (hardy perennial) with purple or pink flowers. It is best grown from cuttings.

Calendula, or *Pot Marigold*, a half-hardy annual with double or single flowers, ranges from pale yellow to a rich gold. Sown in early spring, it should provide plenty of colour in late summer. Height 18 to 30 inches.

Candytuft is grown from seed as a hardy annual or perennial. The average height is 12 inches; the spiked flowers are pink, crimson or lilac.

Cheiranthus, or *Siberian Wallflower*, is available in yellow and orange. Sown in May and transplanted after reaching a height of 2 inches, it flowers the following year. Height 18 inches.

Chrysanthemums are of two kinds. The hardy annuals are sown in the open in spring for summer flowering; the perennials can be grown from cuttings and root division. There are many varieties and shades, and chrysanthemums are the mainstay of the autumn flower-bed. Height 18 inches to 3 feet.

Clarkia is a hardy annual with pastel or white flowers. It is sown in April and grows to about 24 inches in height.

Cornflower, a hardy annual, is easy to grow and has a wide range of colours. Height 2 to 2½ feet.

Crocus is a hardy perennial, yellow, white or purple, with a corm or bulb which is planted in the early autumn for flowering the following spring.

Dahlia is a half-hardy perennial with a tuberous root. It can be raised from seed, and after flowering the tubers can be stored away from frost for replanting the next year. It comes in a variety of colours, and varies in size from 18 inches to 5 feet.

Delphinium is of two varieties. The annual, known as *Larkspur*, is planted as seed in the spring; the perennial is often raised from cuttings planted in spring or autumn. It is usually available in various shades of blue and is from 2 to 6 feet in height.

Dianthus is the family which includes the *Carnation, Pink* and *Sweet William*. Hardy border carnations are propagated by cuttings, and so are pinks. Sweet Williams are grown from seed as biennials.

Gladiolus is a tall flowering plant grown from a corm planted in the spring. In early autumn the corms are lifted and the new offset corms removed and stored to start fresh plants the next spring. The plant grows from 30 inches to 4½ feet in height and is available in a wide variety of colours.

Gypsophila is a pink or white annual, grown from seed in March. A perennial variety can be raised from root division. Height about 18 inches.

Hyacinth is a bulb planted in October for spring flowering, or in pots indoors from August onwards for mid-winter. Available in many colours, it grows to about 12 inches in height.

Iris is a hardy perennial with roots that divide easily for propagation in the late autumn. It is available in a great variety of heights and colours.

Lobelia is best started under glass in early spring. The mass of blue or white flowers it produces is ideal for borders and rockeries.

Love-in-a-Mist is an annual with blue or white flowers, and is sown in the open in March or April. Height 18 inches.

Narcissus is a class of bulb which includes the *Daffodil*. It is planted in the late summer or early autumn for spring flowering, and need not be lifted except when so many new bulbs have formed that splitting becomes necessary.

Nasturtium is sown in the open as soon as the danger of frost is past. There are many varieties, ranging from pale yellow to deep orange in colour.

Phlox is a hardy annual or perennial available in a variety of colours. The annual is sown under glass in spring for summer flowering; the perennial is best increased by cuttings in early spring or October. Height from 1 to 5 feet.

Primula is a member of the family which includes *Primroses* and *Polyanthus*. All varieties can be raised from seed, but the usual method is by splitting old plants after flowering has ended.

Roses are best planted in early November. There are a number of types, such as ramblers, bushes and standards, climbers and polyanthas. Most varieties need pruning for good results. In general, the rule is that strong growers are lightly pruned and weak growers need more severe treatment.

Sweet Pea is a hardy annual grown mainly for cut flowers. Sown in autumn or spring, it requires good, well-manured soil. The more sweet peas are picked, the more they flower. The range of colours and sizes is considerable.

Tulip is a hardy perennial bulb plant for early spring flowering. It is planted in autumn in the open. It can also be grown indoors in pots.

Garden Calendar

January. Take cuttings of chrysanthemums from the bases of old plants and set them in pots containing leaf-mould and old mortar. Sow sweet peas in boxes under glass.

February. Plant onions, leeks, shallots and early peas in the open. Sow spinach, parsnips and early carrots if the ground is not frozen.

March. Plant broccoli, Brussels sprouts, cabbage, carrots, cauliflower, lettuce, peas, potatoes, parsley, radishes and summer cabbages in the open. Plant pinks and carnations, and begin sowing annuals.

April. Plant French beans, cauliflower, beetroot, celery, lettuce, mustard and cress, peas, potatoes, spinach, summer turnips and marrows. Sow remaining annuals, and plant shrubs.

May. Plant further crops of potatoes, lettuce and cabbage. Sow runner beans, further annuals, also sweet William, wallflowers, forget-me-nots and Canterbury bells. Plant early chrysanthemums.

June. Plant tomatoes, sweet corn and cucumber. Plant dahlia tubers and hardy perennials.

July. Plant out winter cabbages. Sow further annuals for autumn flowering, and plant out biennials sown in May.

August. Sow winter spinach, winter Swedes and turnips in the open. Plant crocuses, narcissi and snowdrops, as well as bulbs in fibre for indoor display.

September. Continue sowing winter vegetables. Harvest root crops and gather tomatoes. Plant irises and additional narcissi and crocuses.

October. Plant spring cabbages. Lift dahlias and gladioli. Prepare soil for roses.

November. Sow broad beans. Plant and transplant trees and shrubs. Plant cuttings from perennials and also increase them by root-splitting. Plant roses.

December. Start of the best season for digging. Remove weeds. Prepare trenches for sweet peas. Take chrysanthemum cuttings.

Judging the Weather

The following is a rough guide to judging the weather by means of a household barometer.

1. If the needle or mercury is rising, calm or fair weather can be expected.
2. If the needle or mercury is falling, expect rain and un-settled weather.
3. A rising and falling barometer indicates changeable weather.
4. A steady barometer means that the weather is likely to continue as at the time of reading.
5. A very slow rise or fall indicates the approach of a good or bad settled condition.

Cleaning Up: Simple Ways of Removing Stains

Blood. Use cold water containing soda and salt, or spread a starch mixture on the stain and leave for several hours before washing with soap and warm water.

Cocoa. Wash thoroughly in *cold* water.

Coffee. Wash with warm water and a little borax.

Dye. Some of these can be removed by repeated washing with a very soapy solution, but some dye stains will be permanent.

Fruit. Soak in warm water and borax.

Grease. Magnesia, rubbed on the grease spot when wet, may remove the stain if thoroughly washed afterwards. A standard grease solvent should also be effective.

Ink. If still wet, soak in boiled milk, or, if on woollen materials, rub the surface with a cloth dipped in turpentine. If dry, use a solution made of one teaspoonful of salts of lemon to a pint of warm water. Dry stains will come out of a carpet if rubbed with a mixture of methylated spirit and medicinal fruit salts.

Iodine. Rub with a slice of lemon.

Milk. Wash with soap and water.

Paint. If wet, rub with turpentine (if none available try kitchen detergent). Dry stains should be rubbed with a mixture of ammonia and turpentine.

Tar. Household lard will usually remove these if rubbed in, left for several hours and then washed out.

Tea. Soak in warm water and borax; on china, rub with salt while article is damp.

Wax. With two layers of blotting paper over the stain, iron with a moderate heat until the blotting paper absorbs the melted wax.

Indoor Games

Indoor games can be excellent fun, especially as your skill in mastering them increases. Here are the rules of a few of the standard games:

Chess

The game is for two players, each of whom has sixteen playing pieces. One set is white, the other either red or black. A board of sixty-four black and white squares in eight rows of eight is used, turned so that each player has a white square in the right-hand corner of the row nearest him. Each player then sets up his men on the two back rows nearest him, as follows: back row (l. to r.)—Castle, Knight, Bishop, King, Queen, Bishop, Knight, Castle; second row—the eight Pawns.

White always starts the game, and the players toss to decide which of them shall have the white pieces. The purpose of the game is to capture the opponent's King.

Each player has (in order of importance): a King and a Queen; two Bishops; two Knights; two Castles; eight Pawns. These can make the following moves:

King: one square at a time in any direction (so long as the square is empty).

Queen: as many unoccupied squares as desired, in any direction and either diagonally or straight.

Bishops: diagonally, in either direction, as many unoccupied squares as desired.

Knights: one square straight, then one diagonally, regardless of intervening pieces (provided a Knight does not finish on a square holding one of its own men).

Castles: straight, in either direction, as many squares as desired.

Pawns: one square forward, except in their first move, which may be two squares if wished, and in 'capturing', when they move one forward and one to left or right.

1

It does not matter how many pieces you lose in capturing your opponent's King. This is done by placing him in 'check'—a position in which he could be captured at the next move. He must then move out of check, and if unable to do so he is 'check-mated', and thus defeated. The game can end in a 'stalemate', or draw, when a player's King, though not in check, is unable to move without moving into check and the player has no other piece to move. The game may also be drawn when neither player can capture the other's King.

Once in any game a player may 'castle'. If neither the King nor the Castle in question has moved so far, and the King is not in check, the King may move two squares towards the Castle, which is then placed on the last square passed over by the King. The purpose of this is to move the King to greater safety, and at the same time to bring the Castle into play. You cannot castle if your King is in check, or if opposing pieces are in the way.

A Pawn reaching the eighth line may be exchanged for any other piece.

Draughts

This is played on the black squares of a chess-board, using two sets of 'men', each consisting of twelve black and twelve red or white circular pieces. These are arranged on the black squares of the first three rows at each end of the board, and move one square forward, diagonally. The purpose of the game is to capture all the opponent's pieces, which is done by jumping across them to a vacant square beyond. If, by so doing, the attacker then lands on a square from which it is able to capture again, it does so without waiting for the next move. On reaching the opponent's back line, a piece becomes a King by having a captured piece placed on top, and thenceforward may move forward or back.

Any piece in a position to make a capture but which does not do so is 'huffed'—removed from play.

Marbles

There are several varieties of this game, the best known being Ring Taw, in which one player places his marbles in a circle and the other flicks his in turn towards them from a distance of six feet. A hit wins the marble.

Shove-halfpenny

This is played on a board across which parallel lines have been drawn to divide it into nine equal strips a little wider than a halfpenny. Each player has five halfpennies, and the object of the game is to place three halfpennies in each of the beds, each turn being taken with five shots. 'Cannoning' is allowed. Extra halfpennies placed in any bed in error, above the three required, may be claimed by the opponent towards his own score.

Boys' Organisations

Air Training Corps. This is a voluntary organisation for boys of 14 to 18 whose ambition is to take up flying as a future occupation. It provides first-stage training in aircraft recognition, navigation, aircraft maintenance, aircraft communications, etc., and offers plenty of opportunity for flying experience. Details can be had from R.A.F. stations and recruiting headquarters.

Army Cadet Force. Boys between the ages of 14 and 18 who hope to make the Army their career can get off to a head start by learning rifle-shooting, drill, military tactics and camp-craft in the Cadet Force. Full particulars can be had from any Army recruiting office or from the Headquarters at 16 Buckingham Palace Road, London, S.W.1.

Boys Brigade. The Boys Brigade is first and foremost an organisation for those who enjoy outdoor life, and provides plenty of chances to learn first aid, camping, swimming and all other forms of sport. Each local company of the Brigade is linked with a church in the neighbourhood, and your vicar or curate will be able to supply full details or put you in touch with those who can. The Headquarters are: Abbey House, Westminster, London S.W.1.

Boy Scouts Association. This is the most truly international of all youth organisations. Anybody interested in camping, exploring, signalling, sport and other outdoor activities will find in the Scouts no fewer than seven million others throughout the world with the same enthusiasm. By joining the Cubs while still very young, boys can keep up a continuous membership right through to their twenties. The Headquarters of the Scouts in Britain are at 25 Buckingham Palace Road, London, S.W.1.

Church Lads' Brigade. This is a boys' organisation which maintains a close link with local churches and church activities. Headquarters are at 58 Gloucester Place, London, W.1.

Cyclists Touring Club. This is an association for cyclists of all ages which helps to make life easier for the rider on tour by supplying maps, suggested routes, and details of clean, inexpensive hostels. It also issues free insurance to its members to cover claims against them in road accidents. Its Headquarters are at 3 Craven Hill, London, W.2.
National Federation of Young Farmers' Clubs. Membership is open to anybody between the ages of 10 and 25 who is interested in farming and the countryside. There are more than 1,500 branches in England and Wales. The Headquarters are at 55 Gower Street, London, W C.1.
Sea Cadet Corps. Boys planning to join the Royal or Merchant Navies can take their preliminary training through the Sea Cadet Corps, which admits boys from 12 to 18. Headquarters are at Grand Buildings, Trafalgar Square, London, W.C.2.

Clubs and Meetings

Many leisure activities are best carried out through a club. There may already be one in your district, with sections for interests ranging from cycling to coin collecting, from bird-watching to scientific research. If there isn't then it may be useful to know how to organise one.

The following is a simple way of starting a club:

1. Hold a first, informal meeting with two or three friends who are likely to be interested and to wish to help. Decide what the objects of the club are to be, and make a list of people to approach as possible members.
2. Prepare and send out circulars to all the people on your list, telling them what has been proposed and asking them to meet at a set time and place under your temporary chairmanship.

3. At this meeting, tell everybody once again about the purposes of the club and then suggest the election of a chairman, secretary, treasurer and committee. As the original proposer of the club, you are likely to find yourself elected to one of these posts.

4. Many of the club's activities, once begun, will run themselves almost automatically, but from time to time general meetings are necessary to make major decisions affecting the whole club—such as future plans or money matters. For such a meeting notices should be sent to members, with a list of the business which is to be discussed at the meeting. This list is called the Agenda; it need not be very detailed but should state quite clearly what each item is about.

5. At each meeting the club secretary takes note of the main points discussed, and his final record of this is known as the Minutes. The Minutes should contain full details of all proposals put to the meeting and of any resolutions passed. To ensure that the Minutes are accurate, it is customary for the secretary to read them out at the start of the next meeting, and if nobody protests that they are incorrect they are signed by the chairman and incorporated in the permanent records of the club.

6. Most clubs decide at their first meeting the number of members who must be present at any future meeting to ensure a Quorum — a sufficient number for taking a vote upon any issue. At the start of each meeting, the chairman should satisfy himself that he has a Quorum.

7. Any member wishing the club to adopt an idea of his submits a Resolution. The chairman then asks if anyone else will Second this. If it is Seconded, then the Resolution is debated by the meeting, as a Motion, and a vote is taken. If it is not Seconded, then the Motion lapses.

8. Voting on most matters can be taken by a show of hands, but in cases where feelings run high a secret ballot, using voting papers, is often better.

9. The success of meetings depends entirely upon the skill of the chairman. A good chairman will get through the Agenda without allowing discussion to wander or tempers to rise; he should follow carefully throughout, and be prepared to deal firmly with unnecessary interruptions—in this way he can get through the Agenda in the time allotted.

Secret Codes

The simplest secret codes are made by merely advancing every letter of every word by two, three or four in the alphabet; thus, using a four-stage code, the word 'alphabet' would become 'eptlefix'. Rapid coding and decoding of messages using this system can be done by drawing a large circle and writing the alphabet round it, leaving equal distances between each letter. A smaller circle is cut out of a sheet of paper, and the alphabet written once more round it. This is pinned to the centre of the larger circle, so that it can be rotated. Move it four stages forward, and every letter is moved by the same amount.

But this kind of code can be solved very easily, and for messages of top secrecy a more complicated code can be made with very little trouble. Both the sender and receiver of the code message must agree in advance upon a secret code word. It can be any word, as long as no letter occurs more than once. Let's say, for example, that it is the word 'DIVER'.

Draw a square and divide it into twenty-five small squares. Starting at the top left-hand corner, fill in the letters of the code word, one in each square, and then the remaining letters of the alphabet in correct order, omitting the ones used already and also omitting 'J', because as we have only twenty-five squares the same code symbol has to serve for both 'I' and 'J'.

The method of coding and decoding may at first seem rather complicated, but a little practice will enable you to carry it out rapidly. Begin by dividing your message into pairs of letters. Thus 'DO NOT RETURN TO BASE' would become 'DO NO TR ET UR NT OB AS EQ'. The letter 'Q' is added as a dummy to complete the final pair.

Now your code square, with 'DIVER' as its code word, looks like this:

D	I	V	E	R
A	B	C	F	G
H	K	L	M	N
O	P	Q	S	T
U	W	X	Y	Z

Now, looking at your pairs of letters waiting for coding, you can see that any two letters are either on the same vertical line, such as 'DO', on the same horizontal line, or at opposite corners of a square or rectangle. If the letters are in the same vertical column, each is translated into code by using the next letter above it, the very top letter of a column being coded by the one at the bottom. Thus 'DO' becomes 'UH' in code. A group on the same horizontal line is coded by using for each letter the one immediately on its right, with the end right-hand letter coded by the one at the extreme left. Letters at opposite corners of a square or rectangle are coded by taking the letters at the other corners of the square or rectangle, so that 'NO' becomes 'HT', and 'ET' becomes 'RS'. The original message, 'DO NOT RETURN TO BASE', becomes, in code, 'UH HT NZ RS ZD GN PA FO VS'. To decode this when receiving at the other end, you simply work the whole process in reverse, using a similar code square. The only other factor to be remembered is that it is impossible to code a pair of identical letters, such as 'BB' or 'OO', for obvious reasons, and it is necessary, therefore, to put a 'Q' between them while dividing the message into groups.

There are many other codes in use, but though some of them are very much more complicated, nearly all of them depend upon the principle used in this twenty-five-square system.

Personal Record

The following section is about *you*. We've dealt with facts and figures on hundreds of subjects of world-wide importance; now what about yourself? Where do *you* fit in, and what kind of person are you? Here, then, is the personal record which not only reminds you of facts and figures which may otherwise get lost or forgotten but helps you to find out more about yourself.

Full Name:

Date of Birth:

Address:

Telephone Number:

School: *School Number:*

Savings Book Number:

Club Number:

Medical Card Number:

Position in School:

Term	Year	Class	Position
Spring	19		
Summer	19		
Autumn	19		
Spring	19		
Summer	19		
Autumn	19		
Spring	19		
Summer	19		
Autumn	19		

Weight and Height Charts

These two graphs will help you to note your own progress. As you fill in the dots marking your height and weight at different ages, link them up to form a line from the bottom left corner to the top right of each graph.

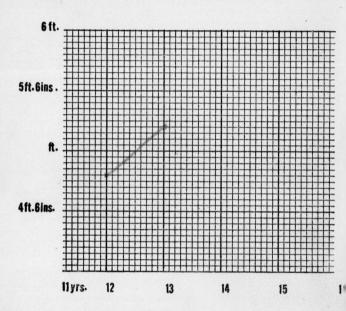

Height

298

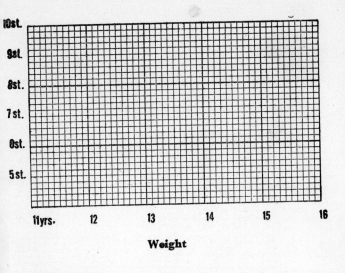

Weight

Athletics Charts

If you want to find out whether you're above or below average in field and track events, try comparing your own performances with this set of standards.

Average Performances for Boys of 12 to 13

Event	Average Performance
100 yards	12.8 s. to 13.4 s.
220 yards	29 s. to 32 s.
70 yards hurdles	12.5 s. to 13.5 s.
4 by 110 yards relay	57 s. to 60 s.
Long jump	13 ft. to 13 ft. 6 in.
High jump	3 ft. 10 in. to 4 ft. 1 in.

Average Performances for Boys of 13 to 14

Event	Average Performance		
100 yards		12.6 s. to	13 s.
220 yards		29 s. to	31 s.
440 yards		67 s. to	74 s.
880 yards	2. m.	40 s. to 2 m.	50 s.
75 yards hurdles		12.9 s. to	13.4 s.
80 yards hurdles		13.1 s. to	13.6 s.
4 by 110 yards relay		54 s. to	57 s.
Long jump	13 ft. 8 in.	to 14 ft.	3 in.
High jump		4 ft. to 4 ft.	3 in.
Discus		roughly	70 ft.
Javelin		roughly	70 ft.
Shot putt		roughly	20 ft.

Average Performances for Boys of 14 to 15

Event	Average Performance		
100 yards		12.3 s. to	12.7 s.
220 yards		28 s. to	30 s.
440 yards		65 s. to	70 s.
880 yards	2 m.	28 s. to 2 m.	35 s.
75 yards hurdles		12.8 s. to	13.5 s.
80 yards hurdles		13 s. to	13.8 s.
4 by 110 yards relay		52 s. to	55 s.
Long jump	14 ft. 9 in.	to 15 ft.	1 in.
High jump	4 ft. 3 in.	to 4 ft.	6 in.
Discus		roughly	90 ft.
Javelin		roughly	95 ft.
Shot putt		roughly	30 ft.

Average Performances for Boys of 15 to 16

Event	Average Performance			
100 yards		11.3 s.	to	12 s.
220 yards		26 s.	to	29 s.
440 yards		61 s.	to	68 s.
880 yards	2 m.	24 s.	to 2 m.	31 s.
110 yards hurdles		16 s.	to	19 s.
Long jump	14 ft.	11 in.	to 15 ft.	9 in.
High jump	4 ft.	6 in.	to 4 ft.	9 in.
Discus		roughly	98 ft.	
Javelin		roughly	100 ft.	
Shot putt		roughly	35 ft.	

Charts such as the ones below show you how to keep records of your own best performances each season, and lines drawn to join each entry to the next will reveal how steady your improvement is.

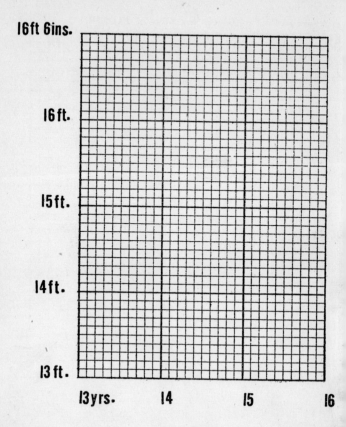

Long Jump

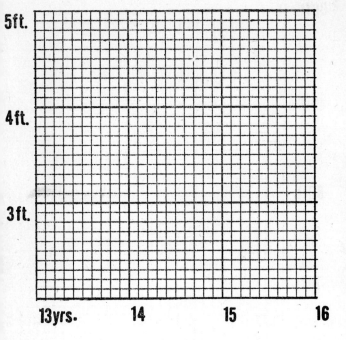

High Jump

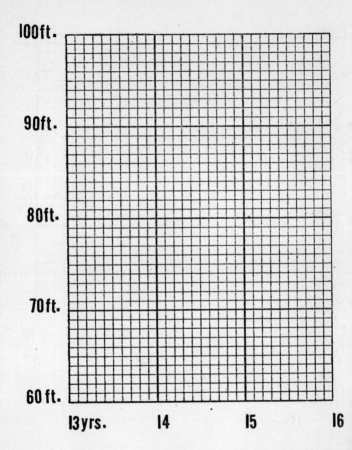

Discus

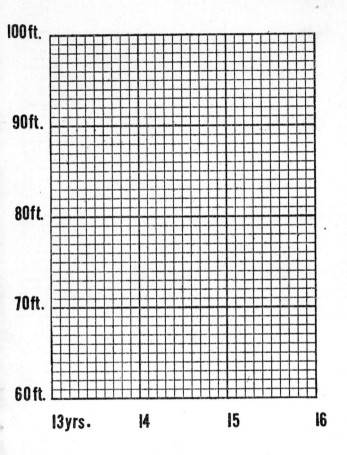

Javelin

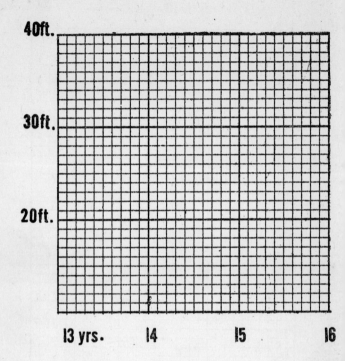

Shot Putt

Sports Awards and Performances

Date	Sport	Award or Performance

Prizes and Certificates Won

At School

Date	Prize

Outside School

Date	Prize

Printed in Czechoslovakia